ANNE FRANK:
THE DIARY OF A YOUNG GIRL

is the true story of a young Jewish girl who lived
with seven other people in a secret nest of rooms in
Amsterdam. Her diary reveals the life of this group
of Jews hiding from the Nazis. It has been called
"one of the most moving documents to come out of
World War II," and is truly a warm, heart-rending
revelation of extreme insight and talent written by
a young adolescent. Translated into nearly a score
of languages, it has been read and loved by more
than five million people all over the world.

The supplemental materials in this Reader's
Enrichment edition have been prepared under the
supervision of an editorial committee directed by
Harry Shefter, Professor of English at New York University and former Vice-Principal of the William
Howard Taft High School, New York City. He is the
author of a number of successful books, including
SHEFTER'S GUIDE TO BETTER COMPOSITIONS. All editorial work and writing has been done by teachers
working as a team.

READER'S ENRICHMENT SERIES

ANNE FRANK:
THE DIARY
OF A
YOUNG GIRL

Translated from the Dutch by
B. M. Mooyaart-Doubleday

WSP

WASHINGTON SQUARE PRESS, INC. • NEW YORK

ANNE FRANK: THE DIARY OF A YOUNG GIRL

A *Reader's Enrichment* edition

1st printing....................November, 1963
6th printing......................August, 1967

The Doubleday edition of *Anne Frank: The Diary of a Young Girl*
was published June, 1952.

Produced as a Broadway Play October 5, 1955
under the title *The Diary of Anne Frank*

Anne Frank: The Diary of a Young Girl has been published in
the following countries: Argentina, Brazil, Czechoslovakia,
Denmark, Finland, France, Germany, Great Britain, Greece,
Iceland, Israel, Italy, Japan, The Netherlands, Norway, Poland,
Portugal, Spain, Sweden, Turkey.

L

Published by
Washington Square Press, Inc., 630 Fifth Avenue, New York, N.Y.

WASHINGTON SQUARE PRESS editions are distributed in the
U.S. by Simon & Schuster, Inc., 630 Fifth Avenue, New
York, N.Y. 10020 and in Canada by Simon & Schuster
of Canada, Ltd., Richmond Hill, Ontario, Canada.

FIRST PUBLISHED IN 1947 IN HOLLAND
BY CONTACT, AMSTERDAM, UNDER THE TITLE *Het Achterhuis*

Het Achterhuis, the Dutch title of this book, refers to that part of the building which served as a hiding place for the two families who took shelter there between 1942 and 1944. *Achter* means "behind" or "in back of" and *huis* is Dutch for "house." In Amsterdam's old buildings the apartments overlooking a garden or court may be divided from those overlooking the street, thus providing two separate suites within the same apartment. Het Achterhuis or, literally, "the house behind" is situated on the Prinsengracht, one of the city's canals.

To simplify the English text, we have called that part of the house the Secret Annexe, although it is not an annex in the proper sense of the word.

Ik zal hoop ik aan jou alles kunnen toevertrouwen, zoals ik het nog aan niemand gekund heb, en ik hoop dat je me een grote steun zult zijn.

Anne Frank. 12 Juni 1942.

I hope I shall be able to confide in you completely, as I have never been able to do in anyone before, and I hope that you will be a great support and comfort to me.

Anne Frank:

THE DIARY OF A YOUNG GIRL

Sunday, 14 June, 1942

On Friday, June 12th, I woke up at six o'clock and no wonder; it was my birthday. But of course I was not allowed to get up at that hour, so I had to control my curiosity until a quarter to seven. Then I could bear it no longer, and went to the dining room, where I received a warm welcome from Moortje (the cat).

Soon after seven I went to Mummy and Daddy and then to the sitting room to undo my presents. The first to greet me was *you*, possibly the nicest of all. Then on the table there were a bunch of roses, a plant, and some peonies, and more arrived during the day.

I got masses of things from Mummy and Daddy, and was thoroughly spoiled by various friends. Among other things I was given *Camera Obscura,* a party game, lots of sweets, chocolates, a puzzle, a brooch, *Tales and Legends of the Netherlands* by Joseph Cohén, *Daisy's Mountain Holiday* (a terrific book), and some money. Now I can buy *The Myths of Greece and Rome*—grand!

Then Lies called for me and we went to school. During recess I treated everyone to sweet biscuits, and then we had to go back to our lessons.

Now I must stop. Bye-bye, we're going to be great pals!

Monday, 15 June, 1942

I had my birthday party on Sunday afternoon. We showed a film *The Lighthouse Keeper* with Rin-Tin-Tin, which my school friends thoroughly enjoyed. We had a lovely time. There were lots of girls and boys. Mummy always wants to

1

know whom I'm going to marry. Little does she guess that it's Peter Wessel; one day I managed, without blushing or flickering an eyelid, to get that idea right out of her mind. For years Lies Goosens and Sanne Houtman have been my best friends. Since then, I've got to know Jopie de Waal at the Jewish Secondary School. We are together a lot and she is now my best girl friend. Lies is more friendly with another girl, and Sanne goes to a different school, where she has made new friends.

Saturday, 20 June, 1942

I haven't written for a few days, because I wanted first of all to think about my diary. It's an odd idea for someone like me to keep a diary; not only because I have never done so before, but because it seems to me that neither I—nor for that matter anyone else—will be interested in the unbosomings of a thirteen-year-old schoolgirl. Still, what does that matter? I want to write, but more than that, I want to bring out all kinds of things that lie buried deep in my heart.

There is a saying that "paper is more patient than man"; it came back to me on one of my slightly melancholy days, while I sat chin in hand, feeling too bored and limp even to make up my mind whether to go out or stay at home. Yes, there is no doubt that paper is patient and as I don't intend to show this cardboard-covered notebook, bearing the proud name of "diary," to anyone, unless I find a real friend, boy or girl, probably nobody cares. And now I come to the root of the matter, the reason for my starting a diary: it is that I have no such real friend.

Let me put it more clearly, since no one will believe that a girl of thirteen feels herself quite alone in the world, nor is it so. I have darling parents and a sister of sixteen. I know about thirty people whom one might call friends—I have strings of boy friends, anxious to catch a glimpse of me and who, failing that, peep at me through mirrors in class. I have relations, aunts and uncles, who are darlings too, a good home, no—I don't seem to lack anything. But it's the same with all my friends, just fun and joking, nothing more. I can never bring myself to talk of anything outside the common round. We don't seem to be able to get any closer, that is the root of the trouble. Perhaps I lack confidence, but anyway, there it is, a stubborn fact and I don't seem to be able to do anything about it.

Hence, this diary. In order to enhance in my mind's eye the picture of the friend for whom I have waited so long, I don't want to set down a series of bald facts in a diary like most people do, but I want this diary itself to be my friend, and I shall call my friend Kitty. No one will grasp what I'm talking about if I begin my letters to Kitty just out of the blue, so albeit unwillingly, I will start by sketching in brief the story of my life.

My father was thirty-six when he married my mother, who was then twenty-five. My sister Margot was born in 1926 in Frankfort-on-Main, I followed on June 12, 1929, and, as we are Jewish, we emigrated to Holland in 1933, where my father was appointed Managing Director of Travies N.V. This firm is in close relationship with the firm of Kolen & Co. in the same building, of which my father is a partner.

The rest of our family, however, felt the full impact of Hitler's anti-Jewish laws, so life was filled with anxiety. In 1938 after the pogroms, my two uncles (my mother's brothers) escaped to the U.S.A. My old grandmother came to us, she was then seventy-three. After May 1940 good times rapidly fled: first the war, then the capitulation, followed by the arrival of the Germans, which is when the sufferings of us Jews really began. Anti-Jewish decrees followed each other in quick succession. Jews must wear a yellow star,[1] Jews must hand in their bicycles, Jews are banned from trains and are forbidden to drive. Jews are only allowed to do their shopping between three and five o'clock and then only in shops which bear the placard "Jewish shop." Jews must be indoors by eight o'clock and cannot even sit in their own gardens after that

---

[1]To distinguish them from others, all Jews were forced by the Germans to wear, prominently displayed, a yellow six-pointed star.

hour. Jews are forbidden to visit theaters, cinemas, and other places of entertainment. Jews may not take part in public sports. Swimming baths, tennis courts, hockey fields, and other sports grounds are all prohibited to them. Jews may not visit Christians. Jews must go to Jewish schools, and many more restrictions of a similar kind.

So we could not do this and were forbidden to do that. But life went on in spite of it all. Jopie used to say to me, "You're scared to do anything, because it may be forbidden." Our freedom was strictly limited. Yet things were still bearable.

Granny died in January 1942; no one will ever know how much she is present in my thoughts and how much I love her still.

In 1934 I went to school at the Montessori Kindergarten and continued there. It was at the end of the school year, I was in form 6B, when I had to say good-by to Mrs. K. We both wept, it was very sad. In 1941 I went, with my sister Margot, to the Jewish Secondary School, she into the fourth form and I into the first.

So far everything is all right with the four of us and here I come to the present day.

Saturday, 20 June, 1942

Dear Kitty,

I'll start straight away. It is so peaceful at the moment, Mummy and Daddy are out and Margot has gone to play ping-pong with some friends.

I've been playing ping-pong a lot myself lately. We ping-pongers are very partial to an ice cream, especially in summer, when one gets warm at the game, so we usually finish up with a visit to the nearest ice-cream shop, Delphi or Oasis, where Jews are allowed. We've given up scrounging for extra pocket money. Oasis is usually full and among our large circle of friends we always manage to find some kindhearted gentleman or boy friend, who presents us with more ice cream than we could devour in a week.

I expect you will be rather surprised at the fact that I should talk of boy friends at my age. Alas, one simply can't seem to avoid it at our school. As soon as a boy asks if he may bicycle home with me and we get into conversation, nine out of ten times I can be sure that he will fall head over heels in love immediately and simply won't allow me out of his sight. After a while it cools down of course, especially as I take little notice of ardent looks and pedal blithely on.

If it gets so far that they begin about "asking Father" I swerve slightly on my bicycle, my satchel falls, the young man is bound to get off and hand it to me, by which time I have introduced a new topic of conversation.

These are the most innocent types; you get some who blow kisses or try to get hold of your arm, but then they are definitely knocking at the wrong door. I get off my bicycle and refuse to go further in their company, or I pretend to be insulted and tell them in no uncertain terms to clear off.

There, the foundation of our friendship is laid, till tomorrow!

Yours, Anne

Sunday, 21 June, 1942

Dear Kitty,

Our whole class B1 is trembling, the reason is that the teachers' meeting is to be held soon. There is much speculation as to who will move up and who will stay put. Miep de Jong and I are highly amused at Wim and Jacques, the two boys behind us. They won't have a florin left for the holidays, it will all be gone on betting. "You'll move up," "Shan't," "Shall," from morning till night. Even Miep pleads for silence and my angry outbursts don't calm them.

According to me, a quarter of the class should stay where they are; there are some absolute cuckoos, but teachers are the greatest freaks on earth, so perhaps they will be freakish in the *right* way for once.

I'm not afraid about my girl friends and myself, we'll

squeeze through somehow, though I'm not too certain about my math. Still we can but wait patiently. Till then, we cheer each other along.

I get along quite well with all my teachers, nine in all, seven masters and two mistresses. Mr. Keptor, the old math master, was very annoyed with me for a long time because I chatter so much. So I had to write a composition with "A Chatterbox" as the subject. A chatterbox! Whatever could one write? However, deciding I would puzzle that out later, I wrote it in my notebook, and tried to keep quiet.

That evening, when I'd finished my other homework, my eyes fell on the title in my notebook. I pondered, while chewing the end of my fountain pen, that anyone can scribble some nonsense in large letters with the words well spaced but the difficulty was to prove beyond doubt the necessity of talking. I thought and thought and then, suddenly having an idea, filled my three allotted sides and felt completely satisfied. My arguments were that talking is a feminine characteristic and that I would do my best to keep it under control, but I should never be cured, for my mother talked as much as I, probably more, and what can one do about inherited qualities? Mr. Keptor had to laugh at my arguments, but when I continued to hold forth in the next lesson, another composition followed. This time it was "Incurable Chatterbox," I handed this in and Keptor made no complaints for two whole lessons. But in the third lesson it was too much for him again. "Anne, as punishment for talking, will do a composition entitled 'Quack, quack, quack, says Mrs. Natterbeak.'" Shouts of laughter from the class. I had to laugh too, although I felt that my inventiveness on this subject was exhausted. I had to think of something else, something entirely original. I was in luck, as my friend Sanne writes good poetry and offered to help by doing the whole composition in verse. I jumped for joy. Keptor wanted to make a fool of me with this absurd theme, I would get my own back and make him the laughing-stock of the whole class. The poem was finished and was perfect. It was about a mother duck and a father swan who had three baby ducklings. The baby ducklings were bitten to death by Father because they chattered too much. Luckily Keptor saw the joke, he read the poem out loud to the class, with comments, and also to various other classes.

Since then I am allowed to talk, never get extra work, in fact Keptor always jokes about it.

Yours, Anne

Wednesday, 24 June, 1942

Dear Kitty,

It is boiling hot, we are all positively melting, and in this heat I have to walk everywhere. Now I can fully appreciate how nice a tram is; but that is a forbidden luxury for Jews—shank's mare is good enough for us. I had to visit the dentist in the Jan Luykenstraat in the lunch hour yesterday. It is a long way from our school in the Stadstimmertuinen; I nearly fell asleep in school that afternoon. Luckily, the dentist's assistant was very kind and gave me a drink—she's a good sort.

We are allowed on the ferry and that is about all. There is a little boat from the Josef Israelskade, the man there took us at once when we asked him. It is not the Dutch people's fault that we are having such a miserable time.

I do wish I didn't have to go to school, as my bicycle was stolen in the Easter holidays and Daddy has given Mummy's to a Christian family for safekeeping. But thank goodness, the holidays are nearly here, one more week and the agony is over. Something amusing happened yesterday, I was passing the bicycle sheds when someone called out to me. I looked around and there was the nice-looking boy I met on the previous evening, at my girl friend Eva's home. He came shyly towards me and introduced himself as Harry Goldberg. I was rather surprised and wondered what he wanted, but I didn't have to wait long. He asked if I would allow him to accompany me to school. "As you're going my way in any case, I will," I replied and so we went together. Harry is sixteen and can tell all kinds of amusing stories. He was waiting for me again this morning and I expect he will from now on.

Yours, Anne

Tuesday, 30 June, 1942

Dear Kitty,

I've not had a moment to write to you until today. I was with friends all day on Thursday. On Friday we had visitors, and so it went on until today. Harry and I have got to know each other well in a week, and he has told me a lot about his life; he came to Holland alone, and is living with his grandparents. His parents are in Belgium.

Harry had a girl friend called Fanny. I know her too, a very soft, dull creature. Now that he has met me, he realizes that he was just daydreaming in Fanny's presence. I seem to act as a stimulant to keep him awake. You see we all have our uses, and queer ones too at times!

Jopie slept here on Saturday night, but she went to Lies on Sunday and I was bored stiff. Harry was to have come in the evening, but he rang up at 6 P.M. I went to the telephone, he said, "Harry Goldberg here, please may I speak to Anne?"
"Yes, Harry, Anne speaking."

"Hullo, Anne, how are you?"
"Very well, thank you."

"I'm terribly sorry I can't come this evening, but I would like to just speak to you; is it all right if I come in ten minutes?"

"Yes, that's fine, good-by!"
"Good-by, I'll be with you soon."
Receiver down.

I quickly changed into another frock and smartened up my hair a bit. Then I stood nervously at the window watching for him. At last I saw *him* coming. It was a wonder I didn't dash down at once; instead I waited patiently until he rang. Then I went down and he positively burst in when I opened the door.

"Anne, my grandmother thinks you are too young to go out

regularly with me, and that I should go to the Leurs, but perhaps you know that I am not going out with Fanny any more!"

"No, why is that, have you quarreled?"

"No, not at all. I told Fanny that we didn't get on well together, so it was better for us not to go out together any more, but she was always welcome in our home, and I hope I should be in hers. You see, I thought Fanny had been going out with another boy and treated her accordingly. But that was quite untrue. And now my uncle says I should apologize to Fanny, but of course I didn't want to do that so I finished the whole affair. That was just one of the many reasons. My grandmother would rather I went with Fanny than you, but I shan't; old people have such terribly old-fashioned ideas at times, but I just can't fall into line. I need my grandparents, but in a sense they need me too. From now on I shall be free on Wednesday evenings. Officially I go to wood-carving lessons to please my grandparents, in actual fact I go to a meeting of the Zionist Movement. I'm not supposed to, because my grandparents are very much against the Zionists. I'm by no means a fanatic, but I have a leaning that way and find it interesting. But lately it has become such a mess there that I'm going to quit, so next Wednesday will be my last time. Then I shall be able to see you on Wednesday evenings, Saturday afternoon, Sunday afternoon, and perhaps more."

"But your grandparents are against it, you can't do it behind their backs!"

"Love finds a way."

Then we passed the bookshop on the corner, and there stood Peter Wessel with two other boys; he said "Hello"—it's the first time he has spoken to me for ages, I was really pleased.

Harry and I walked on and on and the end of it all was that I should meet him at five minutes to seven in the front of his house next evening.

                                                    Yours, Anne

Friday, 3 July, 1942

Dear Kitty,

Harry visited us yesterday to meet my parents. I had bought a cream cake, sweets, tea, and fancy biscuits, quite a spread, but neither Harry nor I felt like sitting stiffly side by side indefinitely, so we went for a walk, and it was already ten past eight when he brought me home. Daddy was very cross, and thought it was very wrong of me because it is dangerous for Jews to be out after eight o'clock, and I had to promise to be in by ten to eight in future.

Tomorrow I've been invited to his house. My girl friend Jopie teases me the whole time about Harry. I'm honestly not in love, oh, no, I can surely have boy friends—no one thinks anything of that—but one boy friend, or beau, as Mother calls him, seems to be quite different.

Harry went to see Eva one evening and she told me that she asked him, "Who do you like best, Fanny or Anne?" He said, "It's nothing to do with you!" But when he left (they hadn't chatted together any more the whole evening), "Now listen, it's Anne, so long, and don't tell a soul." And like a flash he was gone.

It's easy to see that Harry is in love with me, rather fun for a change. Margot would say, "Harry is a decent lad." I agree, but he is more than that. Mummy is full of praise: a good-looking boy, a well-behaved, nice boy. I'm glad that the whole family approve of him. He likes them too, but he thinks my girl friends are very childish, and he's quite right.

Yours, Anne

Sunday morning, 5 July, 1942

Dear Kitty,

Our examination results were announced in the Jewish Theater last Friday. I couldn't have hoped for better. My report is not at all bad, I had one *vix satis*, a five for algebra, two sixes, and the rest were all sevens or eights. They were certainly pleased at home, although over the question of marks my parents are quite different from most. They don't care a bit whether my reports are good or bad as long as I'm well and happy, and not too cheeky: then the rest will come by itself. I am just the opposite. I don't want to be a bad pupil; I should really have stayed in the seventh form in the Montessori School, but was accepted for the Jewish Secondary. When all the Jewish children had to go to Jewish schools, the headmaster took Lies and me conditionally after a bit of persuasion. He relied on us to do our best and I don't want to let him down. My sister Margot has her report too, brilliant as usual. She would move up with *cum laude* if that existed at school, she is so brainy. Daddy has been at home a lot lately, as there is nothing for him to do at business; it must be rotten to feel so superfluous. Mr. Koophuis has taken over Travies and Mr. Kraler the firm Kolen & Co. When we walked across our little square together a few days ago, Daddy began to talk of us going into hiding. I asked him why on earth he was beginning to talk of that already. "Yes, Anne," he said, "you know that we have been taking food, clothes, furniture to other people for more than a year now. We don't want our belongings to be seized by the Germans, but we certainly don't want to fall into their clutches ourselves. So we shall disappear of our own accord and not wait until they come and fetch us."

"But, Daddy, when would it be?" He spoke so seriously that I grew very anxious.

"Don't you worry about it, we shall arrange everything. Make the most of your carefree young life while you can." That was all. Oh, may the fulfillment of these somber words remain far distant yet!

Yours, Anne

Wednesday, 8 July, 1942

Dear Kitty,

Years seem to have passed between Sunday and now. So

much has happened, it is just as if the whole world had turned upside down. But I am still alive, Kitty, and that is the main thing, Daddy says.

Yes, I'm still alive, indeed, but don't ask where or how. You wouldn't understand a word, so I will begin by telling you what happened on Sunday afternoon.

At three o'clock (Harry had just gone, but was coming back later) someone rang the front doorbell. I was lying lazily reading a book on the veranda in the sunshine, so I didn't hear it. A bit later, Margot appeared at the kitchen door looking very excited. "The S.S. have sent a call-up notice for Daddy," she whispered. "Mummy has gone to see Mr. Van Daan already." (Van Daan is a friend who works with Daddy in the business.) It was a great shock to me, a call-up; every one knows what that means. I picture concentration camps and lonely cells—should we allow him to be doomed to this? "Of course he won't go," declared Margot, while we waited together. "Mummy has gone to the Van Daans to discuss whether we should move into our hiding place tomorrow. The Van Daans are going with us, so we shall be seven in all." Silence. We couldn't talk any more, thinking about Daddy, who, little knowing what was going on, was visiting some old people in the Joodse Invalide; waiting for Mummy, the heat and suspense, all made us very overawed and silent.

Suddenly the bell rang again. "That is Harry," I said. "Don't open the door." Margot held me back, but it was not necessary as we heard Mummy and Mr. Van Daan downstairs, talking to Harry, then they came in and closed the door behind them. Each time the bell went, Margot or I had to creep softly down to see if it was Daddy, not opening the door to anyone else.

Margot and I were sent out of the room. Van Daan wanted to talk to Mummy alone. When we were alone together in our bedroom, Margot told me that the call-up was not for Daddy, but for her. I was more frightened than ever and began to cry. Margot is sixteen; would they really take girls of that age away alone? But thank goodness she won't go,

Mummy said so herself; that must be what Daddy meant when he talked about us going into hiding.

Into hiding—where would we go, in a town or the country, in a house or a cottage, when, how, where . . .?

These were questions I was not allowed to ask, but I couldn't get them out of my mind. Margot and I began to pack some of our most vital belongings into a school satchel. The first thing I put in was this diary, then hair curlers, handkerchiefs, schoolbooks, a comb, old letters; I put in the craziest things with the idea that we were going into hiding. But I'm not sorry, memories mean more to me than dresses.

At five o'clock Daddy finally arrived, and we phoned Mr. Koophuis to ask if he could come around in the evening. Van Daan went and fetched Miep. Miep has been in the business with Daddy since 1933 and has become a close friend, likewise her brand-new husband, Henk. Miep came and took some shoes, dresses, coats, underwear, and stockings away in her bag, promising to return in the evening. Then silence fell on the house; not one of us felt like eating anything, it was still hot and everything was very strange. We let our large upstairs room to a certain Mr. Goudsmit, a divorced man in his thirties, who appeared to have nothing to do on this particular evening; we simply could not get rid of him without being rude; he hung about until ten o'clock. At eleven o'clock Miep and Henk Van Santen arrived. Once again, shoes, stockings, books, and underclothes disappeared into Miep's bag and Henk's deep pockets, and at eleven-thirty they too disappeared. I was dog-tired and although I knew that it would be my last night in my own bed, I fell asleep immediately and didn't wake up until Mummy called me at five-thirty the next morning. Luckily it was not so hot as Sunday; warm rain fell steadily all day. We put on heaps of clothes as if we were going to the North Pole, the sole reason being to take clothes with us. No Jew in our situation would have dreamed of going out with a suitcase full of clothing. I had on two vests, three pairs of pants, a dress, on top of that a skirt, jacket, summer coat, two pairs of stockings, lace-up shoes, woolly cap, scarf, and still more; I was nearly stifled before we started, but no one inquired about that.

Margot filled her satchel with schoolbooks, fetched her bicycle, and rode off behind Miep into the unknown, as far as I was concerned. You see I still didn't know where our secret hiding place was to be. At seven-thirty the door closed behind us. Moortje, my little cat, was the only creature to whom I said farewell. She would have a good home with the neighbors. This was all written in a letter addressed to Mr. Goudsmit.

There was one pound of meat in the kitchen for the cat, breakfast things lying on the table, stripped beds, all giving the impression that we had left helter-skelter. But we didn't care about impressions, we only wanted to get away, only escape and arrive safely, nothing else. Continued tomorrow.

                                                          Yours, Anne

                                        Thursday, 9 July, 1942

Dear Kitty,

So we walked in the pouring rain, Daddy, Mummy, and I, each with a school satchel and shopping bag filled to the brim with all kinds of things thrown together anyhow.

We got sympathetic looks from people on their way to work. You could see by their faces how sorry they were they couldn't offer us a lift; the gaudy yellow star spoke for itself.

Only when we were on the road did Mummy and Daddy begin to tell me bits and pieces about the plan. For months as many of our goods and chattels and necessities of life as possible had been sent away and they were sufficiently ready for us to have gone into hiding of our own accord on July 16. The plan had had to be speeded up ten days because of the call-up, so our quarters would not be so well organized, but we had to make the best of it. The hiding place itself would be in the building where Daddy has his office. It will be hard for outsiders to understand, but I shall explain that later on. Daddy didn't have many people working for him: Mr. Kraler,

Koophuis, Miep, and Elli Vossen, a twenty-three-year-old typist who all knew of our arrival. Mr. Vossen, Elli's father, and two boys worked in the warehouse; they had not been told.

I will describe the building: there is a large warehouse on the ground floor which is used as a store. The front door to the house is next to the warehouse door, and inside the front door is a second doorway which leads to a staircase (A). There is another door at the top of the stairs, with a frosted glass window in it, which has "Office" written in black letters across it. That is the large main office, very big, very light, and very full. Elli, Miep, and Mr. Koophuis work there in the daytime. A small dark room containing the safe, a wardrobe, and a large cupboard leads to a small somewhat dark second office. Mr. Kraler and Mr. Van Daan used to sit here, now it is only Mr. Kraler. One can reach Kraler's office from the passage, but only via a glass door which can be opened from the inside, but not easily from the outside.

From Kraler's office a long passage goes past the coal store, up four steps and leads to the showroom of the whole building: the private office. Dark, dignified furniture, linoleum and carpets on the floor, radio, smart lamp, everything first-class. Next door there is a roomy kitchen with a hot-water faucet and a gas stove. Next door the W.C. That is the first floor.

A wooden staircase leads from the downstairs passage to the next floor (B). There is a small landing at the top. There is a door at each end of the landing, the left one leading to a storeroom at the front of the house and to the attics. One of those really steep Dutch staircases runs from the side to the other door opening on to the street (C).

The right-hand door leads to our "Secret Annexe." No one would ever guess that there would be so many rooms hidden behind that plain gray door. There's a little step in front of the door and then you are inside.

There is a steep staircase immediately opposite the entrance (E). On the left a tiny passage brings you into a room which was to become the Frank family's bed-sitting-room,

next door a smaller room, study and bedroom for the two
young ladies of the family. On the right a little room without
windows containing the washbasin and a small W.C. compartment, with another door leading to Margot's and my
room. If you go up the next flight of stairs and open the door,
you are simply amazed that there could be such a big light
room in such an old house by the canal. There is a gas stove
in this room (thanks to the fact that it was used as a labora-

tory) and a sink. This is now the kitchen for the Van Daan couple, besides being general living room, dining room, and scullery.

A tiny little corridor room will become Peter Van Daan's apartment. Then, just as on the lower landing, there is a large attic. So there you are, I've introduced you to the whole of our beautiful "Secret Annexe."

Yours, Anne

Friday, 10 July, 1942

Dear Kitty,

I expect I have thoroughly bored you with my long-winded descriptions of our dwelling. But still I think you should know where we've landed.

But to continue my story—you see, I've not finished yet —when we arrived at the Prinsengracht, Miep took us quickly upstairs and into the "Secret Annexe." She closed the door behind us and we were alone. Margot was already waiting for us, having come much faster on her bicycle. Our living room and all the other rooms were chock-full of rubbish, indescribably so. All the cardboard boxes which had been sent to the office in the previous months lay piled on the floor and the beds. The little room was filled to the ceiling with bedclothes. We had to start clearing up immediately, if we wished to sleep in decent beds that night. Mummy and Margot were not in a fit state to take part; they were tired and lay down on their beds, they were miserable, and lots more besides. But the two "clearers-up" of the family— Daddy and myself—wanted to start at once.

The whole day long we unpacked boxes, filled cupboards, hammered and tidied, until we were dead beat. We sank into clean beds that night. We hadn't had a bit of anything warm the whole day, but we didn't care; Mummy and Margot were too tired and keyed up to eat, and Daddy and I were too busy.

On Tuesday morning we went on where we left off the

day before. Elli and Miep collected our rations for us, Daddy improved the poor blackout, we scrubbed the kitchen floor, and were on the go the whole day long again. I hardly had time to think about the great change in my life until Wednesday. Then I had a chance, for the first time since our arrival, to tell you all about it, and at the same time to realize myself what had actually happened to me and what was still going to happen.

Yours, Anne

Saturday, 11 July, 1942

Dear Kitty,

Daddy, Mummy, and Margot can't get used to the sound of the Westertoren clock yet, which tells us the time every quarter of an hour. I can. I loved it from the start, and especially in the night it's like a faithful friend. I expect you will be interested to hear what it feels like to "disappear"; well, all I can say is that I don't know myself yet. I don't think I shall ever feel really at home in this house, but that does not mean that I loathe it here, it is more like being on vacation in a very peculiar boardinghouse. Rather a mad idea, perhaps, but that is how it strikes me. The "Secret Annexe" is an ideal hiding place. Although it leans to one side and is damp, you'd never find such a comfortable hiding place anywhere in Amsterdam, no, perhaps not even in the whole of Holland. Our little room looked very bare at first with nothing on the walls; but thanks to Daddy who had brought my film-star collection and picture postcards on beforehand, and with the aid of paste pot and brush, I have transformed the walls into one gigantic picture. This makes it look much more cheerful, and, when the Van Daans come, we'll get some wood from the attic, and make a few little cupboards for the walls and other odds and ends to make it look more lively.

Margot and Mummy are a little bit better now. Mummy felt well enough to cook some soup for the first time yesterday, but then forgot all about it, while she was downstairs talking, so the peas were burned to a cinder and utterly refused to leave the pan. Mr. Koophuis has brought me a book called *Young People's Annual*. The four of us went to the private office yesterday evening and turned on the radio. I was so terribly frightened that someone might hear it that I simply begged Daddy to come upstairs with me. Mummy understood how I felt and came too. We are very nervous in other ways, too, that the neighbors might hear us or see something going on. We made curtains straight away on the first day. Really one can hardly call them curtains, they are just light, loose strips of material, all different shapes, quality, and pattern, which Daddy and I sewed together in a most unprofessional way. These works of art are fixed in position with drawing pins, not to come down until we emerge from here.

There are some large business premises on the right of us, and on the left a furniture workshop; there is no one there after working hours but even so, sounds could travel through the walls. We have forbidden Margot to cough at night, although she has a bad cold, and make her swallow large doses of codeine. I am looking for Tuesday when the Van Daans arrive; it will be much more fun and not so quiet. It is the silence that frightens me so in the evenings and at night. I wish like anything that one of our protectors could sleep here at night. I can't tell you how oppressive it is *never* to be able to go outdoors, also I'm very afraid that we shall be discovered and be shot. That is not exactly a pleasant prospect. We have to whisper and tread lightly during the day, otherwise the people in the warehouse might hear us.

Someone is calling me.

Yours, Anne

Friday, 14 August, 1942

Dear Kitty,

I have deserted you for a whole month, but honestly,

there is so little news here that I can't find amusing things
to tell you every day. The Van Daans arrived on July 13. We
thought they were coming on the fourteenth, but between
the thirteenth and sixteenth of July the Germans called up
people right and left which created more and more unrest,
so they played for safety, better a day too early than a day
too late. At nine-thirty in the morning (we were still having
breakfast) Peter arrived, the Van Daans' son, not sixteen
yet, a rather soft, shy, gawky youth; can't expect much from
his company. He brought his cat (Mouschi) with him. Mr.
and Mrs. Van Daan arrived half an hour later, and to our
great amusement she had a large pottie in her hat box. "I
don't feel at home anywhere without my chamber," she
declared, so it was the first thing to find its permanent rest-
ing place under her divan. Mr. Van Daan did not bring his,
but carried a folding tea table under his arm.

From the day they arrived we all had meals cozily together
and after three days it was just as if we were one large
family. Naturally the Van Daans were able to tell us a lot
about the extra week they had spent in the inhabited world.
Among other things we were very interested to hear what
had happened to our house and to Mr. Goudsmit. Mr. Van
Daan told us:

"Mr. Goudsmit phoned at nine o'clock on Monday morning and asked if I could come around. I went immediately
and found G. in a state of great agitation. He let me read a
letter that the Franks had left behind and wanted to take
the cat to the neighbors as indicated in the letter, which
pleased me. Mr. G. was afraid that the house would be
searched so we went through all the rooms, tidied up a bit,
and cleared away the breakfast things. Suddenly I discovered
a writing pad on Mrs. Frank's desk with an address in
Maastricht written on it. Although I knew that this was
done on purpose, I pretended to be very surprised and
shocked and urged Mr. G. to tear up this unfortunate little
piece of paper without delay.

"I went on pretending that I knew nothing of your disappearance all the time, but after seeing the paper, I got a

brain wave. 'Mr. Goudsmit'—I said—'it suddenly dawns on me what this address may refer to. Now it all comes back to me, a high-ranking officer was in the office about six months ago, he appeared to be very friendly with Mr. Frank and offered to help him, should the need arise. He was stationed in Maastricht. I think he must have kept his word and somehow or other managed to get them into Belgium and then on to Switzerland. I should tell this to any friends who may inquire. Don't, of course, mention Maastricht.'

"With these words I left the house. Most of your friends know already, because I've been told myself several times by different people."

We were highly amused at the story and, when Mr. Van Daan gave us further details, laughed still more at the way people can let their imagination run away with them. One family had seen the pair of us pass on bicycles very early in the morning and another lady knew quite definitely that we were fetched by a military car in the middle of the night.

Yours, Anne

Friday, 21 August, 1942

Dear Kitty,

The entrance to our hiding place has now been properly concealed. Mr. Kraler thought it would be better to put a cupboard in front of our door (because a lot of houses are being searched for hidden bicycles), but of course it had to be a movable cupboard that can open like a door.

Mr. Vossen made the whole thing. We had already let him into the secret and he can't do enough to help. If we want to go downstairs, we have to first bend down and then jump, because the step has gone. The first three days we were all going about with masses of lumps on our foreheads, because we all knocked ourselves against the low doorway. Now we have nailed a cloth filled with wood wool against the top of the door. Let's see if that helps!

I'm not working much at present; I'm giving myself holidays until September. Then Daddy is going to give me lessons; it's shocking how much I've forgotten already. There is little change in our life here. Mr. Van Daan and I usually manage to upset each other, it's just the opposite with Margot whom he likes very much. Mummy sometimes treats me just like a baby, which I can't bear. Otherwise things are going better. I still don't like Peter any more, he is so boring; he flops lazily on his bed half the time, does a bit of carpentry, and then goes back for another snooze. What a fool!

It is lovely weather and in spite of everything we make the most we can of it by lying on a camp bed in the attic, where the sun shines through an open window.

Yours, Anne

Wednesday, 2 September, 1942

Dear Kitty,

Mr. and Mrs. Van Daan have had a terrific quarrel, I've never seen anything quite like it before. Mummy and Daddy would never dream of shouting at each other. The cause was so trivial that the whole thing was a pure waste of breath. But, still, everyone to his own liking.

Naturally it is very unpleasant for Peter, who has to stand by. No one takes him seriously, he is so frightfully touchy and lazy. Yesterday he was badly upset because he found that his tongue was blue instead of red; this unusual phenomenon of nature disappeared just as quickly as it had come. Today he is going about with a scarf on, as he has a stiff neck; in addition "M'lord" complains of lumbago. Pains around the heart, kidneys, and lungs are not unusual either, he is a real hypochondria (that's the word for such people, isn't it?)! It is not all honey between Mummy and Mrs. Van Daan; there is plenty of cause for unpleasantness. To give a small example, I will tell you that Mrs. Van Daan has taken all three of her sheets out of the common linen cupboard. She takes it for granted that Mummy's sheets will do for all of us. It will be a nasty surprise for her when she finds that Mummy has followed her good example.

Also, she is thoroughly piqued that her dinner service and not ours is in use. She is always trying to find out where we have actually put our plates; they are closer than she thinks, they are in a cardboard box behind a lot of junk in the attic. Our plates are unget-at-able as long as we are here, and a good thing too. I always have bad luck; I smashed one of Mrs. Van Daan's soup plates into a thousand pieces yesterday. "Oh!" she cried angrily. "Couldn't you be careful for once—that's the last one I've got." Mr. Van Daan is all sugar to me nowadays. Long may it last. Mummy gave me another frightful sermon this morning; I can't bear them. Our ideas are completely opposite. Daddy is a darling, although he can sometimes be angry with me for five minutes on end. Last week we had a little interruption in our monotonous life; it was over a book about women—and Peter. First I must tell you that Margot and Peter are allowed to read nearly all the books that Mr. Koophuis lends us, but the grownups held back this particular book on the subject of women. Peter's curiosity was aroused at once. What was it the two of them were not allowed to read in this book? He got hold of the book on the sly, while his mother was downstairs talking, and disappeared with his booty to the attic. All went well for a few days. His mother knew what he was doing, but didn't tell tales, until Father found out. He was very angry, took the book away, and thought that that would finish the whole business. However, he had not allowed for his son's curiosity, which waxed rather than waned because of his father's attitude. Peter, determined to finish it, thought of a way to get hold of this enthralling book. In the meantime, Mrs. Van Daan had asked Mummy what she thought about it all. Mummy thought this particular book was not suitable for Margot, but she saw no harm in letting her read most books.

"There is a great difference, Mrs. Van Daan," said Mummy, "between Margot and Peter. In the first place, Margot is a girl and girls are always more grownup than boys, secondly, Margot has read quite a lot of serious books, and does not go in search of things that are forbidden her, and thirdly, Margot is far more developed and intelligent, shown by the fact of her being in the fourth form at school." Mrs. Van Daan agreed, but still thought it was wrong in principle to let children read books which were written for grownups.

In the meantime Peter had found a time of the day when no one bothered about him or the book: seven-thirty in the evening—then everyone was in the private office listening to the radio. That was when he took his treasure to the attic again. He should have been downstairs again by eight-thirty, but because the book was so thrilling he forgot the time and was just coming downstairs as his father came into the room. You can imagine the consequences! With a slap and a snatch, the book lay on the table and Peter was in the attic. That's how matters stood as we sat down to table. Peter stayed upstairs—no one bothered about him, and he had to go to bed without any supper. We went on with the meal, chattering gaily, when suddenly we heard a piercing whistle; we all stopped eating and looked with pale changed faces from one to another. Then we heard Peter's voice, calling down the chimney, "I say, I'm not coming down anyway." Mr. Van Daan sprang to his feet, his napkin fell to the floor, and scarlet in the face he shouted, "I've had enough of this." Daddy took his arm, afraid of what might happen, and the two men went together to the attic. After a good deal of resistance and stamping, Peter landed up in his room with the door closed and we went on eating. Mrs. Van Daan wanted to save one slice of bread for the dear boy, but his father stood firm. "If he doesn't apologize soon, he will have to sleep in the attic." Loud protests from the rest of us, as we thought missing supper was quite enough punishment. Besides, Peter might catch cold and we couldn't call a doctor.

Peter did not apologize; he was already in the attic. Mr. Van Daan did nothing more about it, but I noticed the next morning that Peter's bed had been slept in. Peter was back in the attic at seven o'clock, but Daddy managed with a few friendly words to persuade him to come down again. Sour faces and obstinate silences for three days and then everything went smoothly once more.

Yours, Anne

Monday, 21 September, 1942

Dear Kitty,

Today I'm going to tell you our general news.

Mrs. Van Daan is unbearable. I get nothing but "blow-ups" from her for my continuous chatter. She is always pestering us in some way or other. This is the latest: she doesn't want to wash up the pans if there is a fragment left; instead of putting it into a glass dish, as we've always done until now, she leaves it in the pan to go bad.

After the next meal Margot sometimes has about seven pans to wash up and then Madame says: "Well, well, Margot, you have got a lot to do!"

I'm busy with Daddy working out his family tree: as we go along he tells me little bits about everyone—it's terribly interesting. Mr. Koophuis brings a few special books for me every other week. I'm thrilled with the *Joop ter Heul* series. I've enjoyed the whole of Cissy van Marxveldt very much. And I've read *Een Zomerzotheid* four times and I still laugh about some of the ludicrous situations that arise.

Term time has begun again, I'm working hard at my French and manage to pump in five irregular verbs per day. Peter sighs and groans over his English. A few schoolbooks have just arrived; we have a good stock of exercise books, pencils, rubbers, and labels, as I brought these with me. I sometimes listen to the Dutch news from London, heard Prince Bernhard recently. He said that Princess Juliana is expecting a baby about next January. I think it is lovely; it surprises the others that I should be so keen on the Royal Family.

I was being discussed and they decided that I'm not completely stupid after all, which had the effect of making me work extra hard the next day. I certainly don't want to still be in the first form when I'm fourteen or fifteen.

Also the fact that I'm hardly allowed to read any decent books was mentioned. Mummy is reading *Heeren, Vrouwen en Knechten* now, which I'm not allowed (Margot is). First I must be more developed, like my talented sister. Then we talk about my ignorance of philosophy and psychology, about which I know nothing. Perhaps by next year I shall be wiser! (I looked up these difficult words quickly in *Koenen*.)

I have just woken up to the disturbing fact that I have one long-sleeved dress and three cardigans for the winter. I've received permission from Daddy to knit a jumper of white sheep's wool; it's not very nice wool, but as long as it's warm that's all that matters. We have some clothes deposited with friends, but unfortunately we shall not see them until after the war, that is if they are still there then. I had just written something about Mrs. Van Daan when in she came. Slap! I closed the book. "Hey, Anne, can't I just have a look?"

"I'm afraid not."

"Just the last page then?"

"No, I'm sorry."

Naturally it gave me a frightful shock, because there was an unflattering description of her on this particular page.

Yours, Anne

Friday, 25 September, 1942

Dear Kitty,

Yesterday evening I went upstairs and "visited" the Van Daans. I do so occasionally to have a chat. Sometimes it can be quite fun. Then we have some moth biscuits (the biscuit tin is kept in the wardrobe which is full of moth balls) and drink lemonade. We talked about Peter. I told them how Peter often strokes my cheek and that I wished he wouldn't as I don't like being pawed by boys.

In a typical way parents have, they asked if I couldn't get

fond of Peter, because he certainly liked me very much. I thought "Oh dear!" and said: "Oh, no!" Imagine it!

I did say that I thought Peter rather awkward, but that it was probably shyness, as many boys who haven't had much to do with girls are like that.

I must say that the Refuge Committee of the "Secret Annexe" (male section) is very ingenious. I'll tell you what they've done now to get news of us through to Mr. Van Dijk, Travies' chief representative and a friend who has surreptitiously hidden some of our things for us! They typed a letter to a chemist in South Zeeland, who does business with our firm, in such a way that he has to send the enclosed reply back in an addressed envelope. Daddy addressed the envelope to the office. When this envelope arrives from Zeeland, the enclosed letter is taken out, and is replaced by a message in Daddy's handwriting as a sign of life. Like this, Van Dijk won't become suspicious when he reads the note. They specially chose Zeeland because it is so close to Belgium and the letter could have easily been smuggled over the border, in addition no one is allowed into Zeeland without a special permit; so if they thought we were there, he couldn't try and look us up.

Yours, Anne

Sunday, 27 September, 1942

Dear Kitty,

Just had a big bust-up with Mummy for the umpteenth time; we simply don't get on together these days and Margot and I don't hit it off any too well either. As a rule we don't go in for such outbursts as this in our family. Still, it's by no means always pleasant for me. Margot's and Mummy's natures are completely strange to me. I can understand my friends better than my own mother—too bad!

We often discuss postwar problems, for example, how one ought to address servants.

Mrs. Van Daan had another tantrum. She is terribly moody.

She keeps hiding more of her private belongings. Mummy ought to answer each Van Daan "disappearance" with a Frank "disappearance." How some people do adore bringing up other people's children in addition to their own. The Van Daans are that kind. Margot doesn't need it, she is such a goody-goody, perfection itself, but I seem to have enough mischief in me for the two of us put together. You should hear us at mealtimes, with reprimands and cheeky answers flying to and fro. Mummy and Daddy always defend me stoutly. I'd have to give up if it weren't for them. Although they do tell me that I mustn't talk so much, that I must be more retiring and not poke my nose into everything, still I seem doomed to failure. If Daddy wasn't so patient, I'd be afraid I was going to turn out to be a terrific disappointment to my parents and they are pretty lenient with me.

If I take a small helping of some vegetable I detest and make up with potatoes, the Van Daans, and Mevrouw in particular, can't get over it, that any child should be so spoiled.

"Come along, Anne, have a few more vegetables," she says straight away.

"No, thank you, Mrs. Van Daan," I answer, "I have plenty of potatoes."

"Vegetables are good for you, your mother says so too. Have a few more," she says, pressing them on me until Daddy comes to my rescue.

Then we have from Mrs. Van Daan—"You ought to have been in our home, we were properly brought up. It's absurd that Anne's so frightfully spoiled. I wouldn't put up with it if Anne were my daughter."

These are always her first and last words "if Anne were my daughter." Thank heavens I'm not!

But to come back to this "upbringing" business. There was a deadly silence after Mrs. Van Daan had finished speaking yesterday. Then Daddy said, "I think Anne is extremely well brought up; she has learned one thing anyway, and that is to make no reply to your long sermons. As to the vegetables, look at your own plate." Mrs. Van Daan was beaten, well and truly beaten. She had taken a minute helping of vegetables herself. But *she* is not spoiled! Oh, no, too many vegetables in the evening make her constipated. Why on earth doesn't she keep her mouth shut about me, then she wouldn't need to make such feeble excuses. It's gorgeous the way Mrs. Van Daan blushes. I don't and that is just what she hates.

Yours, Anne

Monday, 28 September, 1942

Dear Kitty,

I had to stop yesterday, long before I'd finished. I just must tell you about another quarrel, but before I start on that, something else.

Why do grownups quarrel so easily, so much, and over the most idiotic things? Up till now I thought that only children squabbled and that that wore off as you grew up. Of course, there is sometimes a real reason for a quarrel, but this is just plain bickering. I suppose I should get used to it. But I can't nor do I think I shall, as long as I am the subject of nearly every discussion (they use the word "discussion" instead of quarrel). Nothing, I repeat, nothing about me is right; my general appearance, my character, my manners are discussed from A to Z. I'm expected (by order) to simply swallow all the harsh words and shouts in silence and I am not used to this. In fact, I can't! I'm not going to take all these insults lying down, I'll show them that Anne Frank wasn't born yesterday. Then they'll be surprised and perhaps they'll keep their mouths shut when I let them see that I am going to start educating them. Shall I take up that attitude? Plain barbarism! I'm simply amazed again and again over their awful manners and especially . . . stupidity (Mrs. Van Daan's), but as soon as I get used to this—and it won't be long—then I'll give them some of their own back, and no half measures. Then they'll change their tune!

Am I really so bad-mannered, conceited, headstrong, pushing, stupid, lazy, etc., etc., as they all say? Oh, of course not.

I have my faults, just like everyone else, I know that, but they thoroughly exaggerate everything.

Kitty, if only you knew how I sometimes boil under so many gibes and jeers. And I don't know how long I shall be able to stifle my rage. I shall just blow up one day.

Still, no more of this, I've bored you long enough with all these quarrels. But I simply must tell you of one highly interesting discussion at table. Somehow or other, we got on to the subject of Pim's (Daddy's nickname) extreme modesty. Even the most stupid people have to admit this about Daddy. Suddenly Mrs. Van Daan says, "I too, have an unassuming nature, more so than my husband."

Did you ever! This sentence in itself shows quite clearly how thoroughly forward and pushing she is! Mr. Van Daan thought he ought to give an explanation regarding the reference to himself. "I don't wish to be modest—in my experience it does not pay." Then to me: "Take my advice, Anne, don't be too unassuming, it doesn't get you anywhere."

Mummy agreed with this too. But Mrs. Van Daan had to add, as always, her ideas on the subject. Her next remark was addressed to Mummy and Daddy. "You have a strange outlook on life. Fancy saying such a thing to Anne; it was very different when I was young. And I feel sure that it still is, except in your modern home." This was a direct hit at the way Mummy brings up her daughters.

Mrs. Van Daan was scarlet by this time. Mummy calm and cool as a cucumber. People who blush get so hot and excited, it is quite a handicap in such a situation. Mummy, still entirely unruffled, but anxious to close the conversation as soon as possible, thought for a second and then said: "I find, too, Mrs. Van Daan, that one gets on better in life if one is not overmodest. My husband, now, and Margot, and Peter are exceptionally modest, whereas your husband, Anne, you, and I, though not exactly the opposite, don't allow ourselves to be completely pushed to one side." Mrs. Van Daan: "But, Mrs. Frank, I don't understand you; I'm so very modest and retiring, how can you think of calling me anything else?" Mummy: "I did not say you were exactly forward, but no one could say you had a retiring disposition." Mrs. Van Daan: "Let us get this matter cleared up, once and for all. I'd like to know in what way I am pushing? I know one thing, if I didn't look after myself, I'd soon be starving."

This absurd remark in self-defense just made Mummy rock with laughter. That irritated Mrs. Van Daan, who added a string of German-Dutch, Dutch-German expressions, until she became completely tongue-tied; then she rose from her chair and was about to leave the room.

Suddenly her eye fell on me. You should have seen her. Unfortunately, at the very moment that she turned round, I was shaking my head sorrowfully—not on purpose, but quite involuntarily, for I had been following the whole conversation so closely.

Mrs. Van Daan turned round and began to reel off a lot of harsh German, common, and ill-mannered, just like a coarse, red-faced fishwife—it was a marvelous sight. If I could draw, I'd have liked to catch her like this; it was a scream, such a stupid, foolish little person!

Anyhow, I've learned one thing now. You only really get to know people when you've had a jolly good row with them. Then and then only can you judge their true characters!

Yours, Anne

Tuesday, 29 September, 1942

Dear Kitty,

Extraordinary things can happen to people who go into hiding. Just imagine, as there is no bath, we use a washtub and because there is hot water in the office (by which I always mean the whole of the lower floor) all seven of us take it in turns to make use of this great luxury.

But because we are all so different and some are more modest than others, each member of the family has found his own place for carrying out the performance. Peter uses the kitchen in spite of its glass door. When he is going to have a bath, he goes to each one of us in turn and tells us that we must not walk past the kitchen for half an hour. He seems to think this is sufficient. Mr. Van Daan goes right upstairs; to him it is worth the bother of carrying hot water all that way, so as to have the seclusion of his own room. Mrs. Van Daan simply doesn't bathe at all at present; she is waiting to see which is the best place. Daddy has his bath in the private office, Mummy behind a fire guard in the kitchen; Margot and I have chosen the front office for our scrub. The curtains there are drawn on Saturday afternoons, so we wash ourselves in semi-darkness.

However, I don't like this place any longer, and since last week I've been on the lookout for more comfortable quarters. Peter gave me an idea and that was to try the large office W.C. There I can sit down, have the light on, lock the door, pour my own bath water away, and I'm safe from prying eyes.

I tried my beautiful bathroom on Sunday for the first time and although it sounds mad, I think it is the best place of all. Last week the plumber was at work downstairs to move the drains and water pipes from the office W.C. to the passage. This change is a precaution against frozen pipes, in case we should have a cold winter. The plumber's visit was far from pleasant for us. Not only were we unable to draw water the whole day, but we could not go to the W.C. either. Now it is rather indecent to tell you what we did to overcome this difficulty, however, I'm not such a prude that I can't talk about these things.

The day we arrived here, Daddy and I improvised a pottie for ourselves; not having a better receptacle, we sacrificed a glass preserving jar for this purpose. During the plumber's visit, nature's offerings were deposited in these jars in the sitting room during the day. I don't think this was nearly as bad as having to sit still and not talk the whole day. You can't imagine what a trial that was for "Miss Quack-Quack." I have to whisper on ordinary days; but not being able to speak or move was ten times worse. After being flattened by three days of continuous sitting, my bottom was very stiff and painful. Some exercises at bedtime helped.

                                                                Yours, Anne

Thursday, 1 October, 1942

Dear Kitty,

I got a terrible shock yesterday. Suddenly at eight o'clock the bell rang loudly. Of course, I thought that someone had come: you'll guess who I mean. But I calmed down a bit when everyone said it must be some urchins or perhaps the postman.

The days are becoming very quiet here. Lewin, a small Jewish chemist and dispenser, works for Mr. Kraler in the kitchen. He knows the whole building well and therefore we are always afraid that he'll take it into his head to have a peep in the old laboratory. We are as quiet as mice. Who, three months ago, would ever have guessed that quicksilver Anne would have to sit still for hours—and, what's more, could?

The twenty-ninth was Mrs. Van Daan's birthday. Although it could not be celebrated in a big way, we managed a little party in her honor, with a specially nice meal, and she received some small presents and flowers. Red carnations from her husband; that seems to be a family tradition. To pause for a moment on the subject of Mrs. Van Daan, I must tell you that her attempts to flirt with Daddy are a source of continual irritation for me. She strokes his face and hair, pulls her skirt right up, and makes so-called witty remarks, trying in this way to attract Pim's attention. Pim, thank goodness, doesn't find her either attractive or funny, so he doesn't play ball. Mummy doesn't behave like that with Mr. Van Daan, I've said that to Mrs. Van Daan's face.

Now and then Peter comes out of his shell and can be quite funny. We have one thing in common, from which everyone usually gets a lot of amusement: we both love dressing up. He appeared in one of Mrs. Van Daan's very narrow dresses and I put on his suit. He wore a hat and I a cap. The grownups were doubled up with laughter and we enjoyed ourselves as much as they did. Elli has bought new skirts for Margot and me at Bijenkorf's. The material is rotten, just like sacking, and they cost 24.00 florins and 7.50 florins respectively. What a difference compared with before the war!

Another nice thing I've been keeping up my sleeve. Elli has

written to some secretarial school or other and ordered a correspondence course in shorthand for Margot, Peter, and me. You wait and see what perfect experts we shall be by next year. In any case it's extremely important to be able to write in a code.

Yours, Anne

Saturday, 3 October, 1942

Dear Kitty,

There was another dust-up yesterday. Mummy kicked up a frightful row and told Daddy just what she thought of me. Then she had an awful fit of tears so, of course, off I went too; and I'd got such an awful headache anyway. Finally I told Daddy that I'm much more fond of him than Mummy, to which he replied that I'd get over that. But I don't believe it. I have to simply force myself to stay calm with her. Daddy wishes that I would sometimes volunteer to help Mummy, when she doesn't feel well or has a headache; but I shan't. I am working hard at my French and am now reading *La Belle Nivernaise*.

Yours, Anne

Friday, 9 October, 1942

Dear Kitty,

I've only got dismal and depressing news for you today. Our many Jewish friends are being taken away by the dozen. These people are treated by the Gestapo without a shred of decency, being loaded into cattle trucks and sent to Westerbork, the big Jewish camp in Drente. Westerbork sounds terrible: only one washing cubicle for a hundred people and not nearly enough lavatories. There is no separate accommodation. Men, women, and children all sleep together. One hears of frightful immorality because of this;

and a lot of the women, and even girls, who stay there any length of time are expecting babies.

It is impossible to escape; most of the people in the camp are branded as inmates by their shaven heads and many also by their Jewish appearance.

If it is as bad as this in Holland whatever will it be like in the distant and barbarous regions they are sent to? We assume that most of them are murdered. The English radio speaks of their being gassed.

Perhaps that is the quickest way to die. I feel terribly upset. I couldn't tear myself away while Miep told these dreadful stories; and she herself was equally wound up for that matter. Just recently for instance, a poor old crippled Jewess was sitting on her doorstep; she had been told to wait there by the Gestapo, who had gone to fetch a car to take her away. The poor old thing was terrified by the guns that were shooting at English planes overhead, and by the glaring beams of the searchlights. But Miep did not dare take her in; no one would undergo such a risk. The Germans strike without the slightest mercy. Elli too is very quiet: her boy friend has got to go to Germany. She is afraid that the airmen who fly over our homes will drop their bombs, often weighing a million kilos, on Dirk's head. Jokes such as "he's not likely to get a million" and "it only takes one bomb" are in rather bad taste. Dirk is certainly not the only one who has to go: trainloads of boys leave daily. If they stop at a small station en route, sometimes some of them manage to get out unnoticed and escape; perhaps a few manage it. This, however, is not the end of my bad news. Have you ever heard of hostages? That's the latest thing in penalties for sabotage. Can you imagine anything so dreadful?

Prominent citizens—innocent people—are thrown into prison to await their fate. If the saboteur can't be traced, the Gestapo simply put about five hostages against the wall. Announcements of their deaths appear in the papers frequently. These outrages are described as "fatal accidents." Nice people, the Germans! To think that I was once one of them too! No, Hitler took away our nationality long ago.

In fact, Germans and Jews are the greatest enemies in the world.

Yours, Anne

Friday, 16 October, 1942

Dear Kitty,

I'm terribly busy. I've just translated a chapter out of *La Belle Nivernaise* and made notes of new words. Then a perfectly foul math problem and three pages of French grammar. I flatly refuse to do these math problems every day. Daddy agrees that they're vile. I'm almost better at them than he is, though neither of us are much good and we often have to fetch Margot. I'm the furthest on of the three of us in shorthand.

Yesterday I finished *The Assault*. It's quite amusing, but doesn't touch *Joop ter Heul*. As a matter of fact, I think Cissy van Marxveldt is a first-rate writer. I shall definitely let my children read her books. Mummy, Margot, and I are as thick as thieves again. It's really much better. Margot and I got in the same bed together last evening; it was a frightful squash, but that was just the fun of it. She asked if she could read my diary. I said "Yes—at least, bits of it"; and then I asked if I could read hers and she said "Yes." Then we got on to the subject of the future. I asked her what she wanted to be. But she wouldn't say and made a great secret of it. I gathered something about teaching; I'm not sure if I'm right, but I think so. Really, I shouldn't be so curious!

This morning I was lying on Peter's bed, having chased him off at first. He was furious with me, not that I cared very much. He might be a bit more friendly with me for once; after all I did give him an apple yesterday.

I asked Margot if she thought I was very ugly. She said that I was quite attractive and that I had nice eyes. Rather vague, don't you think?

Till next time,

Yours, Anne

Tuesday, 20 October, 1942

Dear Kitty,

My hand still shakes, although it's two hours since we had the shock. I should explain that there are five fire extinguishers in the house. We knew that someone was coming to fill them, but no one had warned us when the carpenter, or whatever you call him, was coming.

The result was that we weren't making any attempt to keep quiet, until I heard hammering outside on the landing opposite our cupboard door. I thought of the carpenter at once and warned Elli, who was having a meal with us, that she shouldn't go downstairs. Daddy and I posted ourselves at the door so as to hear when the man left. After he'd been working for a quarter of an hour, he laid his hammer and tools down on top of our cupboard (as we thought) and knocked at our door. We turned absolutely white. Perhaps he had heard something after all and wanted to investigate our secret den. It seemed like it. The knocking, pulling, pushing, and wrenching went on. I nearly fainted at the thought that this utter stranger might discover our beautiful secret hiding place. And just as I thought my last hour was at hand, I heard Mr. Koophuis say, "Open the door, it's only me." We opened it immediately. The hook that holds the cupboard, which can be undone by people who know the secret, had got jammed. That was why no one had been able to warn us about the carpenter. The man had now gone downstairs and Koophuis wanted to fetch Elli, but couldn't open the cupboard again. It was a great relief to me, I can tell you. In my imagination the man who I thought was trying to get in had been growing and growing in size until in the end he appeared to be a giant and the greatest fascist that ever walked the earth.

Well! Well! Luckily everything was okay this time. Meanwhile we had great fun on Monday. Miep and Henk spent the night here. Margot and I went in Mummy and Daddy's room for the night, so that the Van Santens could have our room. The meal tasted divine. There was one small interruption. Daddy's lamp blew a fuse, and all of a sudden we were sitting in darkness. What was to be done? There was some fuse wire in the house, but the fuse box is right at the very back of the dark storeroom—not such a nice job after dark. Still the men ventured forth and after ten minutes we were able to put the candles away again.

I got up early this morning. Henk had to leave at half past eight. After a cozy breakfast Miep went downstairs. It was pouring and she was glad not to have to cycle to the office. Next week Elli is coming to stay for a night.

Yours, Anne

Thursday, 29 October, 1942

Dear Kitty,

I am awfully worried, Daddy is ill. He has a high temperature and a red rash, it looks like measles. Think of it, we can't even call a doctor! Mummy is letting him have a good sweat. Perhaps that will send his temperature down.

This morning Miep told us that all the furniture has been removed from the Van Daans' home. We haven't told Mrs. Van Daan yet. She's such a bundle of nerves already, and we don't feel like listening to another moan over all the lovely china and beautiful chairs that she left at home. *We* had to leave almost all our nice things behind; so what's the good of grumbling about it now?

I'm allowed to read more grown-up books lately. I'm now reading *Eva's Youth* by Nico van Suchtelen. I can't see much difference between this and the schoolgirl love stories. It is true there are bits about women selling themselves to unknown men in back streets. They ask a packet of money for it. I'd die of shame if anything like that happened to me. Also it says that Eva has a monthly period. Oh, I'm so longing to have it too; it seems so important.

Daddy has brought the plays of Goethe and Schiller from the big cupboard. He is going to read to me every evening. We've started with *Don Carlos*.

Following Daddy's good example, Mummy has pressed

her prayer book into my hand. For decency's sake I read some of the prayers in German; they are certainly beautiful but they don't convey much to me. Why does she force me to be pious, just to oblige her?

Tomorrow we are going to light the fire for the first time. I expect we shall be suffocated with smoke. The chimney hasn't been swept for ages, let's hope the thing draws.

Yours, Anne

Saturday, 7 November, 1942

Dear Kitty,

Mummy is frightfully irritable and that always seems to herald unpleasantness for me. Is it just a chance that Daddy and Mummy never rebuke Margot and that they always drop on me for everything? Yesterday evening, for instance: Margot was reading a book with lovely drawings in it; she got up and went upstairs, put the book down ready to go on with it later. I wasn't doing anything, so picked up the book and started looking at the pictures. Margot came back, saw "her" book in my hands, wrinkled her forehead and asked for the book back. Just because I wanted to look a little further on, Margot got more and more angry. Then Mummy joined in: "Give the book to Margot; she was reading it," she said. Daddy came into the room. He didn't even know what it was all about, but saw the injured look on Margot's face and promptly dropped on me: "I'd like to see what you'd say if Margot ever started looking at one of your books!" I gave way at once, laid the book down, and left the room—offended, as they thought. It so happened I was neither offended nor cross, just miserable. It wasn't right of Daddy to judge without knowing what the squabble was about. I would have given Margot the book myself, and much more quickly, if Mummy and Daddy hadn't interfered. They took Margot's part at once, as though she were the victim of some great injustice.

It's obvious that Mummy would stick up for Margot; she and Margot always do back each other up. I'm so used to that that I'm utterly indifferent to both Mummy's jawing and Margot's moods.

I love them; but only because they are Mummy and Margot. With Daddy it's different. If he holds Margot up as an example, approves of what she does, praises and caresses her, then something gnaws at me inside, because I adore Daddy. He is the one I look up to. I don't love anyone in the world but him. He doesn't notice that he treats Margot differently from me. Now Margot is just the prettiest, sweetest, most beautiful girl in the world. But all the same I feel I have some right to be taken seriously too. I have always been the dunce, the ne'er-do-well of the family, I've always had to pay double for my deeds, first with the scolding and then again because of the way my feelings are hurt. Now I'm not satisfied with this apparent favoritism any more. I want something from Daddy that he is not able to give me.

I'm not jealous of Margot, never have been. I don't envy her good looks or her beauty. It is only that I long for Daddy's real love: not only as his child, but for me—Anne, myself.

I cling to Daddy because it is only through him that I am able to retain the remnant of family feeling. Daddy doesn't understand that I need to give vent to my feelings over Mummy sometimes. He doesn't want to talk about it; he simply avoids anything which might lead to remarks about Mummy's failings. Just the same, Mummy and her failings are something I find harder to bear than anything else. I don't know how to keep it all to myself. I can't always be drawing attention to her untidiness, her sarcasm, and her lack of sweetness, neither can I believe that I'm always in the wrong.

We are exact opposites in everything; so naturally we are bound to run up against each other. I don't pronounce judgment on Mummy's character, for that is something I can't judge. I only look at her as a mother, and she just doesn't succeed in being that to me; I have to be my own mother. I've drawn myself apart from them all; I am my own skipper and later on I shall see where I come to land. All this comes about particularly because I have in my mind's eye an image of what a perfect mother and wife should be; and in her whom I must call "Mother" I find no trace of that image.

I am always making resolutions not to notice Mummy's bad example. I want to see only the good side of her and to seek in myself what I cannot find in her. But it doesn't work; and the worst of it is that neither Daddy nor Mummy understands this gap in my life, and I blame them for it. I wonder if anyone can ever succeed in making their children absolutely content.

Sometimes I believe that God wants to try me, both now and later on; I must become good through my own efforts, without examples and without good advice. Then later on I shall be all the stronger. Who besides me will ever read these letters? From whom but myself shall I get comfort? As I need comforting often, I frequently feel weak, and dissatisfied with myself; my shortcomings are too great. I know this, and every day I try to improve myself, again and again.

My treatment varies so much. One day Anne is so sensible and is allowed to know everything; and the next day I hear that Anne is just a silly little goat who doesn't know anything at all and imagines that she's learned a wonderful lot from books. I'm not a baby or a spoiled darling any more, to be laughed at, whatever she does. I have my own views, plans, and ideas, though I can't put them into words yet. Oh, so many things bubble up inside me as I lie in bed, having to put up with people I'm fed up with, who always misinterpret my intentions. That's why in the end I always come back to my diary. That is where I start and finish, because Kitty is always patient. I'll promise her that I shall persevere, in spite of everything, and find my own way through it all, and swallow my tears. I only wish I could see the results already or occasionally receive encouragement from someone who loves me.

Don't condemn me; remember rather that sometimes I too can reach the bursting point.

Yours, Anne

Monday, 9 November, 1942

Dear Kitty,

Yesterday was Peter's birthday, he was sixteen. He had some nice presents. Among other things a game of Monopoly, a razor, and a lighter. Not that he smokes much; it's really just for show.

The biggest surprise came from Mr. Van Daan when, at one o'clock, he announced that the British had landed in Tunis, Algiers, Casablanca, and Oran. "This is the beginning of the end," everyone was saying, but Churchill, the British Prime Minister, who had probably heard the same thing in England, said: "This is not the end. It is not even the beginning of the end. But it is, perhaps, the end of the beginning." Do you see the difference? There is certainly reason for optimism. Stalingrad, the Russian town which they've already been defending for three months, still hasn't fallen into German hands.

But to return to affairs in our secret den. I must tell you something about our food supply. As you know, we have some real greedy pigs on the top floor. We get our bread from a nice baker, a friend of Koophuis. We don't get so much as we used to at home, naturally. But it's sufficient. Four ration cards have also been bought illegally. Their price is going up all the time; it has now gone up from twenty-seven florins to thirty-three. And all that for a little slip of printed paper! In order to have something in the house that will keep, apart from our 150 tins of vegetables, we have bought 270 pounds of dried peas and beans. They are not all for us, some are for the office people. They are in sacks which hang on hooks in our little passage (inside the hidden door). Owing to the weight of the contents, a few stitches in the sacks burst open. So we decided it would be better to put our winter store in the attic and Peter was given the job of dragging it all up there.

He had managed to get five of the six sacks upstairs intact, and he was just busy pulling up number six, when the bottom seam of the sack split and a shower—no, a positive hailstorm of brown beans came pouring down and rattled down the stairs. There were about fifty pounds in the sack and the noise was enough to waken the dead. Downstairs they thought the old house with all its contents was coming down on them. (Thank God there were no strangers in the house.) It gave Peter a moment's fright. But he was soon roaring with laughter, especially when he saw me standing at the bottom of the stairs, like a little island in the middle of a sea of beans! I was entirely surrounded up to my ankles in beans. Quickly we started to pick them up. But beans are so slippery and small that they seemed to roll into all the possible and impossible corners and holes. Now, every time anyone goes downstairs they bend down once or twice, in order to be able to present Mrs. Van Daan with a handful of beans.

I'd almost forgotten to mention that Daddy is quite better again.

Yours, Anne

P.S. The news has just come over the radio that Algiers has fallen. Morocco, Casablanca, and Oran have been in British hands for several days. Now we're waiting for Tunis.

Tuesday, 10 November, 1942

Dear Kitty,

Great news—we want to take in an eighth person. Yes, really! We've always thought that there was quite enough room and food for one more. We were only afraid of giving Koophuis and Kraler more trouble. But now that the appalling stories we hear about Jews are getting even worse, Daddy got hold of the two people who had to decide, and they thought it was an excellent plan. "It is just as dangerous for seven as for eight," they said, and quite rightly. When this was settled, we ran through our circle of friends, trying to think of a single person who would fit in well with our "family." It wasn't difficult to hit on someone. After Daddy had refused all members of the Van Daan family, we chose a

dentist called Albert Dussel, whose wife was fortunate enough
to be out of the country when war broke out. He is known
to be quiet, and so far as we and Mr. Van Daan can judge
from a superficial acquaintance, both families think he is a
congenial person. Miep knows him too, so she will be able to
make arrangements for him to join us. If he comes, he will
have to sleep in my room instead of Margot, who will use the
camp bed.

Yours, Anne

Thursday, 12 November, 1942

Dear Kitty,
Dussel was awfully pleased when Miep told him that she
had got a hiding place for him. She urged him to come as
soon as possible. Preferably Saturday. He thought that this
was rather doubtful, since he had to bring his card index up
to date first, see to a couple of patients, and settle his accounts. Miep came to us with this news this morning. We
thought it was unwise of him to put it off. All these preparations entail explanations to a number of people, whom we
would rather keep out of it. Miep is going to ask if he can't
manage to come on Saturday after all.

Dussel said no; now he is coming on Monday. I must say I
think it's pretty crazy that he doesn't jump at the proposal—
whatever it is. If he were to get picked up outside, would he
still be able to do his card index, settle his finances, and see to
his patients? Why delay then? I think it's stupid of Daddy to
have given in. No other news——

Yours, Anne

Tuesday, 17 November, 1942

Dear Kitty,
Dussel has arrived. All went well. Miep had told him that
he must be at a special place in front of the Post Office at
eleven o'clock, where a man would meet him. Dussel was

standing at the rendezvous dead on time. Mr. Koophuis, who knows Dussel too, went up to him and told him that the said gentleman could not come, but asked whether he would just go to Miep at the office. Koophuis got into a tram and went back to the office, while Dussel walked in the same direction. At twenty past eleven Dussel tapped at the office door. Miep helped him off with his coat, so that the yellow star would not be seen, and took him to the private office, where Koophuis engaged him in conversation until the charwoman had gone. Then Miep went upstairs with Dussel under the pretext that the private office was needed for something, opened the swinging cupboard, and stepped inside before the eyes of the dumfounded Dussel.

We all sat around the table upstairs, waiting with coffee and cognac to greet the newcomer. Miep showed him into our sitting room first. He recognized our furniture at once, and had not the remotest idea that we were there, above his head. When Miep told him he nearly passed out with surprise. But luckily Miep didn't give him much time and took him straight upstairs.

Dussel sank into a chair, speechless, and looked at us all for a while, as if he had to really take it all in first. After a while he stuttered "But . . . *aber, sind* you not in Belgium then? *Ist der Militar nicht* come, *das Auto,* the escape is *sie nicht* successful?"

We explained everything to him, that we had spread the story about the soldiers and the car on purpose to put people, and especially the Germans, on the wrong track, should they try to find us.

Dussel was again struck dumb by such ingenuity and, when he had explored further our superpractical exquisite little "Secret Annexe," he could do nothing but gaze about him in astonishment.

We all had lunch together. Then he had a little nap and joined us for tea, tidied up his things a bit (Miep had brought them beforehand), and began to feel more at home. Especially when he received the following typed "Secret Annexe Rules" (Van Daan product).

PROSPECTUS AND GUIDE TO THE "SECRET ANNEXE"

Special institution as temporary residence
for Jews and suchlike.

Open all the year round. Beautiful, quiet, free from woodland
surroundings, in the heart of Amsterdam. Can be reached
by trams 13 and 17, also by car or bicycle. In special cases
also on foot, if the Germans prevent the use of transport.

Board and lodging: Free.

Special fat-free diet.

Running water in the bathroom (alas, no bath) and down various
inside and outside walls.

Ample storage room for all types of goods.

Own radio center, direct communication with London, New
York, Tel Aviv, and numerous other stations. This ap-
pliance is only for residents' use after six o'clock in the evening. No stations are forbidden, on the understanding that
German stations are only listened to in special cases, such
as classical music and the like.

Rest hours: 10 o'clock in the evening until 7:30 in the morning.
10:15 on Sundays. Residents may rest during the day, conditions permitting, as the directors indicate. For reasons of
public security rest hours must be strictly observed! !

Holidays (outside the home): postponed indefinitely.

Use of language: Speak softly at all times, by order! All civilized
languages are permitted, therefore no German!

Lessons: One written shorthand lesson per week. English, French,
Mathematics, and History at all times.

Small Pets—Special Department (permit is necessary): Good
treatment available (vermin excepted).

Mealtimes: breakfast, every day except Sundays and Bank Holidays, 9 A.M. Sundays and Bank Holidays, 11:30 A.M. approximately.

Lunch: (not very big): 1:15 P.M. to 1:45 P.M.

Dinner: cold and/or hot: no fixed time (depending on the news
broadcast).

Duties: Residents must always be ready to help with office work.

Baths: The washtub is available for all residents from 9 A.M. on
Sundays. The W.C. kitchen, private office or main office,
whichever preferred, are available.

Alcoholic Beverages: only with doctor's prescription.

END

Yours, Anne

Thursday, 19 November, 1942

Dear Kitty,

Dussel is a very nice man, just as we had all imagined. Of course he thought it was all right to share my little room.

Quite honestly I'm not so keen that a stranger should use my things, but one must be prepared to make some sacrifices for a good cause, so I shall make my little offering with a good will. "If we can save someone, then everything else is of secondary importance," says Daddy, and he's absolutely right.

The first day that Dussel was here, he immediately asked me all sorts of questions: When does the charwoman come? When can one use the bathroom? When is one allowed to use the lavatory? You may laugh, but these things are not so simple in a hiding place. During the day we mustn't make any noise that might be heard downstairs; and if there is some stranger—such as the charwoman for example—then we have to be extra careful. I explained all this carefully to Dussel. But one thing amazed me: he is very slow on the uptake. He asks everything twice over and still doesn't seem to remember. Perhaps that will wear off in time, and it's only that he's thoroughly upset by the sudden change.

Apart from that, all goes well. Dussel has told us a lot about the outside world, which we have missed for so long now. He had very sad news. Countless friends and acquaintances have gone to a terrible fate. Evening after evening the green and gray army lorries trundle past. The Germans ring at every front door to inquire if there are any Jews living in the house. If there are, then the whole family has to go at once. If they don't find any, they go on to the next house. No one has a chance of evading them unless one goes into hiding. Often they go around with lists, and only ring when they know they can get a good haul. Sometimes they let them off for cash—so much per head. It seems like the slave hunts of olden times. But it's certainly no joke; it's much too tragic for that. In the evenings when it's dark, I often see rows of good, innocent people accompanied by crying children, walking on and on, in charge of a couple of these chaps, bullied

and knocked about until they almost drop. No one is spared
—old people, babies, expectant mothers, the sick—each and
all join in the march of death.

How fortunate we are here, so well cared for and undisturbed. We wouldn't have to worry about all this misery were
it not that we are so anxious about all those dear to us whom
we can no longer help.

I feel wicked sleeping in a warm bed, while my dearest
friends have been knocked down or have fallen into a gutter
somewhere out in the cold night. I get frightened when I
think of close friends who have now been delivered into the
hands of the cruelest brutes that walk the earth. And all because they are Jews!

Yours, Anne

Friday, 20 November, 1942

Dear Kitty,

None of us really knows how to take it all. The news about
the Jews had not really penetrated through to us until now,
and we thought it best to remain as cheerful as possible.
Every now and then, when Miep lets out something about
what has happened to a friend, Mummy and Mrs. Van Daan
always begin to cry, so Miep thinks it better not to tell us any
more. But Dussel was immediately plied with questions from
all sides, and the stories he told us were so gruesome and
dreadful that one can't get them out of one's mind.

Yet we shall still have our jokes and tease each other, when
these horrors have faded a bit in our minds. It won't do us
any good, or help those outside, to go on being as gloomy as
we are at the moment. And what would be the object of making our "Secret Annexe" into a "Secret Annexe of Gloom"?
Must I keep thinking about those other people, whatever I
am doing? And if I want to laugh about something, should I
stop myself quickly and feel ashamed that I am cheerful?
Ought I then to cry the whole day long? No, that I can't do.
Besides, in time this gloom will wear off.

Added to this misery there is another, but of a purely per-

sonal kind; and it pales into insignificance beside all the
wretchedness I've just told you about. Still, I can't refrain
from telling you that lately I have begun to feel deserted. I
am surrounded by too great a void. I never used to feel like
this, my fun and amusements, and my girl friends, completely
filled my thoughts. Now I either think about unhappy things,
or about myself. And at long last I have made the discovery
that Daddy, although he's such a darling, still cannot take
the place of my entire little world of bygone days. But why
do I bother you with such foolish things? I'm very ungrateful, Kitty; I know that. But it often makes my head swim if
I'm jumped upon too much, and then on top of that have to
think about all those other miseries!

                                             Yours, Anne

                        Saturday, 28 November, 1942

Dear Kitty,
    We have used too much electricity, more than our ration.
Result: the utmost economy and the prospect of having it
cut off. No light for a fortnight; a pleasant thought, that, but
who knows, perhaps it won't happen after all! It's too dark to
read in the afternoons after four or half past. We pass the
time in all sorts of crazy ways: asking riddles, physical train-
ing in the dark, talking English and French, criticizing books.
But it all begins to pall in the end. Yesterday evening I discovered something new: to peer through a powerful pair of
field glasses into the lighted rooms of the houses at the back.
In the daytime we can't allow even as much as a centimeter's
chink to appear between our curtains, but it can't do any
harm after dark. I never knew before that neighbors could be
such interesting people. At any rate, ours are. I found one
couple having a meal, one family was in the act of taking a
home movie; and the dentist opposite was just attending to
an old lady, who was awfully scared.
    It was always said about Mr. Dussel that he could get on
wonderfully with children and that he loved them all. Now

he shows himself in his true colors; a stodgy, old-fashioned disciplinarian, and preacher of long, drawn-out sermons on manners.

As I have the unusual good fortune (!) to share my bedroom—alas, a small one—with His Lordship, and as I'm generally considered to be the most badly behaved of the three young people, I have a lot to put up with and have to pretend to be deaf in order to escape the old, much-repeated tickings-off and warnings. All this wouldn't be too bad, if he wasn't such a frightful sneak and he didn't pick on Mummy of all people to sneak to every time. When I've already just had a dose from him, Mummy goes over it all again, so I get a gale aft as well as fore. Then, if I'm really lucky, I'm called on to give an account of myself to Mrs. Van Daan and then I get a veritable hurricane!

Honestly, you needn't think it's easy to be the "badly brought-up" central figure of a hypercritical family in hiding. When I lie in bed at night and think over the many sins and shortcomings attributed to me, I get so confused by it all that I either laugh or cry: it depends what sort of mood I am in.

Then I fall asleep with a stupid feeling of wishing to be different from what I am or from what I want to be; perhaps to behave differently from the way I want to behave, or do behave. Oh, heavens above, now I'm getting you in a muddle too. Forgive me, but I don't like crossing things out, and in these days of paper shortage we are not allowed to throw paper away. Therefore I can only advise you not to read the last sentence again, and certainly not to try to understand it, because you won't succeed anyhow!

Yours, Anne

Monday, 7 December, 1942

Dear Kitty,

Chanuka and St. Nicholas Day came almost together this year—just one day's difference. We didn't make much fuss about Chanuka: we just gave each other a few little presents and then we had the candles. Because of the shortage of candles we only had them alight for ten minutes, but it is all right as long as you have the song. Mr. Van Daan has made a wooden candlestick, so that too was all properly arranged.

Saturday, the evening of St. Nicholas Day, was much more fun. Miep and Elli had made us very inquisitive by whispering all the time with Daddy, so naturally we guessed that something was on.

And so it was. At eight o'clock we all filed down the wooden staircase through the passage in pitch-darkness (it made me shudder and wish that I was safely upstairs again) into the little dark room. There, as there are no windows, we were able to turn on a light. When that was done, Daddy opened the big cupboard. "Oh! how lovely," we all cried. A large basket decorated with St. Nicholas paper stood in the corner and on top there was a mask of Black Peter.

We quickly took the basket upstairs with us. There was a nice little present for everyone, with a suitable poem attached. I got a doll, whose skirt is a bag for odds and ends; Daddy got book ends, and so on. In any case it was a nice idea and as none of us had ever celebrated St. Nicholas, it was a good way of starting.

Yours, Anne

Thursday, 10 December, 1942

Dear Kitty,

Mr. Van Daan used to be in the meat, sausage, and spice business. It was because of his knowledge of this trade that he was taken on in Daddy's business. Now he is showing the sausagy side of himself, which, for us, is by no means disagreeable.

We had ordered a lot of meat (under the counter, of course) for preserving in case we should come upon hard times. It was fun to watch, first the way the pieces of meat went through the mincer, two or three times, then how all the accompanying ingredients were mixed with the minced meat, and then how the intestine was filled by means of a spout, to make the sausages. We fried the sausage meat and ate it with sauerkraut for supper that evening, but the Gelderland sausages had to be thoroughly dried first, so we hung them over a stick tied to the ceiling with string. Everyone who came into the room began to laugh when they caught a glimpse of the row of sausages on show. They looked terribly funny!

The room was in a glorious mess. Mr. Van Daan was wearing one of his wife's aprons swathed round his substantial person (he looked fatter than he is!) and was busy with the meat. Hands smothered in blood, red face, and the soiled apron, made him look like a butcher. Mrs. Van Daan was trying to do everything at once, learning Dutch from a book, stirring the soup, watching the meat being done, sighing and complaining about her injured rib. That's what happens to elderly ladies (!) who do such idiotic exercises to reduce their large behinds!

Dussel had inflammation in one eye and was bathing it with camomile tea by the fire. Pim, who was sitting on a chair in a beam of sunlight that shone through the window, kept being pushed from one side to the other. In addition, I think his rheumatism was bothering him, because he sat rather hunched up with a miserable look on his face, watching Mr. Van Daan at work. He looked exactly like some shriveled-up old man from an old people's home. Peter was doing acrobatics round the room with his cat. Mummy, Margot, and I were peeling potatoes; and, of course, all of us were doing everything wrong because we were so busy watching Mr. Van Daan.

Dussel has opened his dental practice. For the fun of it, I must tell you about his first patient. Mummy was ironing; and Mrs. Van Daan was the first to face the ordeal. She went and sat on a chair in the middle of the room. Dussel began to unpack his case in an awfully important way, asked for some eau de cologne as a disinfectant and vaseline to take the place of wax.

He looked in Mrs. Van Daan's mouth and found two teeth

which, when touched, just made her crumple up as if she was
going to pass out, uttering incoherent cries of pain. After a
lengthy examination (in Mrs. Van Daan's case, lasting in
actual fact not more than two minutes) Dussel began to
scrape away at one of the holes. But, no fear—it was out of
the question—the patient flung her arms and legs about
wildly in all directions until at one point Dussel let go of the
scraper—that remained stuck in Mrs. Van Daan's tooth.

Then the fat was really in the fire! She cried (as far as it
was possible with such an instrument in one's mouth), tried
to pull the thing out of her mouth, and only succeeded in
pushing it further in. Mr. Dussel stood with his hands against
his sides calmly watching the little comedy. The rest of the
audience lost all control and roared with laughter. It was
rotten of us, because I for one am quite sure that I should
have screamed even louder. After much turning, kicking,
screaming, and calling out, she got the instrument free at last
and Mr. Dussel went on with his work, as if nothing had happened!

This he did so quickly that Mrs. Van Daan didn't have
time to start any fresh tricks. But he'd never had so much
help in all his life before. Two assistants are pretty useful:
Van Daan and I performed our duties well. The whole scene
looked like a picture from the Middle Ages entitled "A
Quack at Work." In the meantime, however, the patient
hadn't much patience; she had to keep an eye on "her" soup
and "her" meal. One thing is certain. Mrs. Van Daan won't
be in such a hurry to allow herself to be treated again!

                                                    Yours, Anne

Sunday, 13 December, 1942

Dear Kitty,

I'm sitting cozily in the main office, looking outside
through a slit in the curtain. It is dusk but still just light
enough to write to you.

It is a very queer sight, as I watch the people walking by;
it looks just as if they are all in a terrible hurry and nearly

trip over their own toes. With cyclists, now, one simply can't keep pace with their speed. I can't even see what sort of person is riding on the machine.

The people in this neighborhood don't look very attractive. The children especially are so dirty you wouldn't want to touch them with a barge pole. Real slum kids with running noses. I can hardly understand a word they say.

Yesterday afternoon Margot and I were having a bath here and I said, "Supposing we were to take the children who are walking past, one by one, hoist them up with a fishing rod, give them each a bath, wash and mend their clothes, and then let them go again, then . . ." Margot interrupted me, "By tomorrow they would look just as filthy and ragged as before."

But I'm just talking nonsense; besides, there are other things to see—cars, boats, and rain. I like particularly the screech of the trams as they go by.

There is no more variety in our thoughts than there is for ourselves. They go round and round like a roundabout—from Jews to food and from food to politics. By the way, talking of Jews, I saw two Jews through the curtain yesterday. I could hardly believe my eyes; it was a horrible feeling, just as if I'd betrayed them and was now watching them in their misery. There is a houseboat immediately opposite, where a bargeman lives with his family. He has a small yapping dog. We only know the little dog by his bark and his tail, which we can see when he runs round the deck. Ugh! Now it's started to rain and most of the people are hidden under umbrellas. I see nothing but raincoats and occasionally the back of someone's hat. Really I don't need to see more. I'm gradually getting to know all the women at a glance, blown out with potatoes, wearing a red or a green coat, trodden-down heels and with a bag under their arms. Their faces either look grim or kind—depending on their husbands' dispositions.

Yours, Anne

Tuesday, 22 December, 1942

Dear Kitty,

The "Secret Annexe" has heard the joyful news that each person will receive an extra quarter of a pound of butter for Christmas. It says half a pound in the newspapers, but that's only for the lucky mortals who get their ration books from the government, not for Jews who have gone into hiding, who can only afford to buy four illegal ration books, instead of eight.

We are all going to bake something with our butter. I made some biscuits and two cakes this morning. Everyone is very busy upstairs and Mummy has told me I must not go there to work or read, until the household jobs are done.

Mrs. Van Daan is in bed with her bruised rib, complains the whole day long, allows herself to be given fresh dressings all the time, and isn't satisfied with anything. I shall be glad when she's on her feet again and tidies up her own things, because I must say this for her; she's exceptionally industrious and tidy, all the while she is healthy in mind and body. She is cheerful too.

Just as if I didn't hear enough "ssh-ssh" during the day, for making too much noise, my gentleman bedroom companion now repeatedly calls out "ssh-ssh" to me at night too. According-ing to him, I am not even allowed to turn over! I refuse to take the slightest notice of him, and shall go "ssh-ssh" back at him the next time.

He makes me furious, on Sundays especially, when he turns the light on early to do his exercises. It seems to take simply hours, while I, poor tormented creature, feel the chairs, which are placed at the head of my bed to lengthen it, slide back-wards and forwards continually under my sleepy head. When he has ended with a couple of violent arm-waving exercises to loosen his muscles, His Lordship begins his toilet. His pants are hanging up, so to and fro he must go to collect them. But he forgets his tie, which is lying on the table. Therefore once more he pushes and bumps past the chairs to get it.

But I won't bore you any longer on the subject of old men.
It won't make things any better and all my plans of revenge
(such as disconnecting the lamp, shutting the door, hiding
his clothes) must be abandoned in order to keep the peace.
Oh, I'm becoming so sensible! One must apply one's reason
to everything here, learning to obey, to hold your tongue, to
help, to be good, to give in, and I don't know what else. I'm
afraid I shall use up all my brains too quickly, and I haven't
got so very many. Then I shall not have any left for when the
war is over.

Yours, Anne

Wednesday, 13 January, 1943

Dear Kitty,
Everything has upset me again this morning, so I wasn't
able to finish a single thing properly.

It is terrible outside. Day and night more of those poor
miserable people are being dragged off, with nothing but a
rucksack and a little money. On the way they are deprived
even of these possessions. Families are torn apart, the men,
women, and children all being separated. Children coming
home from school find that their parents have disappeared.
Women return from shopping to find their homes shut up
and their families gone.

The Dutch people are anxious too, their sons are being sent
to Germany. Everyone is afraid.

And every night hundreds of planes fly over Holland and
go to German towns, where the earth is plowed up by their
bombs, and every hour hundreds and thousands of people are
killed in Russia and Africa. No one is able to keep out of it,
the whole globe is waging war and although it is going better
for the Allies, the end is not yet in sight.

And as for us, we are fortunate. Yes, we are luckier than
millions of people. It is quiet and safe here, and we are, so to
speak, living on capital. We are even so selfish as to talk about
"after the war," brighten up at the thought of having new

clothes and new shoes, whereas we really ought to save every penny, to help other people, and save what is left from the wreckage after the war.

The children here run about in just a thin blouse and clogs; no coat, no hat, no stockings, and no one helps them. Their tummies are empty, they chew an old carrot to stay the pangs, go from their cold homes out into the cold street and, when they get to school, find themselves in an even colder class-room. Yes, it has even got so bad in Holland that countless children stop the passers-by and beg for a piece of bread. I could go on for hours about all the suffering the war has brought, but then I would only make myself more dejected. There is nothing we can do but wait as calmly as we can till the misery comes to an end. Jews and Christians wait, the whole earth waits; and there are many who wait for death.

Yours, Anne

Saturday, 30 January, 1943

Dear Kitty,

I'm boiling with rage, and yet I mustn't show it. I'd like to stamp my feet, scream, give Mummy a good shaking, cry, and I don't know what else, because of the horrible words, mocking looks, and accusations which are leveled at me repeatedly every day, and find their mark, like shafts from a tightly strung bow, and which are just as hard to draw from my body.

I would like to shout to Margot, Van Daan, Dussel—and Daddy too—"Leave me in peace, let me sleep one night at least without my pillow being wet with tears, my eyes burning and my head throbbing. Let me get away from it all, preferably away from the world!" But I can't do that, they mustn't know my despair, I can't let them see the wounds which they have caused, I couldn't bear their sympathy and their kindhearted jokes, it would only make me want to scream all the more. If I talk, everyone thinks I'm showing off; when I'm silent they think I'm ridiculous; rude if I answer, sly if I get a good idea, lazy if I'm tired, selfish if I eat a mouthful more than I should, stupid, cowardly, crafty, etc., etc. The whole day long I hear nothing else but that I am an insufferable baby, and although I laugh about it and pretend not to take any notice, I *do* mind. I would like to ask God to give me a different nature, so that I didn't put everyone's back up. But that can't be done. I've got the nature that has been given to me and I'm sure it can't be bad. I do my very best to please everybody, far more than they'd ever guess. I try to laugh it all off, because I don't want to let them see my trouble. More than once, after a whole string of undeserved rebukes, I have flared up at Mummy: "I don't care what you say anyhow. Leave me alone: I'm a hopeless case anyway." Naturally, I was then told I was rude and was virtually ignored for two days; and then, all at once, it was quite forgotten, and I was treated like everyone else again. It is impossible for me to be all sugar one day and spit venom the next. I'd rather choose the golden mean (which is not so golden), keep my thoughts to myself, and try for *once* to be just as disdainful to them as they are to me. Oh, if only I could!

Yours, Anne

Friday, 5 February, 1943

Dear Kitty,

Although I haven't written anything about our rows for a long time, there still isn't any change. The discord, long accepted by us, struck Mr. Dussel as a calamity at first. But he is getting used to it now and tries not to think about it. Margot and Peter aren't a bit what you would call "young," they are both so staid and quiet. I show up terribly against them and am always hearing, "You don't find Margot and Peter doing that—why don't you follow their example?" I simply loathe it. I might tell you I don't want to be in the least like Margot. She is much too soft and passive for my liking and allows everyone to talk her around, and gives in about everything. I want to be a stronger character! But I keep such ideas to myself: they would only laugh at me, if I came along with this as an explanation of my attitude. The atmosphere at table is usually strained, though luckily the outbursts are sometimes checked by "the soup eaters"! The "soup eaters" are the people from the office who come in and are served with a cup of soup. This afternoon Mr. Van Daan was talking about Margot eating so little again. "I suppose you do it to keep slim," he added, teasing her. Mummy, who always defends Margot, said loudly: "I can't bear your stupid chatter any longer." Mr. Van Daan turned scarlet, looked straight in front of him, and said nothing. We often laugh about things; just recently Mrs. Van Daan came out with some perfect nonsense. She was recalling the past, how well she and her father got on together and what a flirt she was. "And do you know," she went on, "if a man gets a bit aggressive, my father used to say, then you must say to him, 'Mr. So and So, remember I am a lady!' and he will know what you mean." We thought that was a good joke and burst out laughing. Peter too, although usually so quiet, sometimes gives cause for mirth. He is blessed with a passion for foreign words, although he does not always know their meaning. One afternoon we couldn't go to the lavatory because there were visitors in the office; however, Peter had to pay an urgent call. So he didn't pull the plug. He put a notice up on the lavatory door to warn us, with "S.V.P. gas" on it. Of course he meant to put "Beware of gas"; but he thought the other looked more genteel. He hadn't got the faintest notion it meant "if you please."

Yours, Anne

Saturday, 27 February, 1943

Dear Kitty,

Pim is expecting the invasion any day. Churchill has had pneumonia, but is improving slowly. The freedom-loving Gandhi of India is holding his umpteenth fast. Mrs. Van

Daan claims to be fatalistic. But who is the most scared when the guns go off? No one else but Petronella.

Henk brought a copy of the bishop's letter to churchgoers for us to read. It was very fine and inspiring. "Do not rest, people of the Netherlands, everyone is fighting with his own weapons to free the country, the people, and their religion." "Give help, be generous, and do not dismay!" is what they cry from the pulpit, just like that. Will it help? It won't help the people of our religion.

You'd never guess what has happened to us now. The owner of these premises has sold the house without informing Kraler and Koophuis. One morning the new owner arrived with an architect to have a look at the house. Luckily, Mr. Koophuis was present and showed the gentlemen everything except the "Secret Annexe." He professed to have forgotten the key of the communicating door. The new owner didn't question any further. It will be all right as long as he doesn't come back and want to see the "Secret Annexe," because then it won't look too good for us.

Daddy has emptied a card index box for Margot and me, and put cards in it. It is to be a book card system; then we both write down which books we have read, who they are by, etc. I have procured another little notebook for foreign words.

Lately Mummy and I have been getting on better together, but we still *never* confide in each other. Margot is more catty than ever and Daddy has got something he is keeping to himself, but he remains the same darling.

New butter and margarine rationing at table! Each person has their little bit of fat put on their plate. In my opinion the Van Daans don't divide it at all fairly. However, my parents are much too afraid of a row to say anything about it. Pity, I think you should always give people like them tit for tat.

Yours, Anne

Wednesday, 10 March, 1943

Dear Kitty,

We had a short circuit last evening, and on top of that the guns kept banging away all the time. I still haven't got over my fear of everything connected with shooting and planes, and I creep into Daddy's bed nearly every night for comfort. I know it's very childish but you don't know what it is like. The A.A. guns roar so loudly that you can't hear yourself speak. Mrs. Van Daan, the fatalist, was nearly crying, and said in a very timid little voice, "Oh, it is so unpleasant! Oh, they are shooting so hard," by which she really means "I'm so frightened."

It didn't seem nearly so bad by candlelight as in the dark. I was shivering, just as if I had a temperature, and begged Daddy to light the candle again. He was relentless, the light remained off. Suddenly there was a burst of machine-gun fire, and that is ten times worse than guns. Mummy jumped out of bed and, to Pim's annoyance, lit the candle. When he complained her answer was firm: "After all, Anne's not exactly a veteran soldier." And that was the end of it.

Have I already told you about Mrs. Van Daan's other fears? I don't think so. If I am to keep you informed of all that happens in the "Secret Annexe," you must know about this too. One night Mrs. Van Daan thought she heard burglars in the attic; she heard loud footsteps and was so frightened that she woke her husband. Just at that moment the burglars disappeared and the only sounds that Mr. Van Daan could hear were the heartbeats of the frightened fatalist herself. "Oh, Putti [Mr. Van Daan's nickname], they are sure to have taken the sausages and all our peas and beans. And Peter, I wonder if he is still safely in bed?" "They certainly won't have stolen Peter. Listen, don't worry and let me go to sleep." But nothing came of that. Mrs. Van Daan was far too nervous to sleep another wink. A few nights after that the whole Van Daan family was woken by ghostly sounds. Peter went up to the attic with a torch—and scamper—scamper! What do you think it was running away? A swarm of enormous rats! When we knew

who the thieves were, we let Mouschi sleep in the attic and
the uninvited guests didn't come back again; at least not during the night.

Peter went up to the loft a couple of evenings ago to fetch
some old newspapers. He had to hold the trap door firmly to
get down the steps. He put his hand down without looking
. . . and went tumbling down the ladder from the sudden
shock and pain. Without knowing it he had put his hand on
a large rat, and it had bitten him hard. By the time he
reached us, as white as a sheet and with his knees knocking,
the blood had soaked through his pajamas. And no wonder;
it's not very pleasant to stroke a large rat; and to get bitten into
the bargain is really dreadful.

Yours, Anne

Friday, 12 March, 1943

Dear Kitty,

May I introduce someone to you: Mama Frank, champion
of youth! Extra butter for the young; the problems of modern youth; Mummy defends youth in everything and after a
certain amount of squabbling she always gets her way. A bottle of preserved sole has gone bad; gala dinner for Mouschi
and Boche. You haven't met Boche yet, although she was here
before we went into hiding. She is the warehouse and office
cat and keeps down the rats in the storerooms. Her odd political name requires an explanation. For some time the firm
had two cats; one for the warehouse and one for the attic.
Now it occasionally happened that the two cats met; and the
result was always a terrific fight. The aggressor was always
the warehouse cat; yet it was always the attic cat who managed to win—just like among nations. So the storehouse cat
was named the German or "Boche" and the attic cat the English or "Tommy." Tommy was got rid of later; we are all entertained by Boche when we go downstairs.

We have eaten so many kidney beans and haricot beans
that I can't bear the sight of them any more. The mere thought

of them makes me feel quite sick. Bread is no longer served in the evenings now. Daddy has just said that he doesn't feel in a good mood. His eyes look so sad again—poor soul!

I can't drag myself away from a book called *The Knock at the Door* by Ina Boudier-Bakker. The story of the family is exceptionally well written. Apart from that, it is about war, writers, the emancipation of women; and quite honestly I'm not awfully interested.

Horrible air raids on Germany. Mr. Van Daan is in a bad mood; the cause—cigarette shortage. Discussions over the question of whether we should, or should not, use our canned vegetables ended in our favor.

I can't get into a single pair of shoes any more, except ski boots, which are not much use about the house. A pair of rush sandals costing 6.50 florins lasted me just one week, after which they were out of action. Perhaps Miep will scrounge something under the counter. I must cut Daddy's hair. Pim maintains that he will never have another barber after the war, as I do the job so well. If only I didn't snip his ear so often!

Yours, Anne

Thursday, 18 March, 1943

Dear Kitty,

Turkey is in the war. Great excitement. Waiting in suspense for the news.

Yours, Anne

Friday, 19 March, 1943

Dear Kitty,

An hour later joy was followed by disappointment. Turkey is not in the war yet. It was only a cabinet minister talking about them soon giving up their neutrality. A newspaper in the Dam[1] was crying, "Turkey on England's side." The newspapers were torn out of his hands. This is how the joyful news

[1] A square in front of the Royal Palace.

reached us too; 500- and 1000-guilder notes have been declared no longer valid. It is a trap for black marketeers and suchlike, but even more for people who have got other kinds of "black" money, and for people in hiding. If you wish to hand in a 1000-guilder note you must be able to declare, and prove, exactly how you got it. They may still be used to pay taxes, but only until next week. Dussel has received an old-fashioned foot-operated dentist's drill, I expect he'll soon give me a thorough check-over. The "Führer aller Germanen" has been talking to wounded soldiers. Listening-in to it was pitiful. Question and answer went something like this:

"My name is Heinrich Scheppel."

"Wounded where?"

"Near Stalingrad."

"What kind of wound?"

"Two feet frozen off and a broken joint in the left arm."

This is exactly what the frightful puppet show on the radio was like. The wounded seemed to be proud of their wounds —the more the better. One of them felt so moved at being able to shake hands with the Führer (that is, if he still had a hand!) that he could hardly get the words out of his mouth.

Yours, Anne

Thursday, 25 March, 1943

Dear Kitty,

Yesterday Mummy, Daddy, Margot, and I were sitting pleasantly together when suddenly Peter came in and whispered something in Daddy's ear. I heard something about "a barrel fallen over in the warehouse" and "someone fumbling about at the door." Margot had heard it too; but when Daddy and Peter went off immediately, she tried to calm me down a bit, because I was naturally as white as a sheet and very jittery.

The three of us waited in suspense. A minute or two later Mrs. Van Daan came upstairs; she'd been listening to the wireless in the private office. She told us that Pim had asked her to turn off the wireless and go softly upstairs. But you know what that's like, if you want to be extra quiet, then each step of the old stairs creaks twice as loudly. Five minutes later Pim and Peter appeared again, white to the roots of their hair, and told us their experiences.

They had hidden themselves under the stairs and waited, with no result at first. But suddenly, yes, I must tell you, they heard two loud bumps, just as if two doors were banged here in the house. Pim was upstairs in one leap. Peter warned Dussel first, who finally landed upstairs with a lot of fuss and noise. Then we all went up in stockinged feet to the Van Daans on the next floor. Mr. Van Daan had a bad cold and had already gone to bed, so we all drew up closely around his bed and whispered our suspicions to him.

Each time Mr. Van Daan coughed loudly, Mrs. Van Daan and I were so scared that we thought we were going to have a fit. That went on until one of us got the bright idea of giving him some codeine, which soothed the cough at once. Again we waited and waited, but we heard no more and finally we all came to the conclusion that the thieves had taken to their heels when they heard footsteps in the house, which was otherwise so silent.

Now it was unfortunate that the wireless downstairs was still tuned to England, and that the chairs were neatly arranged round it. If the door had been forced, and the air-raid wardens had noticed and warned the police, then the results might have been very unpleasant. So Mr. Van Daan got up and put on his coat and hat and followed Daddy cautiously downstairs, Peter took up the rear, armed with a large hammer in case of emergencies. The ladies upstairs (including Margot and me) waited in suspense, until the gentlemen reappeared five minutes later and told us that all was quiet in the house.

We arranged that we would not draw any water or pull the plug in the lavatory. But as the excitement had affected most of our tummies, you can imagine what the atmosphere was like when we had each paid a visit in succession.

When something like that happens, heaps of other things seem to come at the same time, as now. Number One was that the clock at the Westertoren, which I always find so reassuring, did not strike. Number Two was that, Mr. Vossen having left earlier than usual the previous evening, we didn't know definitely whether Elli had been able to get hold of the key, and had perhaps forgotten to shut the door. It was still evening and we were still in a state of uncertainty, although we certainly did feel a bit reassured by the fact that from about eight o'clock, when the burglar had alarmed the house, until half past ten we had not heard a sound. On further reflection it also seemed very unlikely to us that a thief would have forced open a door so early in the evening, while there were still people about in the street. Moreover, one of us got the idea that it was possible that the caretaker of the warehouse next door was still at work since, in the excitement, and with the thin walls, one can easily make a mistake, and what's more, one's imagination can play a big part at such critical moments.

So we all went to bed; but none of us could get to sleep. Daddy as well as Mummy and Mr. Dussel were awake, and without much exaggeration I can say that I hardly slept a wink. This morning the men went downstairs to see whether the outside door was still shut, and everything turned out to be quite safe. We gave everyone a detailed description of the nerve-racking event. They all made fun of it, but it is easy to laugh at such things afterwards. Elli was the only one who took us seriously.

Yours, Anne

Saturday, 27 March, 1943

Dear Kitty,

We have finished our shorthand course; now we are beginning to practice speed. Aren't we getting clever? I must tell you more about my time-killing subjects (I call them such, because we have got nothing else to do but make the days go by as quickly as possible, so that the end of our time here comes more quickly); I'm mad on Mythology and especially the Gods of Greece and Rome. They think here that it is just a passing craze, they've never heard of an adolescent kid of my age being interested in Mythology. Well, then, I shall be the first!

Mr. Van Daan has a cold, or rather he has a little tickle in his throat. He makes a tremendous fuss about it. Gargling with camomile tea, painting his throat with tincture of myrrh, rubbing eucalyptus all over his chest, nose, teeth, and tongue; and then getting into an evil mood on top of it all.

Rauter, one of the German big shots, has made a speech. "All Jews must be out of the German-occupied countries before July 1. Between April 1 and May 1 the province of Utrecht must be cleaned out [as if the Jews were cockroaches]. Between May 1 and June 1 the provinces of North and South Holland." These wretched people are sent to filthy slaughterhouses like a herd of sick, neglected cattle. But I won't talk about it, I only get nightmares from such thoughts.

One good little piece of news is that the German department of the Labor Exchange has been set on fire by saboteurs. A few days after, the Registrar's Office went the same way. Men in German police uniforms gagged the guards and managed to destroy important papers.

Yours, Anne

Thursday, 1 April, 1943

Dear Kitty,

I'm really not April-fooling (see the date), but the opposite; today I can easily quote the saying: "Misfortunes never come singly." To begin with, Mr. Koophuis, the one who always cheers us up, has had hemorrhage of the stomach and has got to stay in bed for at least three weeks. Secondly, Elli has flu. Thirdly, Mr. Vossen is going to the hospital next week. He has probably got an abdominal ulcer. And fourthly, some important business conferences, the main points of which Daddy had discussed in detail with Mr. Koophuis, were due to be held, but now there isn't time to explain everything thoroughly to Mr. Kraler.

The gentlemen who had been expected duly arrived; even before they came Daddy was trembling with anxiety as to how the talks would go. "If only I could be there, if only I was downstairs," he cried. "Why don't you go and lie with one ear pressed against the floor, then you'll be able to hear everything." Daddy's face cleared, and at half past ten yesterday morning Margot and Pim (two ears are better than one!) took up their positions on the floor. The talks were not finished in the morning, but by the afternoon Daddy was not in a fit state to continue the listening campaign. He was half paralyzed from remaining in so unusual and uncomfortable a position. I took his place at half past two, as soon as we heard voices in the passage. Margot kept me company. The talk at times was so long-winded and boring that quite suddenly I fell asleep on the cold hard linoleum floor. Margot did not dare to touch me for fear they might hear us, and talking was out of the question. I slept for a good half hour and then woke with a shock, having forgotten every word of the important discussions. Luckily Margot had paid more attention.

Yours, Anne

Friday, 2 April, 1943

Dear Kitty,

Oh dear: I've got another terrible black mark against my name. I was lying in bed yesterday evening waiting for Daddy to come and say my prayers with me, and wish me good night, when Mummy came into my room, sat on my bed, and asked very nicely, "Anne, Daddy can't come yet, shall I say your prayers with you tonight?" "No, Mummy," I answered.

Mummy got up, paused by my bed for a moment, and walked slowly towards the door. Suddenly she turned around, and with a distorted look on her face said, "I don't want to be cross, love cannot be forced." There were tears in her eyes as she left the room.

I lay still in bed, feeling at once that I had been horrible to push her away so rudely. But I knew too that I couldn't have answered differently. It simply wouldn't work. I felt sorry for Mummy; very, very sorry, because I had seen for the first time in my life that she minds my coldness. I saw the look of sorrow on her face when she spoke of love not being forced. It is hard to speak the truth, and yet it is the truth: she herself has pushed me away, her tactless remarks and her crude jokes, which I don't find at all funny, have now made me insensitive to any love from her side. Just as I shrink at her hard words, so did her heart when she realized that the love between us was gone. She cried half the night and hardly slept at all. Daddy doesn't look at me and if he does for a second, then I read in his eyes the words: "How can you be so unkind, how can you bring yourself to cause your mother such sorrow?"

They expect me to apologize; but this is something I can't apologize for because I spoke the truth and Mummy will have to know it sooner or later anyway. I seem, and indeed am, indifferent both to Mummy's tears and Daddy's looks, because for the first time they are both aware of something which I have always felt. I can only feel sorry for Mummy, who has now had to discover that I have adopted her own attitude. For myself, I remain silent and aloof; and I shall not shrink from the truth any longer, because the longer it is put off, the more difficult it will be for them when they do hear it.

Yours, Anne

Tuesday, 27 April, 1943

Dear Kitty,

Such quarrels that the whole house thunders! Mummy and I, the Van Daans and Daddy, Mummy and Mrs. Van Daan, everyone is angry with everyone else. Nice atmosphere, isn't it? Anne's usual list of failings has been brought out again and fully ventilated.

Mr. Vossen is already in the Binnengasthuis hospital. Mr. Koophuis is up again, the hemorrhage having stopped sooner than usual. He told us that the Registrar's Office received additional damage from the Fire Service who, instead of just quenching the flames, soaked the whole place with water. I'm glad!

The Carlton Hotel is smashed to bits. Two British planes loaded with incendiary bombs fell right on top of the "Offiziersheim."[1] The whole Vijzelstraat-Singel corner is burned down. The air raids on German towns are growing in strength every day. We don't have a single quiet night. I've got dark rings under my eyes from lack of sleep. Our food is miserable. Dry bread and coffee substitute for breakfast. Dinner: spinach or lettuce for a fortnight on end. Potatoes twenty centimeters long and tasting sweet and rotten. Whoever wants to follow a slimming course should stay in the "Secret Annexe"! They complain bitterly upstairs, but we don't regard it as such a tragedy. All the men who fought in 1940 or were mobilized have been called up to work for "der Führer" as prisoners of war. Suppose they're doing that as a precaution against invasion.

Yours, Anne

Saturday, 1 May, 1943

Dear Kitty,

If I just think of how we live here, I usually come to the conclusion that it is a paradise compared with how other Jews who are not in hiding must be living. Even so, later on, when everything is normal again, I shall be amazed to think that we, who were so spick and span at home, should have sunk to such a low level. By this I mean that our manners have declined. For instance, ever since we have been here, we have had one oilcloth on our table which, owing to so much use, is not one of the cleanest. Admittedly I often try to clean it with a dirty dishcloth, which is more hole than cloth. The table doesn't do

[1] German Officers' Club.

us much credit either, in spite of hard scrubbing. The Van Daans have been sleeping on the same flannelette sheet the whole winter; one can't wash it here because the soap powder we get on the ration isn't sufficient, and besides it's not good enough. Daddy goes about in frayed trousers and his tie is beginning to show signs of wear too. Mummy's corsets have split today and are too old to be repaired, while Margot goes about in a brassiere two sizes too small for her.

Mummy and Margot have managed the whole winter with three vests between them, and mine are so small that they don't even reach my tummy.

Certainly, these are all things which can be overcome. Still, I sometimes realize with a shock: "How are we, now going about in worn-out things, from my pants down to Daddy's shaving brush, ever going to get back to our prewar standards?"

They were banging away so much last night that four times I gathered all my belongings together. Today I have packed a suitcase with the most necessary things for an escape. But Mummy quite rightly says: "Where will you escape to?" The whole of Holland is being punished for the strikes which have been going on in many parts of the country. Therefore a state of siege has been declared and everyone gets one butter coupon less. What naughty little children!

Yours, Anne

Tuesday, 18 May, 1943

Dear Kitty,

I witnessed a terrific air battle between German and British planes. Unfortunately a couple of the Allies had to jump from burning machines. Our milkman, who lives in Halfweg, saw four Canadians sitting by the roadside, one of them spoke fluent Dutch. He asked the milkman to give him a light for his cigarette, and told him that the crew had consisted of six men. The pilot was burned to death, and their fifth man had hidden himself somewhere. The German police came and fetched the four perfectly fit men. I wonder how they managed to have such clear brains after that terrifying parachute trip.

Although it is fairly warm, we have to light our fires every other day, in order to burn vegetable peelings and refuse. We can't put anything in the garbage pails, because we must always think of the warehouse boy. How easily one could be betrayed by being a little careless!

All students who wish either to get their degrees this year, or continue their studies, are compelled to sign that they are in sympathy with the Germans and approve of the New Order. Eighty per cent have refused to go against their consciences. Naturally they had to bear the consequences. All the students who do not sign have to go to a labor camp in Germany. What will be left of the youth of the country if they have all got to do hard labor in Germany? Mummy shut the window last night because of all the banging; I was in Pim's bed. Suddenly Mrs. Van Daan jumped out of bed above us, just as if Mouschi had bitten her. A loud clap followed immediately. It sounded just as if an incendiary bomb had fallen beside my bed. I shrieked out, "Light, light!" Pim turned on the lamp. I expected nothing less than to see the room ablaze within a few minutes. Nothing happened. We all hurried upstairs to see what was going on. Mr. and Mrs. Van Daan had seen a red glow through the open window. He thought that there was a fire in the neighborhood and she thought that our house had caught fire. When the clap came Mrs. Van Daan was already on her feet with her knees knocking. But nothing more happened and we all crept back into our beds.

Before a quarter of an hour had passed the shooting started up again. Mrs. Van Daan sat bolt upright at once and then went downstairs to Mr. Dussel's room, seeking there the rest which she could not find with her spouse. Dussel received her with the words, "Come into my bed, my child!" which sent us off into uncontrollable laughter. The gunfire troubled us no longer, our fear was banished!

Yours, Anne

Sunday, 13 June, 1943

Dear Kitty,

My birthday poem from Daddy is too good to keep from you. As Pim usually writes verses in German, Margot volunteered to translate it. Judge for yourself whether Margot didn't do it brilliantly. After the usual summary of the events of the year, this is how it ran:

> *Though youngest here, you are no longer small,*
> *But life is very hard, since one and all*
> *Aspire to be your teacher, thus and thus:*
> *"We have experience, take a tip from us."*
> *"We know because we did it long ago."*
> *"Elders are always better, you must know."*
> *At least that's been the rule since life began!*
> *Our personal faults are much too small to scan*
> *This makes it easier to criticize*
> *The faults of others, which seem double size.*
> *Please bear with us, your parents, for we try*
> *To judge you fairly and with sympathy.*
> *Correction sometimes take against your will,*
> *Though it's like swallowing a bitter pill,*
> *Which must be done if we're to keep the peace,*
> *While time goes by till all this suffering cease.*
> *You read and study nearly all the day,*
> *Who might have lived in such a different way.*
> *You're never bored and bring us all fresh air.*
> *Your only moan is this: "What can I wear?*
> *I have no knickers, all my clothes are small,*
> *My vest might be a loincloth, that is all!*
> *To put on shoes would mean to cut off toes,*
> *Oh dear, I'm worried by so many woes!"*

There was also a bit about food that Margot could not translate into rhyme, so I shall leave it out. Don't you think my birthday poem is good? I have been thoroughly spoiled in other ways and received a lot of lovely things. Among other things a fat book on my pet subject—the mythology of Greece and Rome. I can't complain of a shortage of sweets either—everyone has broken into their last reserves. As the Benjamin of the family in hiding, I am really more honored than I deserve.

Yours, Anne

Tuesday, 15 June, 1943

Dear Kitty,

Lots of things have happened, but I often think that all my uninteresting chatter bores you very much and that you are glad not to receive too many letters. So I shall give you the news in brief.

Mr. Vossen has not been operated on for his duodenal ulcer. When he was on the operating table and they had opened him up, the doctors saw that he had cancer, which was far too advanced to operate. So they stitched him up again, kept him in bed for three weeks and gave him good food, and finally sent him home again. I do pity him terribly and think it is rotten that we can't go out, otherwise I should certainly visit him frequently to cheer him up. It is a disaster for us that good old Vossen won't be able to keep us in touch with all that goes on, and all he hears in the warehouse. He was our best helper and security adviser; we miss him very much indeed.

It will be our turn to hand in our radio next month. Koophuis has a clandestine baby set at home that he will let us have to take the place of our big Phillips. It certainly is a shame to have to hand in our lovely set, but in a house where people are hiding, one daren't, under any circumstances, take wanton risks and so draw the attention of the authorities. We shall have the little radio upstairs. On top of hidden Jews, clandestine money and clandestine buying, we can add a clandestine radio. Everyone is trying to get hold of an old set and to hand that in instead of their "source of courage." It is really true that as the news from outside gets worse, so the radio with its miraculous voice helps us to keep up our morale and to say again, "Chins up, stick it out, better times will come!"

Yours, Anne

Sunday, 11 July, 1943

Dear Kitty,

To return to the "upbringing" theme for the umpteenth time, I must tell you that I really am trying to be helpful, friendly, and good, and to do everything I can so that the rain of rebukes dies down to a light summer drizzle. It is mighty difficult to be on such model behavior with people you can't bear, especially when you don't mean a word of it. But I do really see that I get on better by shamming a bit, instead of my old habit of telling everyone exactly what I think (although no one ever asked my opinion or attached the slightest importance to it).

I often lose my cue and simply can't swallow my rage at some injustice, so that for four long weeks we hear nothing but an everlasting chatter about the cheekiest and most shameless girl on earth. Don't you think that sometimes I've cause for complaint? It's a good thing I'm not a grouser, because then I might get sour and bad-tempered.

I have decided to let my shorthand go a bit, firstly to give me more time for my other subjects and secondly because of my eyes. I'm so miserable and wretched as I've become very shortsighted and ought to have had glasses for a long time already (phew, what an owl I shall look!) but you know, of course, in hiding one cannot. Yesterday everyone talked of nothing but Anne's eyes, because Mummy had suggested sending me to the oculist with Mrs. Koophuis. I shook in my shoes somewhat at this announcement, for it is no small thing to do. Go out of doors, imagine it, in the street—doesn't bear thinking about! I was petrified at first, then glad. But it doesn't go as easily as that, because all the people who would have to approve such a step could not reach an agreement quickly. All the difficulties and risks had first to be carefully weighed, although Miep would have gone with me straight away.

In the meantime I got out my gray coat from the cupboard, but it was so small that it looked as if it belonged to my younger sister.

I am really curious to know what will come of it all, but I

don't think the plan will come off because the British have landed in Sicily now and Daddy is once again hoping for a "quick finish."

Elli gives Margot and me a lot of office work; it makes us both feel quite important and is a great help to her. Anyone can file away correspondence and write in the sales book, but we take special pains.

Miep is just like a pack mule, she fetches and carries so much. Almost every day she manages to get hold of some vegetables for us and brings everything in shopping bags on her bicycle. We always long for Saturdays when our books come. Just like little children receiving a present.

Ordinary people simply don't know what books mean to us, shut up here. Reading, learning, and the radio are our amusements.

                                                         Yours, Anne

                                               Tuesday, 13 July, 1943

Dear Kitty,

Yesterday afternoon, with Daddy's permission, I asked Dussel whether he would please be so good (being really very polite) as to allow me to use the little table in our room twice a week in the afternoons, from four o'clock till half past five. I sit there every day from half past two till four, while Dussel sleeps, but otherwise the room plus table are out of bounds. Inside, in our common room, there is much too much going on; it is impossible to work there, and besides, Daddy likes to sit at the writing table and work too sometimes.

So it was quite a reasonable request, and the question was put very politely. Now honestly what do you think the very learned Dussel replied: "No." Just plain "No!" I was indignant and refused to be put off like that, so I asked him the reason for his "No." But I was sent away with a flea in my ear. This was the barrage which followed:

"I have to work too, and if I can't work in the afternoons, then there is no time left for me at all. I must finish my task, otherwise I've started it all for nothing. Anyway, you don't work seriously at anything. Your mythology, now just what kind of work is that; knitting and reading are not work either. I am at the table and shall stay there." My reply was:

"Mr. Dussel, I do work seriously and there is nowhere else for me to work in the afternoons. I beg of you to kindly reconsider my request!"

With these words the offended Anne turned her back on the very learned doctor, ignoring him completely. I was seething with rage, and thought Dussel frightfully rude (which he certainly was) and myself very friendly. In the evening when I could get hold of Pim, I told him how it had gone off and discussed what I should do next, because I was not going to give in, and preferred to clear it up myself. Pim told me how I ought to tackle the problem, but warned me that it would be better to leave it till the next day, as I was so het up. I let this advice go to the winds, and waited for Dussel after the dishes were done. Pim sat in the room next to us, which had a calming influence on me. I began: "Mr. Dussel, I don't suppose you see any point in discussing the matter any more, but I must ask you to do so." Dussel then remarked with his sweetest smile: "I am always, and at all times, prepared to discuss this matter, but it has already been settled."

I went on talking, though continually interrupted by Dussel. "When you first came here we arranged that this room should be for both of us; if we were to divide it fairly, you would have the morning and I all the afternoon! But I don't even ask that much, and I think that my two afternoons are really perfectly reasonable." At this Dussel jumped up as if someone had stuck a needle into him. "You can't talk about your rights here at all. And where am I to go, then? I shall ask Mr. Van Daan whether he will build a little compartment in the attic, then I can go and sit there. I simply can't work anywhere. With you one always gets trouble. If your sister Margot, who after all has more reason to ask such a thing, would have come to me with the same questions, I should not think of refusing, but you . . ." Then followed the business about the mythology and the knitting, and Anne was insulted again. However, she did not show it and let Dussel finish speaking: "But you, one simply can't talk to you. You are so outrageously selfish, as long as you can get what you want, you don't mind pushing everyone else to one side, I've never seen such a child. But after all, I suppose I shall be obliged to give you your own way, because otherwise I shall be told later on that Anne Frank failed her exam because Mr. Dussel would not give up the table for her."

It went on and on and finally it was such a torrent I could hardly keep pace with it. At one moment I thought, "In a minute I'll give him such a smack in the face that he'll fly up to the ceiling together with his lies," but the next moment I said to myself, "Keep calm! Such a fellow isn't worth getting worked up about."

After giving final vent to his fury, Master Dussel left the room with an expression of mixed wrath and triumph, his coat stuffed with food. I dashed to Daddy and told him all that he had not already heard of the story. Pim decided to talk to Dussel the same evening, which he did. They talked for over half an hour. The theme of the conversation was something like this: first of all they talked about whether Anne should sit at the table, yes or no. Daddy said that he and Dussel had already discussed the subject once before, when he had professed to agree with Dussel, in order not to put him in the wrong in front of the young. But Daddy had not thought it fair then. Dussel thought that I should not speak as if he was an intruder who tried to monopolize everything, but Daddy stuck up for me firmly over that, because he had heard for himself that I had not breathed a word of such a thing.

To and fro it went, Daddy defending my selfishness and my "trifling" work, Dussel grumbling continually.

Finally, Dussel had to give in after all, and I had the opportunity of working undisturbed until five o'clock for two afternoons a week. Dussel looked down his nose very much, didn't speak to me for two days and still had to go and sit at the table from five till half past—frightfully childish.

A person of fifty-four who is still so pedantic and small-minded must be so by nature, and will never improve.

Yours, Anne

Friday, 16 July, 1943

Dear Kitty,

Burglars again, but real this time! This morning Peter went to the warehouse at seven o'clock as usual, and at once noticed that both the warehouse door and the door opening on to the street were ajar. He told Pim, who tuned the radio in the private office to Germany and locked the door. Then they went upstairs together.

The standing orders for such times were observed as usual: no taps to be turned on; therefore, no washing, silence, everything to be finished by eight o'clock and no lavatory. We were all very glad that we had slept so well and not heard anything. Not until half past eleven did we learn from Mr. Koophuis that the burglars had pushed in the outer door with a crowbar and had forced the warehouse door. However, they did not find much to steal, so they tried their luck upstairs. They stole two cashboxes containing forty florins, postal orders and checkbooks and then, worst of all, all the coupons for 150 kilos of sugar.

Mr. Koophuis thinks that they belonged to the same gang as the ones who tried all three doors six weeks ago. They were unsuccessful then.

It has caused rather a stir in the building, but the "Secret Annexe" can't seem to go on without sensations like this. We were very glad that the typewriters and money in our wardrobe, where they are brought upstairs every evening, were safe.

Yours, Anne

ANNE FRANK

Monday, 19 July, 1943

Dear Kitty,

North Amsterdam was very heavily bombed on Sunday. The destruction seems to be terrible. Whole streets lie in ruins, and it will take a long time before all the people are dug out. Up till now there are two hundred dead and countless wounded; the hospitals are crammed. You hear of children lost in the smoldering ruins, looking for their parents. I shudder when I recall the dull droning rumble in the distance, which for us marked the approaching destruction.

Yours, Anne

Friday, 23 July, 1943

Dear Kitty,

Just for fun I'm going to tell you each person's first wish, when we are allowed to go outside again. Margot and Mr. Van Daan long more than anything for a hot bath filled to overflowing and want to stay in it for half an hour. Mrs. Van Daan wants most to go and eat cream cakes immediately. Dussel thinks of nothing but seeing Lotje, his wife; Mummy of her cup of coffee; Daddy is going to visit Mr. Vossen first; Peter the town and a cinema, while I should find it so blissful, I shouldn't know where to start! But most of all, I long for a home of our own, to be able to move freely and to have some help with my work again at last, in other words—school.

Elli has offered to get us some fruit. It costs next to nothing—grapes f.5.00 per kilo, gooseberries f.0.70 per pound, *one* peach f.0.50, one kilo melon f.1.50.[1] Then you see in the newspapers every evening in bold letters, "Play fair and keep prices down!"

Yours, Anne

[1]Equivalent prices, in order, would be approximately $1.40, twenty-one cents, fourteen cents, and forty-two cents.

Monday, 26 July, 1943

Dear Kitty,

Nothing but tumult and uproar yesterday, we are still very het up about it all. You might really ask, does a day go by without some excitement?

We had the first warning siren while we were at breakfast, but we don't give a hoot about that, it only means that the planes are crossing the coast.

After breakfast I went and lay down for an hour as I had a bad headache, then I went downstairs. It was about two o'clock. Margot had finished her office work at half past two: she had not packed her things together when the sirens began to wail, so upstairs I went again with her. It was high time, for we had not been upstairs five minutes when they began shooting hard, so much so that we went and stood in the passage. And yes, the house rumbled and shook, and down came the bombs.

I clasped my "escape bag" close to me, more because I wanted to have something to hold than with an idea of escaping, because there's nowhere we can go. If ever we come to the extremity of fleeing from here, the street would be just as dangerous as an air raid. This one subsided after half an hour, but the activity in the house increased. Peter came down from his lookout post in the attic, Dussel was in the main office, Mrs. Van Daan felt safe in the private office, Mr. Van Daan had been watching from the loft, and we on the little landing dispersed ourselves too: I went upstairs to see rising above the harbor the columns of smoke Mr. Van Daan had told us about. Before long you could smell burning, and outside it looked as if a thick mist hung everywhere. Although such a big fire is not a pleasant sight, luckily for us it was all over, and we went about our respective tasks. That evening at dinner: another air raid alarm! It was a nice meal, but my hunger vanished, simply at the sound of the alarm. Nothing happened and three quarters of an hour later it was all clear. The dishes were stacked ready to be done: air-raid warning, ack-ack fire, an awful lot of planes.

"Oh, dear me, twice in one day, that's too much," we all thought, but that didn't help at all; once again the bombs rained down, the other side this time, on Schiphol,[1] according to the British. The planes dived and climbed, we heard the hum of their engines and it was very gruesome. Each moment I thought: "One's falling now. Here it comes."

I can assure you that when I went to bed at nine o'clock I couldn't hold my legs still. I woke up at the stroke of twelve: planes. Dussel was undressing. I didn't let that put me off, and at the first shot, I leaped out of bed, wide awake. Two hours with Daddy and still they kept coming. Then they ceased firing and I was able to go to bed. I fell asleep at half past two.

Seven o'clock. I sat up in bed with a start. Mr. Van Daan was with Daddy. Burglars was my first thought. I heard Mr. Van Daan say "everything." I thought that everything had been stolen. But no, this time it was wonderful news, such as we have not heard for months, perhaps in all the war years. "Mussolini has resigned, the King of Italy has taken over the government." We jumped for joy. After the terrible day yesterday, at last something good again and—hope. Hope for it to end, hope for peace.

Kraler called in and told us that Fokkers has been badly damaged. Meanwhile we had another air-raid alarm with planes overhead and one more warning siren. I'm just about choked with alarms, very tired and don't feel a bit like work. But now the suspense over Italy will awaken the hope that it will soon end, perhaps even this year.

Yours, Anne

Thursday, 29 July, 1943

Dear Kitty,

Mrs. Van Daan, Dussel, and I were doing the dishes and I was extraordinarily quiet, which hardly ever happens, so they would have been sure to notice.

[1]Amsterdam airport.

In order to avoid questions I quickly sought a fairly neutral topic, and thought that the book *Henry from the Other Side* would meet the need. But I had made a mistake. If Mrs. Van Daan doesn't pounce on me, then Mr. Dussel does. This was what it came to: Mr. Dussel had specially recommended us this book as being excellent. Margot and I thought it was anything but excellent. The boy's character was certainly well drawn, but the rest—I had better gloss over that. I said something to that effect while we were washing the dishes, but that brought me a packet of trouble.

"How can you understand the psychology of a man! Of a child is not so difficult (!). You are much too young for a book like that; why, even a man of twenty would not be able to grasp it." (Why did he so especially recommend this book to Margot and me?) Now Dussel and Mrs. Van Daan continued together: "You know much too much about things that are unsuitable for you, you've been brought up all wrong. Later on, when you are older, you won't enjoy anything, then you'll say: 'I read that in books twenty years ago.' You had better make haste, if you want to get a husband or fall in love—or everything is sure to be a disappointment to you. You are already proficient in the theory, it's only the practice that you still lack!"

I suppose it's their idea of a good upbringing to always try to set me against my parents, because that is what they often do. And to tell a girl of my age nothing about "grown-up" subjects is an equally fine method! I see the results of that kind of upbringing frequently and all too clearly.

I could have slapped both their faces at that moment as they stood there making a fool of me. I was beside myself with rage and I'm just counting the days until I'm rid of "those" people.

Mrs. Van Daan is a nice one! She sets a fine example . . . she certainly sets one—a bad one. She is well known as being very pushing, selfish, cunning, calculating, and is never content. I can also add vanity and coquetry to the list. There is no question about it, she is an unspeakably disagreeable person. I could write whole chapters about Madame, and who knows, perhaps I will someday. Anyone can put on a fine coat of varnish outside. Mrs. Van Daan is friendly to strangers and especially men, so it is easy to make a mistake when you have only known her for a short time. Mummy thinks she is too stupid to waste words over, Margot too unimportant, Pim too ugly (literally and figuratively), and I, after long observation—for I was never prejudiced from the start—have come to the conclusion that she is all three and a lot more! She has so many bad qualities, why should I even begin about one of them?

Yours, Anne

P.S.—Will the reader take into consideration that when this story was written the writer had not cooled down from her fury!

Tuesday, 3 August, 1943

Dear Kitty,

Political news excellent. In Italy the Fascist party has been banned. The people are fighting the Fascists in many places—even the army is actually taking part in the battle. Can a country like that wage war against England?

We've just had a third air raid; I clenched my teeth together to make myself feel courageous. Mrs. Van Daan, who has always said, "A terrible end is better than no end at all," is the greatest coward of us all now. She was shaking like a leaf this morning and even burst into tears. When her husband, with whom she has just made it up after a week's squabbling, comforted her, the expression on her face alone almost made me feel sentimental.

Mouschi has proved that keeping cats has disadvantages as well as advantages. The whole house is full of fleas, and the plague gets worse every day. Mr. Koophuis has scattered yellow powder in every nook and corner, but the fleas don't seem to mind a bit. It's making us all quite nervous; one keeps imagining an itch on one's arms, legs, and various parts of the body, which is why quite a lot of us are doing gymnastics, so as to be able to look at the back of our necks or legs while standing up. Now we're being paid back for not being more supple—we're too stiff to even turn our heads properly. We gave up real gymnastics long ago.

Yours, Anne

Wednesday, 4 August, 1943

Dear Kitty,

Now that we have been in the "Secret Annexe" for over a year, you know something of our lives, but some of it is quite indescribable. There is so much to tell, everything is so different from ordinary times and from ordinary people's lives. But still, to give you a closer look into our lives, now and again I intend to give you a description of an ordinary day. Today I'm beginning with the evening and night.

Nine o'clock in the evening. The bustle of going to bed in the "Secret Annexe" begins and it is always really quite a business. Chairs are shoved about, beds are pulled down, blankets unfolded, nothing remains where it is during the day. I sleep on the little divan, which is not more than one and a half meters long. So chairs have to be used to lengthen it. An eiderdown, sheets, pillows, blankets, are all fetched from Dussel's bed where they remain during the day. One hears terrible creaking in the next room: Margot's concertina-bed being pulled out. Again, divan, blankets, and pillows, everything is done to make the wooden slats a bit more comfortable. It sounds like thunder above, but it is only Mrs. Van Daan's bed. This is shifted to the window, you see, in order to give Her Majesty in the pink bed jacket fresh air to tickle her dainty nostrils!

After Peter's finished, I step into the washing cubicle, where I give myself a thorough wash and general toilet; it occasionally happens (only in the hot weeks or months) that there is a tiny flea floating in the water. Then teeth

cleaning, hair curling, manicure, and my cotton-wool pads
with hydrogen peroxide (to bleach black mustache hairs)—
all this under half an hour.

Half past nine. Quickly into dressing gown, soap in one
hand, pottie, hairpins, pants, curlers, and cotton wool in
the other, I hurry out of the bathroom; but usually I'm
called back once for the various hairs which decorate the
washbasin in graceful curves, but which are not approved of
by the next person.

Ten o'clock. Put up the blackout. Good night! For at
least a quarter of an hour there is creaking of beds and a
sighing of broken springs, then all is quiet, at least that is if
our neighbors upstairs don't quarrel in bed.

Half past eleven. The bathroom door creaks. A narrow
strip of light falls into the room. A squeak of shoes, a large
coat, even larger than the man inside it—Dussel returns
from his night work in Kraler's office. Shuffling on the floor
for ten minutes, crackle of paper (that is the food which has
to be stowed away), and a bed is made. Then the form disappears again and one only hears suspicious noises from the
lavatory from time to time.

Three o'clock. I have to get up for a little job in the metal
pot under my bed, which is on a rubber mat for safety's sake
in case of leakage. When this has to take place, I always
hold my breath, as it clatters into the tin like a brook from
a mountain. Then the pot is returned to its place and the
figure in the white nightgown, which evokes the same cry
from Margot every evening: "Oh, that indecent nightdress!"
steps back into bed.

Then a certain person lies awake for about a quarter of
an hour, listening to the sounds of the night. Firstly, to
whether there might not be a burglar downstairs, then to
the various beds, above, next door, and in my room, from
which one is usually able to make out how the various members of the household are sleeping, or how they pass the night
in wakefulness.

The latter is certainly not pleasant, especially when it concerns a member of the family by the name of Dussel. First,

I hear a sound like a fish gasping for breath, this is repeated nine or ten times, then with much ado and interchanged with little smacking sounds, the lips are moistened, followed by a lengthy twisting and turning in bed and rearranging of pillows. Five minutes' perfect peace and then the same sequence of events unfolds itself at least three times more, after the doctor has soothed himself to sleep again for a little while. It can also happen that we get a bit of shooting in the night, varying between one o'clock and four. I never really realize it, until from habit I am already standing at my bedside. Sometimes I'm so busy dreaming that I'm thinking about French irregular verbs or a quarrel upstairs. It is some time before I begin to realize that guns are firing and that I am still in the room. But it usually happens as described above. I quickly grab a pillow and handkerchief, put on my dressing gown and slippers, and scamper to Daddy, like Margot wrote in this birthday poem:

> The first shot sounds at dead of night.
> Hush, look! A door creaks open wide,
> A little girl glides into sight,
> Clasping a pillow to her side.

Once landed in the big bed, the worst is over, except if the firing gets very bad.

Quarter to seven. Trrrrr—the alarm clock that raises its voice at any hour of the day (if one asks for it and sometimes when one doesn't). Crack—ping—Mrs. Van Daan has turned it off. Creak—Mr. Van Daan gets up. Puts on water and then full speed to the bathroom.

Quarter past seven. The door creaks again. Dussel can go to the bathroom. Once alone, I take down the blackout—and a new day in the "Secret Annexe" has begun.

Yours, Anne

Thursday, 5 August, 1943

Dear Kitty,

Today I am going to take lunchtime.

It is half past twelve. The whole mixed crowd breathes again. The warehouse boys have gone home now. Above one can hear the noise of Mrs. Van Daan's vacuum cleaner on her beautiful, and only, carpet. Margot goes with a few books under her arm for her Dutch lesson "for children who make no progress," because that's Dussel's attitude. Pim goes into a corner with his inseparable Dickens to try and find peace somewhere. Mummy hurries upstairs to help the industrious housewife, and I go to the bathroom to tidy it up a bit, and myself at the same time.

Quarter to one. The place is filling up. First Mr. Van Santen, then Koophuis or Kraler, Elli and sometimes Miep as well.

One o'clock. We're all sitting listening to the B.B.C., seated around the baby wireless; these are the only times when the members of the "Secret Annexe" do not interrupt each other, because now someone is speaking whom even Mr. Van Daan can't interrupt.

Quarter past one. The great share-out. Everyone from below gets a cup of soup and if there is ever a pudding, some of that as well. Mr. Van Santen is happy and goes to sit on the divan or lean against the writing table. Newspaper, cup, and usually the cat, beside him. If one of the three is missing he's sure to protest. Koophuis tells us the latest news from town, he is certainly an excellent source of information. Kraler comes helter-skelter upstairs—a short, firm knock on the door and in he comes rubbing his hands, according to his mood, in a good temper and talkative, or bad-tempered and quiet.

Quarter to two. Everyone rises from the table and goes about his own business. Margot and Mummy to the dishes. Mr. and Mrs. Van Daan to their divan. Peter up to the attic. Daddy to the divan downstairs. Dussel to his bed and Anne to her work. Then follows the most peaceful hour; everyone is asleep, no one is disturbed. Dussel dreams of lovely food —the expression on his face gives this away, but I don't look long because the time goes so fast and at four o'clock the pedantic doctor is standing, clock in hand, because I'm one minute late in clearing the table for him.

Yours, Anne

Monday, 9 August, 1943

Dear Kitty,

To continue the "Secret Annexe" daily timetable. I shall now describe the evening meal:

Mr. Van Daan begins. He is first to be served, takes a lot of everything if it is what he likes. Usually talks at the same time, always gives his opinion as the only one worth listening to, and once he has spoken it is irrevocable. Because if anyone *dares* to question it, then he flares up at once. Oh, he can spit like a cat—I'd rather not argue, I can tell you—if you've *once* tried you don't try again. He has the best opinion, he knows the most about everything. All right then, he has got brains, but "self-satisfaction" has reached a high grade with this gentleman.

Madame. Really, I should remain silent. Some days, especially if there is a bad mood coming on, you can't look at her face. On closer examination, she is the guilty one in all the arguments. Not the subject! Oh, no, everyone prefers to remain aloof over that, but one could perhaps call her the "kindler." Stirring up trouble, that's fun. Mrs. Frank against Anne; Margot against Daddy doesn't go quite so easily.

But now at table, Mrs. Van Daan doesn't go short, although she thinks so at times. The tiniest potatoes, the sweetest mouthful, the best of everything; picking over is her system. The others will get their turn, as long as I have the best. Then talking. Whether anyone is interested, whether they are listening or not, that doesn't seem to matter. I suppose she thinks: "Everyone is interested in what Mrs. Van Daan says." Coquettish smiles, behaving as if one knew

everything, giving everyone a bit of advice and encouragement, that's *sure* to make a good impression. But if you look
longer, then the good soon wears off.

One, she is industrious, two, gay, three, a coquette—and,
occasionally, pretty. This is Petronella Van Daan.

The third table companion. One doesn't hear much from
him. Young Mr. Van Daan is very quiet and doesn't draw
much attention to himself. As for appetite: a Danaïdean
vessel, which is never full and after the heartiest meal declares
quite calmly that he could have eaten double.

Number four—Margot. Eats like a little mouse and doesn't
talk at all. The only things that go down are vegetables and
fruit. "Spoiled" is the Van Daans' judgment; "not enough
fresh air and games" our opinion.

Beside her—Mummy. Good appetite, very talkative. No
one has the impression, as Mrs. Van Daan: this is the housewife. What is the difference? Well, Mrs. Van Daan does the
cooking, and Mummy washes up and polishes.

Numbers six and seven. I won't say much about Daddy
and me. The former is the most unassuming of all at table.
He looks first to see if everyone else has something. He needs
nothing himself, for the best things are for the children. He
is the perfect example, and sitting beside him, the "Secret
Annexe's" "bundle of nerves."

Dr. Dussel. Helps himself, never looks up, eats and doesn't
talk. And if one must talk, then for heaven's sake let it be
about food. You don't quarrel about it, you only brag. Enormous helpings go down and the word "No" is never heard,
never when the food is good, and not often when it's bad.
Trousers wrapping his chest, red coat, black bedroom slippers,
and horn-rimmed spectacles. That is how one sees him at the
little table, always working, alternated only by his afternoon
nap, food, and—his favorite spot—the lavatory. Three, four,
five times a day someone stands impatiently in front of the
door and wriggles, hopping from one foot to the other,
hardly able to contain himself. Does it disturb him? Not a
bit! From quarter past seven till half past, from half past
twelve till one o'clock, from two till quarter past, from four

till quarter past, from six till quarter past, and from half past eleven until twelve. One can make a note of it—these are the regular "sitting times." He won't come off or pay any heed to an imploring voice at the door, giving warning of approaching disaster!

Number nine isn't a member of the "Secret Annexe" family, but rather a companion in the house and at table. Elli has a healthy appetite. Leaves nothing on her plate and is not picky-and-choosy. She is easy to please and that is just what gives us pleasure. Cheerful and good-tempered, willing and good-natured, these are her characteristics.

Yours, Anne

Tuesday, 10 August, 1943

Dear Kitty,

New idea. I talk more to myself than to the others at mealtimes, which is to be recommended for two reasons. Firstly, because everyone is happy if I don't chatter the whole time, and secondly, I needn't get annoyed about other people's opinions. I don't think my opinions are stupid and the others do; so it is better to keep them to myself. I do just the same if I have to eat something that I simply can't stand. I put my plate in front of me, pretend that it is something delicious, look at it as little as possible, and before I know where I am, it is gone. When I get up in the morning, also a very unpleasant process, I jump out of bed thinking to myself: "You'll be back in a second," go to the window, take down the blackout, sniff at the crack of the window until I feel a bit of fresh air, and I'm awake. The bed is turned down as quickly as possible and then the temptation is removed. Do you know what Mummy calls this sort of thing? "The Art of Living"—that's an odd expression. For the last week we've all been in a bit of a muddle about time, because our dear and beloved Westertoren clock bell has apparently been taken away for war purposes, so that neither by day nor night do we ever know the exact time. I still have some hope that they will think up a substitute (tin, copper or some such thing) to remind the neighborhood of the clock.

Whether I'm upstairs or down, or wherever I am, my feet are the admiration of all, glittering in a pair of (for these days) exceptionally fine shoes. Miep managed to get hold of them secondhand for 27.50 florins, wine-colored suede leather with fairly high wedge heels. I feel as if I'm on stilts and look much taller than I am.

Dussel has indirectly endangered our lives. He actually let Miep bring a forbidden book for him, one which abuses Mussolini and Hitler. On the way she happened to be run into by an S.S. car. She lost her temper, shouted, "Miserable wretches," and rode on. It is better not to think of what might have happened if she had had to go to their headquarters.

Yours, Anne

Wednesday, 18 August, 1943

Dear Kitty,

The title for this piece is: "The communal task of the day: potato peeling!"

One person fetches the newspapers, another the knives (keeping the best for himself, of course), a third potatoes, and the fourth a pan of water.

Mr. Dussel begins, does not always scrape well, but scrapes incessantly, glancing right and left. Does everyone do it the way he does? No! "Anne, look here; I take the knife in my hand like this, scrape from the top downwards! No, not like that—like this!"

"I get on better like *this*, Mr. Dussel," I remark timidly.

"But still this is the best way. But *du kannst* take *dies* from me. Naturally I don't care a bit, *aber du* must know for yourself." We scrape on. I look slyly once in my neighbor's direction. He shakes his head thoughtfully once more (over me, I suppose) but is silent.

I scrape on again. Now I look to the other side, where Daddy is sitting; for him scraping potatoes is not just a little odd job, but a piece of precision work. When he reads, he has a deep wrinkle at the back of his head, but if he helps prepare potatoes, beans, or any other vegetables, then it seems as if nothing else penetrates. Then he has on his "potato face," and he would never hand over an imperfectly scraped potato; it's out of the question when he makes that face!

I work on again and then just look up for a second; I know it already. Mrs. Van Daan is trying to attract Dussel's attention. First she looks in his direction and Dussel appears not to notice anything. Then she winks an eye; Dussel works on. Then she laughs, Dussel doesn't look up. Then Mummy laughs too; Dussel takes no notice. Mrs. Van Daan has not achieved anything, so she has to think of something else. A pause and then: "Putti, do put on an apron! Tomorrow I shall have to get all the spots out of your suit!"

"I'm not getting myself dirty!"

Another moment's silence.

"Putti, why don't you sit down?"

"I'm comfortable standing up and prefer it!" Pause.

"Putti, look, *du spatst schon!*" ("You are making a mess!")

"Yes, Mammy, I'm being careful."

Mrs. Van Daan searches for another subject. "I say, Putti, why aren't there any English air raids now?"

"Because the weather is bad, Kerli."

"But it was lovely yesterday, and they didn't fly then either."

"Let's not talk about it."

"Why, surely one can talk about it, or give one's opinion?"

"No."

"Why ever not?"

"Do be quiet, mammi'chen."

"Mr. Frank always answers his wife, doesn't he?"

Mr. Van Daan wrestles with himself. This is his tender spot, it's something he can't take and Mrs. Van Daan begins again: "The invasion seems as if it will never come!"

Mr. Van Daan goes white; when Mrs. Van Daan sees this, she turns red, but goes on again: "The British do nothing!" The bomb explodes!

"And now hold your tongue, *donnerwetter-noch-einmal!*"

Mummy can hardly hold back her laughter. I look straight in front of me.

This sort of thing happens nearly every day, unless they have just had a very bad quarrel, because then they both keep their mouths shut.

I have to go up to the attic to fetch some potatoes. Peter is busy there delousing the cat. He looks up, the cat notices —pop—he has disappeared through the open window into the gutter. Peter swears. I laugh and disappear.

Yours, Anne

Friday, 20 August, 1943

Dear Kitty,

The men in the warehouse go home sharp at half past five and then we are free.

Half past five. Elli comes to give us our evening freedom. Immediately we begin to make some headway with our work. First, I go upstairs with Elli, where she usually begins by having a bite from our second course.

Before Elli is seated, Mrs. Van Daan begins thinking of things she wants. It soon comes out: "Oh, Elli, I have only one little wish. . . ." Elli winks at me; whoever comes upstairs, Mrs. Van Daan never misses a single opportunity of letting them know what she wants. That must be one of the reasons why none of them like coming upstairs.

Quarter to six. Elli departs. I go two floors down to have a look around. First to the kitchen, then to the private office, after that the coalhole, to open the trap door for Mouschi. After a long tour of inspection I land up in Kraler's room. Van Daan is looking in all the drawers and portfolios to find the day's post. Peter is fetching the warehouse key and Boche; Pim is hauling the typewriters upstairs; Margot is looking for a quiet spot to do her office work; Mrs. Van Daan puts a kettle on the gas ring; Mummy is coming downstairs with a pan of potatoes; each one knows his own job.

Peter soon returns from the warehouse. The first question is—bread. This is always put in the kitchen cupboard by the Ladies; but it is not there. Forgotten? Peter offers to look in the main office. He crouches in front of the door to make himself as small as possible and crawls towards the steel lockers on hands and knees, so as not to be seen from outside, gets the bread, which had been put there, and disappears; at least, he wants to disappear, but before he quite realizes what has happened, Mouschi has jumped over him and gone and sat right under the writing table.

Peter looks all around—aha, he sees him there, he crawls into the office again and pulls the animal by its tail. Mouschi spits, Peter sighs. What has he achieved? Now Mouschi is sitting right up by the window cleaning himself, very pleased to have escaped Peter. Now Peter is holding a piece of bread under the cat's nose as a last decoy. Mouschi will not be tempted and the door closes. I stood and watched it all through the crack of the door. We work on. Rat, tat, tat. Three taps means a meal!

Yours, Anne

Monday, 23 August, 1943

Dear Kitty,

Continuation of the "Secret Annexe" daily timetable. As the clock strikes half past eight in the morning, Margot and Mummy are jittery: "Ssh . . . Daddy, quiet, Otto, ssh . . . Pim." "It is half past eight, come back here, you can't run any more water; walk quietly!" These are the various cries to Daddy in the bathroom. As the clock strikes half past eight, he has to be in the living room. Not a drop of water, no lavatory, no walking about, everything quiet. As long as none of the office staff are there, everything can be heard in the warehouse. The door is opened upstairs at twenty minutes past eight and shortly after there are three taps on the floor:

Anne's porridge. I climb upstairs and fetch my "puppy-dog" plate. Down in my room again, everything goes at terrific speed: do my hair, put away my noisy tin pottie, bed in place. Hush, the clock strikes! Upstairs Mrs. Van Daan has changed her shoes and is shuffling about in bedroom slippers. Mr. Van Daan, too; all is quiet.

Now we have a little bit of real family life. I want to read or work, Margot as well, also Daddy and Mummy. Daddy is sitting (with Dickens and the dictionary, naturally) on the edge of the sagging, squeaky bed, where there aren't even any decent mattresses: two bolsters on top of each other will also serve the purpose, then he thinks: "Mustn't have them, then I'll manage without!"

Once he is reading he doesn't look up, or about him, laughs every now and then, takes awful trouble to get Mummy interested in a little story. Answer: "I haven't got time now." Looks disappointed for just a second, then reads on again; a little later, when he comes to something extra amusing, he tries it again: "You must read this, Mummy!" Mummy sits on the "Opklap"[1] bed, reads, sews, knits, or works, whatever she feels like. She suddenly thinks of something. Just says it quickly: "Anne, do you know . . . Margot, just jot down . . . !" After a while peace returns once more.

Margot closes her book with a clap. Daddy raises his eyebrows into a funny curve, his reading wrinkle deepens again, and he is lost in his book once more; Mummy begins to chatter with Margot, I become curious and listen too! Pim is drawn into the discussion . . . nine o'clock! Breakfast!

Yours, Anne

Friday, 10 September, 1943

Dear Kitty,

Every time I write to you something special seems to have happened, but they are more often unpleasant than

[1] Dutch type of bed, which folds against the wall to look like a bookcase with curtains hanging before it.

pleasant things. However, now there is something wonderful going on. Last Wednesday evening, 8 September, we sat around listening to the seven o'clock news and the first thing we heard was: "Here follows the best news of the whole war. Italy has capitulated!" Italy's unconditional surrender! The Dutch program from England began at quarter past eight. "Listeners, an hour ago, I had just finished writing the chronicle of the day when the wonderful news of Italy's capitulation came in. I can tell you that I have never deposited my notes in the wastepaper basket with such joy!" "God Save the King," the American national anthem, and the "Internationale" were played. As always, the Dutch program was uplifting, but not too optimistic.

Still we have troubles, too; it's about Mr. Koophuis. As you know, we are all very fond of him, he is always cheerful and amazingly brave, although he is never well, has a lot of pain, and is not allowed to eat much or do much walking. "When Mr. Koophuis enters, the sun begins to shine," Mummy said just recently, and she is quite right. Now he has had to go into the hospital for a very unpleasant abdominal operation and will have to stay there for at least four weeks. You really ought to have seen how he said good-by to us just as usual—he might have simply been going out to do a bit of shopping.

Yours, Anne

Thursday, 16 September, 1943

Dear Kitty,

Relations between us here are getting worse all the time. At mealtimes, no one dares to open their mouths (except to allow a mouthful of food to slip in) because whatever is said you either annoy someone or it is misunderstood. I swallow Valerian pills every day against worry and depression, but it doesn't prevent me from being even more miserable the next day. A good hearty laugh would help more than ten Valerian pills, but we've almost forgotten how to

laugh. I feel afraid sometimes that from having to be so
serious I'll grow a long face and my mouth will droop at
the corners. The others don't get any better either, everyone looks with fear and misgivings towards that great terror,
winter. Another thing that does not cheer us up is the fact
that the warehouseman, V.M., is becoming suspicious about
the "Secret Annexe." We really wouldn't mind what V.M.
thought of the situation if he wasn't so exceptionally inquisitive, difficult to fob off, and, moreover, not to be trusted.
One day Kraler wanted to be extra careful, put on his coat
at ten minutes to one, and went to the chemist round the
corner. He was back in less than five minutes, and sneaked
like a thief up the steep stairs that lead straight to us. At a
quarter past one he wanted to go again, but Elli came to
warn him that V.M. was in the office. He did a right-about
turn and sat with us until half past one. Then he took off
his shoes and went in stockinged feet to the front attic
door, went downstairs step by step, and, after balancing
there for a quarter of an hour to avoid creaking, he landed
safely in the office, having entered from the outside. Elli
had been freed of V.M. in the meantime, and came up to us
to fetch Kraler, but he had already been gone a long time;
he was still on the staircase with his shoes off. Whatever
would the people in the street have thought if they had
seen the Manager putting on his shoes outside? Gosh! the
Manager in his socks!

Yours, Anne

Wednesday, 29 September, 1943

Dear Kitty,

It is Mrs. Van Daan's birthday. We gave her a pot of jam,
as well as coupons for cheese, meat, and bread. From her
husband, Dussel, and our protectors she received things
to eat and flowers. Such are the times we live in!

Elli had a fit of nerves this week; she had been sent out
so often; time and again she had been asked to go and fetch

something quickly, which meant yet another errand or made her feel that she had done something wrong. If you just think that she still has to finish her office work downstairs, that Koophuis is ill, Miep at home with a cold, and that she herself has a sprained ankle, love worries, and a grumbling father, then it's no wonder she's at her wit's end. We comforted her and said that if she puts her foot down once or twice and says she has no time, then the shopping lists will automatically get shorter.

There is something wrong with Mr. Van Daan again, I can see it coming on already! Daddy is very angry for some reason or other. Oh, what kind of explosion is hanging over us now? If only I wasn't mixed up so much with all these rows! If I could only get away! They'll drive us crazy before long!

Yours, Anne

Sunday, 17 October, 1943

Dear Kitty,

Koophuis is back again, thank goodness! He still looks rather pale, but in spite of this sets out cheerfully to sell clothes for Van Daan. It is an unpleasant fact that the Van Daans have run right out of money. Mrs. Van Daan won't part with a thing from her pile of coats, dresses, and shoes. Mr. Van Daan's suit isn't easily disposed of, because he wants too much for it. The end of the story is not yet in sight. Mrs. Van Daan will certainly have to part with her fur coat. They've had a terrific row upstairs about it, and now the reconciliation period of "oh, darling Putti" and "precious Kerli" has set in.

I am dazed by all the abusive exchanges that have taken place in this virtuous house during the past month. Daddy goes about with his lips tightly pursed; when anyone speaks to him, he looks up startled, as if he is afraid he will have to patch up some tricky relationship again. Mummy has red patches on her cheeks from excitement. Margot complains of headaches. Dussel can't sleep. Mrs. Van Daan grouses the whole day and I'm going completely crazy! Quite honestly, I sometimes forget who we are quarreling with and with whom we've made it up.

The only way to take one's mind off it all is to study, and I do a lot of that.

Yours, Anne

Friday, 29 October, 1943

Dear Kitty,

There have been resounding rows again between Mr. and Mrs. Van Daan. It came about like this: as I have already told you, the Van Daans are at the end of their money. One day, some time ago now, Koophuis spoke about a furrier with whom he was on good terms; this gave Van Daan the idea of selling his wife's fur coat. It's a fur coat made from rabbit skins, and she has worn it seventeen years. He got 325 florins for it—an enormous sum. However, Mrs. Van Daan wanted to keep the money to buy new clothes after the war, and it took some doing before Mr. Van Daan made it clear to her that the money was urgently needed for the household.

The yells and screams, stamping and abuse—you can't possibly imagine it! It was frightening. My family stood at the bottom of the stairs, holding their breath, ready if necessary to drag them apart! All this shouting and weeping and nervous tension are so unsettling and such a strain, that in the evening I drop into my bed crying, thanking heaven that I sometimes have half an hour to myself.

Mr. Koophuis is away again; his stomach gives him no peace. He doesn't even know whether it has stopped bleeding yet. For the first time, he was very down when he told us that he didn't feel well and was going home.

All goes well with me on the whole, except that I have no appetite. I keep being told: "You don't look at all well." I must say that they are doing their very best to keep me up to the mark. Grape sugar, cod-liver oil, yeast tablets, and calcium have all been lined up.

My nerves often get the better of me: it is especially on Sundays that I feel rotten. The atmosphere is so oppressive, and sleepy and as heavy as lead. You don't hear a single bird singing outside, and a deadly close silence hangs everywhere, catching hold of me as if it will drag me down deep into an underworld.

At such times Daddy, Mummy, and Margot leave me cold. I wander from one room to another, downstairs and up again, feeling like a songbird whose wings have been clipped and who is hurling himself in utter darkness against the bars of his cage. "Go outside, laugh, and take a breath of fresh air," a voice cries within me, but I don't even feel a response any more; I go and lie on the divan and sleep, to make the time pass more quickly, and the stillness and the terrible fear, because there is no way of killing them.

Yours, Anne

Wednesday, 3 November, 1943

Dear Kitty,

In order to give us something to do, which is also educational, Daddy applied for a prospectus from the Teachers' Institute in Leiden. Margot nosed through the thick book at least three times without finding anything to her liking or to suit her purse. Daddy was quicker, and wants a letter written to the Institute asking for a trial lesson in "Elementary Latin."

To give me something new to begin as well, Daddy asked Koophuis for a children's Bible so that I could find out something about the New Testament at last. "Do you want to give Anne a Bible for Chanuka?" asked Margot, somewhat perturbed. "Yes—er, I think St. Nicholas Day is a better occasion," answered Daddy; "Jesus just doesn't go with Chanuka."[1]

Yours, Anne

[1] See entry for 7 December, 1942.

Monday evening, 8 November, 1943

Dear Kitty,

If you were to read my pile of letters one after another, you would certainly be struck by the many different moods in which they are written. It annoys me that I am so dependent on the atmosphere here, but I'm certainly not the only one—we all find it the same. If I read a book that impresses me, I have to take myself firmly in hand, before I mix with other people; otherwise they would think my mind rather queer. At the moment, as you've probably noticed, I'm going through a spell of being depressed. I really couldn't tell you why it is, but I believe it's just because I'm a coward, and that's what I keep bumping up against.

This evening, while Elli was still here, there was a long, loud, penetrating ring at the door. I turned white at once, got a tummy-ache and heart palpitations, all from fear. At night, when I'm in bed, I see myself alone in a dungeon, without Mummy and Daddy. Sometimes I wander by the roadside or our "Secret Annexe" is on fire, or they come and take us away at night. I see everything as if it is actually taking place, and this gives me the feeling that it may all happen to me very soon! Miep often says she envies us for possessing such tranquillity here. That may be true, but she is not thinking about all our fears. I simply can't imagine that the world will ever be normal for us again. I do talk about "after the war," but then it is only a castle in the air, something that will never really happen. If I think back to our old house, my girl friends, the fun at school, it is just as if another person lived it all, not me.

I see the eight of us with our "Secret Annexe" as if we were a little piece of blue heaven, surrounded by heavy black rain clouds. The round, clearly defined spot where we stand is still safe, but the clouds gather more closely about us and the circle which separates us from the approaching danger closes more and more tightly. Now we are so surrounded by danger and darkness that we bump against each other, as we search desperately for a means of escape. We all look down below, where people are fighting each other, we look above, where it is quiet and beautiful, and meanwhile we are cut off by the great dark mass, which will not let us go upwards, but which stands before us as an impenetrable wall; it tries to crush us, but cannot do so yet. I can only cry and implore: "Oh, if only the black circle could recede and open the way for us!"

Yours, Anne

Thursday, 11 November, 1943

Dear Kitty,
    I have a good title for this chapter:

ODE TO MY FOUNTAIN PEN

IN MEMORIAM

My fountain pen has always been one of my most priceless possessions; I value it highly, especially for its thick nib, for I can only really write neatly with a thick nib. My fountain pen has had a very long and interesting pen-life, which I will briefly tell you about.

When I was nine, my fountain pen arrived in a packet (wrapped in cotton wool) as "sample without value" all the way from Aachen, where my Grandmother, the kind donor, used to live. I was in bed with flu, while February winds howled round the house. The glorious fountain pen had a red leather case and was at once shown around to all my friends. I, Anne Frank, the proud owner of a fountain pen! When I was ten I was allowed to take the pen to school and the mistress went so far as to permit me to write with it.

When I was eleven, however, my treasure had to be put away again, because the mistress in the sixth form only allowed us to use school pens and inkpots.

When I was twelve and went to the Jewish Lyceum,[1] my

[1] A type of secondary school specializing in the classics, common in most continental countries.

fountain pen received a new case in honor of the great occasion; it could take a pencil as well, and as it closed with a zipper looked much more impressive.

At thirteen the fountain pen came with us to the "Secret Annexe," where it has raced through countless diaries and compositions for me.

Now I am fourteen, we have spent our last year together.

It was on a Friday afternoon after five o'clock. I had come out of my room and wanted to go and sit at the table to write, when I was roughly pushed on one side and had to make room for Margot and Daddy, who wanted to practice their "Latin." The fountain pen remained on the table unused while, with a sigh, its owner contented herself with a tiny little corner of the table and started rubbing beans. "Bean rubbing" is making moldy beans decent again. I swept the floor at a quarter to six and threw the dirt, together with the bad beans, into a newspaper and into the stove. A terrific flame leaped out and I thought it was grand that the fire should burn up so well when it was practically out. All was quiet again, the "Latinites" had finished, and I went and sat at the table to clear up my writing things, but look as I might, my fountain pen was nowhere to be seen. I looked again, Margot looked, but there was not a trace of the thing. "Perhaps it fell into the stove together with the beans," Margot suggested. "Oh, no, of course not!" I answered. When my fountain pen didn't turn up that evening, however, we all took it that it had been burned, all the more as celluloid is terribly inflammable.

And so it was, our unhappy fears were confirmed; when Daddy did the stove the following morning the clip used for fastening was found among the ashes. Not a trace of the gold nib was found. "Must have melted and stuck to some stone or other," Daddy thought.

I have one consolation, although a slender one: my fountain pen has been cremated, just what I want later!

Yours, Anne

Wednesday, 17 November, 1943

Dear Kitty,

Shattering things are happening. Diphtheria reigns in Elli's home, so she is not allowed to come into contact with us for six weeks. It makes it very awkward over food and shopping, not to mention missing her companionship. Koophuis is still in bed and has had nothing but porridge and milk for three weeks. Kraler is frantically busy.

The Latin lessons Margot sends in are corrected by a teacher and returned, Margot writing in Elli's name. The teacher is very nice, and witty, too. I expect he is glad to have such a clever pupil.

Dussel is very put out, none of us knows why. It began by his keeping his mouth closed upstairs; he didn't utter a word to either Mr. or Mrs. Van Daan. Everyone was struck by it, and when it lasted a couple of days, Mummy took the opportunity of warning him about Mrs. Van Daan, who, if he went on like this, could make things very disagreeable for him.

Dussel said that Mr. Van Daan started the silence, so he was not going to be the one to break it.

Now I must tell you that yesterday was the sixteenth of November, the day he had been exactly one year in the "Secret Annexe." Mummy received a plant in honor of the occasion, but Mrs. Van Daan, who for weeks beforehand had made no bones about the fact that she thought Dussel should treat us to something, received nothing.

Instead of expressing, for the first time, his thanks for our unselfishness in taking him in, he didn't say a word. And when I asked him, on the morning of the sixteenth, whether I should congratulate or condole, he answered that it didn't matter to him. Mummy, who wanted to act as peacemaker, didn't get one step further, and finally the situation remained as it was.

Der Man hat einen grossen Geist
Und ist so klein von Taten![1]

Yours, Anne

[1] (The spirit of the man is great,
How puny are his deeds!)

Saturday, 27 November, 1943

Dear Kitty,

Yesterday evening, before I fell asleep, who should suddenly appear before my eyes but Lies!

I saw her in front of me, clothed in rags, her face thin and worn. Her eyes were very big and she looked so sadly and reproachfully at me that I could read in her eyes: "Oh, Anne, why have you deserted me? Help, oh, help me, rescue me from this hell!"

And I cannot help her, I can only look on, how others suffer and die, and can only pray to God to send her back to us.

I just saw Lies, no one else, and now I understand. I misjudged her and was too young to understand her difficulties. She was attached to a new girl friend, and to her it seemed as though I wanted to take her away. What the poor girl must have felt like, I know; I know the feeling so well myself!

Sometimes, in a flash, I saw something of her life, but a moment later I was selfishly absorbed again in my own pleasures and problems. It was horrid of me to treat her as I did, and now she looked at me, oh so helplessly, with her pale face and imploring eyes. If only I could help her!

Oh, God, that I should have all I could wish for and that she should be seized by such a terrible fate. I am not more virtuous than she; she, too, wanted to do what was right, why should I be chosen to live and she probably to die? What was the difference between us? Why are we so far from each other now?

Quite honestly, I haven't thought about her for months, yes, almost for a year. Not completely forgotten her, but still I had never thought about her like this, until I saw her before me in all her misery.

Oh, Lies, I hope that, if you live until the end of the war, you will come back to us and that I shall be able to take you in and do something to make up for the wrong I did you.

But when I am able to help her again, then she will not need my help so badly as now. I wonder if she ever thinks of me; if so, what would she feel?

Good Lord, defend her, so that at least she is not alone. Oh, if only You could tell her that I think lovingly of her and with sympathy, perhaps that would give her greater endurance.

I must not go on thinking about it, because I don't get any further. I only keep seeing her great big eyes, and cannot free myself from them. I wonder if Lies has real faith in herself, and not only what has been thrust upon her?

I don't even know, I never took the trouble to ask her!

Lies, Lies, if only I could take you away, if only I could let you share all the things I enjoy. It is too late now, I can't help, or repair the wrong I have done. But I shall never forget her again, and I shall always pray for her.

Yours, Anne

Monday, 6 December, 1943

Dear Kitty,

When St. Nicholas' Day approached, none of us could help thinking of the prettily decorated basket we had last year and I, especially, thought it would be very dull to do nothing at all this year. I thought a long time about it, until I invented something, something funny.

I consulted Pim, and a week ago we started composing a little poem for each person.

On Sunday evening at a quarter to eight we appeared upstairs with the large laundry basket between us, decorated with little figures, and bows of pink and blue carbon copy paper. The basket was covered with a large piece of brown paper, on which a letter was pinned. Everyone was rather astonished at the size of the surprise package.

I took the letter from the paper and read:

> "Santa Claus has come once more,
> Though not quite as he came before;
> We can't celebrate his day
> In last year's fine and pleasant way.
> For then our hopes were high and bright,
> All the optimists seemed right,

> *None supposing that this year*
> *We would welcome Santa here.*
> *Still, we'll make his spirit live,*
> *And since we've nothing left to give,*
> *We've thought of something else to do*
> *Each please look inside his shoe."*

As each owner took his shoe from the basket there was a resounding peal of laughter. A little paper package lay in each shoe with the address of the shoe's owner on it.

Yours, Anne

Wednesday, 22 December, 1943

Dear Kitty,

A bad attack of flu has prevented me from writing to you until today. It's wretched to be ill here. When I wanted to cough—one, two, three—I crawled under the blankets and tried to stifle the noise. Usually the only result was that the tickle wouldn't go away at all; and milk and honey, sugar or lozenges had to be brought into operation. It makes me dizzy to think of all the cures that were tried on me. Sweating, compresses, wet cloths on my chest, dry cloths on my chest, hot drinks, gargling, throat painting, lying still, cushion for extra warmth, hot-water bottles, lemon squashes, and, in addition, the thermometer every two hours!

Can anyone really get better like this? The worst moment of all was certainly when Mr. Dussel thought he'd play doctor, and came and lay on my naked chest with his greasy head, in order to listen to the sounds within. Not only did his hair tickle unbearably, but I was embarrassed, in spite of the fact that he once, thirty years ago, studied medicine and has the title of Doctor. Why should the fellow come and lie on my heart? He's not my lover, after all! For that matter, he wouldn't hear whether it's healthy or unhealthy inside me anyway; his ears need syringing first, as he's becoming alarmingly hard of hearing.

But that is enough about illness. I'm as fit as a fiddle again, one centimeter taller, two pounds heavier, pale, and with a real appetite for learning.

There is not much news to tell you. We are all getting on well together for a change! There's no quarreling—we haven't had such peace in the home for at least half a year. Elli is still parted from us.

We received extra oil for Christmas, sweets and syrup; the "chief present" is a brooch, made out of a two-and-a-half-cent piece, and shining beautifully. Anyway, lovely, but indescribable. Mr. Dussel gave Mummy and Mrs. Van Daan a lovely cake which he had asked Miep to bake for him. With all her work, she has to do that as well! I have also something for Miep and Elli. For at least two months I have saved the sugar from my porridge, you see, and with Mr. Koophuis's help I'll have it made into fondants.

It is drizzly weather, the stove smells, the food lies heavily on everybody's tummy, causing thunderous noises on all sides! The war at a standstill, morale rotten.

Yours, Anne

Friday, 24 December, 1943

Dear Kitty,

I have previously written about how much we are affected by atmospheres here, and I think that in my own case this trouble is getting much worse lately.

"Himmelhoch jauchzend und zum Tode betrübt"[1] certainly fits here. I am *"Himmelhoch jauchzend"* if I only think how lucky we are here compared with other Jewish children, and *"zum Tode betrübt"* comes over me when, as happened today, for example, Mrs. Koophuis comes and tells us about her daughter Corry's hockey club, canoe trips, theatrical performances, and friends. I don't think I'm jealous of Corry, but I couldn't help feeling a great longing to have lots of fun myself for once, and to laugh until my tummy ached. Especially

[1] A famous line from Goëthe: "On top of the world, or in the depths of despair."

at this time of the year with all the holidays for Christmas and the New Year, and we are stuck here like outcasts. Still, I really ought not to write this, because it seems ungrateful and I've certainly been exaggerating. But still, whatever you think of me, I can't keep everything to myself, so I'll remind you of my opening words—"Paper is patient."

When someone comes in from outside, with the wind in their clothes and the cold on their faces, then I could bury my head in the blankets to stop myself thinking: "When will we be granted the privilege of smelling fresh air?" And because I must not bury my head in the blankets, but the reverse—I must keep my head high and be brave, the thoughts will come, not once, but oh, countless times. Believe me, if you have been shut up for a year and a half, it can get too much for you some days. In spite of all justice and thankfulness, you can't crush your feelings. Cycling, dancing, whistling, looking out into the world, feeling young, to know that I'm free— that's what I long for; still, I mustn't show it, because I sometimes think if all eight of us began to pity ourselves, or went about with discontented faces, where would it lead us? I sometimes ask myself, "Would anyone, either Jew or non-Jew, understand this about me, that I am simply a young girl badly in need of some rollicking fun?" I don't know, and I couldn't talk about it to anyone, because then I know I should cry. Crying can bring such relief.

In spite of all my theories, and however much trouble I take, each day I miss having a real mother who understands me. That is why with everything I do and write I think of the "Mumsie" that I want to be for my children later on. The "Mumsie" who doesn't take everything that is said in general conversation so seriously, but who does take what *I* say seriously. I have noticed, though I can't explain how, that the word "Mumsie" tells you everything. Do you know what I've found? To give me the feeling of calling Mummy something which sounds like "Mumsie" I often call her "Mum"; then from that comes "Mums": the incomplete "Mumsie," as it were, whom I would so love to honor with the extra "ie" and yet who does not realize it. It's a good thing, because it would only make her unhappy.

That's enough about that, writing has made my *"zum Tode betrübt"* go off a bit.

Yours, Anne

Saturday, 25 December, 1943

Dear Kitty,

During these days, now that Christmas is here, I find myself thinking all the time about Pim, and what he told me about the love of his youth. Last year I didn't understand the meaning of his words as well as I do now. If he'd only talk about it again, perhaps I would be able to show him that I understand.

I believe that Pim talked about it because he who "knows the secrets of so many other hearts" had to express his own feelings for once; because otherwise Pim never says a word about himself, and I don't think Margot has any idea of all Pim has had to go through. Poor Pim, he can't make *me* think that he has forgotten everything. He will never forget this. He has become very tolerant. I hope that I shall grow a bit like him, without having to go through all that.

Yours, Anne

Monday, 27 December, 1943

Dear Kitty,

On Friday evening for the first time in my life I received something for Christmas. Koophuis, Kraler and the girls had prepared a lovely surprise again. Miep has made a lovely Christmas cake, on which was written "Peace 1944." Elli had provided a pound of sweet biscuits of prewar quality. For Peter, Margot, and me a bottle of yoghourt, and a bottle of beer for each of the grownups. Everything was so nicely done up, and there were pictures stuck on the different packages. Otherwise Christmas passed by quickly for us.

Yours, Anne

Wednesday, 29 December, 1943

Dear Kitty,

I was very unhappy again last evening. Granny and Lies came into my mind. Granny, oh, darling Granny, how little we understood of what she suffered, or how sweet she was. And besides all this, she knew a terrible secret which she carefully kept to herself the whole time.[1] How faithful and good Granny always was; she would never have let one of us down. Whatever it was, however naughty I had been, Granny always stuck up for me.

Granny, did you love me or didn't you understand me either? I don't know. No one ever talked about themselves to Granny. How lonely Granny must have been, how lonely in spite of us! A person can be lonely even if he is loved by many people, because he is still not the "One and Only" to anyone.

And Lies, is she still alive? What is she doing? Oh, God, protect her and bring her back to us. Lies, I see in you all the time what my lot might have been, I keep seeing myself in your place. Why then should I often be unhappy over what happens here? Shouldn't I always be glad, contented, and happy, except when I think about her and her companions in distress? I am selfish and cowardly. Why do I always dream and think of the most terrible things—my fear makes me want to scream out loud sometimes. Because still, in spite of everything, I have not enough faith in God. He has given me so much—which I certainly do not deserve—and I still do so much that is wrong every day. If you think of your fellow creatures, then you only want to cry, you could really cry the whole day long. The only thing to do is to pray that God will perform a miracle and save some of them. And I hope that I am doing that enough.

Yours, Anne

[1] A severe internal disease.

Sunday, 2 January, 1944

Dear Kitty,

This morning when I had nothing to do I turned over some of the pages of my diary and several times I came across letters dealing with the subject "Mummy" in such a hotheaded way that I was quite shocked, and asked myself: "Anne, is it really you who mentioned hate? Oh, Anne, how could you!" I remained sitting with the open page in my hand, and thought about it and how it came about that I should have been so brimful of rage and really so filled with such a thing as hate that I had to confide it all in you. I have been trying to understand the Anne of a year ago and to excuse her, because my conscience isn't clear as long as I leave you with these accusations, without being able to explain, on looking back, how it happened.

I suffer now—and suffered then—from moods which kept my head under water (so to speak) and only allowed me to see the things subjectively without enabling me to consider quietly the words of the other side, and to answer them as the words of one whom I, with my hotheaded temperament, had offended or made unhappy.

I hid myself within myself, I only considered myself and quietly wrote down all my joys, sorrows, and contempt in my diary. This diary is of great value to me, because it has become a book of memoirs in many places, but on a good many pages I could certainly put "past and done with."

I used to be furious with Mummy, and still am sometimes. It's true that she doesn't understand me, but I don't understand her either. She did love me very much and she was tender, but as she landed in so many unpleasant situations through me, and was nervous and irritable because of other worries and difficulties, it is certainly understandable that she snapped at me.

I took it much too seriously, was offended, and was rude and aggravating to Mummy, which, in turn, made her unhappy. So it was really a matter of unpleasantness and misery rebounding all the time. It wasn't nice for either of us, but it is passing.

I just didn't want to see all this, and pitied myself very much; but that, too, is understandable. Those violent outbursts on paper were only giving vent to anger which in a normal life could have been worked off by stamping my feet a couple of times in a locked room, or calling Mummy names behind her back.

The period when I caused Mummy to shed tears is over. I have grown wiser and Mummy's nerves are not so much on edge. I usually keep my mouth shut if I get annoyed, and so does she, so we appear to get on much better together. I can't really love Mummy in a dependent childlike way—I just don't have that feeling.

I soothe my conscience now with the thought that it is better for hard words to be on paper than that Mummy should carry them in her heart.

Yours, Anne

Wednesday, 5 January, 1944

Dear Kitty,

I have two things to confess to you today, which will take a long time. But I must tell someone and you are the best one to tell, as I know that, come what may, you always keep a secret.

The first is about Mummy. You know that I've grumbled a lot about Mummy, yet still tried to be nice to her again. Now it is suddenly clear to me what she lacks. Mummy herself has told us that she looked upon us more as her friends than her daughters. Now that is all very fine, but still, a friend can't take a mother's place. I need my mother as an example which I can follow, I want to be able to respect her. I have the feeling that Margot thinks differently about these things and would never be able to understand what I've just told you. And Daddy avoids all arguments about Mummy.

I imagine a mother as a woman who, in the first place,

shows great tact, especially towards her children when they reach our age, and who does not laugh at me if I cry about something—not pain, but other things—like "Mums" does.

One thing, which perhaps may seem rather fatuous, I have never forgiven her. It was on a day that I had to go to the dentist. Mummy and Margot were going to come with me, and agreed that I should take my bicycle. When we had finished at the dentist, and were outside again, Margot and Mummy told me that they were going into the town to look at something or buy something—I don't remember exactly what. I wanted to go, too, but was not allowed to, as I had my bicycle with me. Tears of rage sprang into my eyes, and Mummy and Margot began laughing at me. Then I became so furious that I stuck my tongue out at them in the street just as an old woman happened to pass by, who looked very shocked! I rode home on my bicycle, and I know I cried for a long time.

It is queer that the wound that Mummy made then still burns, when I think of how angry I was that afternoon.

The second is something that is very difficult to tell you, because it is about myself.

Yesterday I read an article about blushing by Sis Heyster. This article might have been addressed to me personally. Although I don't blush very easily, the other things in it certainly all fit me. She writes roughly something like this—that a girl in the years of puberty becomes quiet within and begins to think about the wonders that are happening to her body.

I experience that, too, and that is why I get the feeling lately of being embarrassed about Margot, Mummy, and Daddy. Funnily enough, Margot, who is much more shy than I am, isn't at all embarrassed.

I think what is happening to me is so wonderful, and not only what can be seen on my body, but all that is taking place inside. I never discuss myself or any of these things with anybody; that is why I have to talk to myself about them.

Each time I have a period—and that has only been three times—I have the feeling that in spite of all the pain, unpleasantness, and nastiness, I have a sweet secret, and that is why, although it is nothing but a nuisance to me in a way, I always long for the time that I shall feel that secret within me again.

Sis Heyster also writes that girls of this age don't feel quite certain of themselves, and discover that they themselves are individuals with ideas, thoughts, and habits. After I came here, when I was just fourteen, I began to think about myself sooner than most girls, and to know that I am a "person." Sometimes, when I lie in bed at night, I have a terrible desire to feel my breasts and to listen to the quiet rhythmic beat of my heart.

I already had these kinds of feelings subconsciously before I came here, because I remember that once when I slept with a girl friend I had a strong desire to kiss her, and that I did do so. I could not help being terribly inquisitive over her body, for she had always kept it hidden from me. I asked her whether, as a proof of our friendship, we should feel one another's breasts, but she refused. I go into ecstasies every time I see the naked figure of a woman, such as Venus, for example. It strikes me as so wonderful and exquisite that I have difficulty in stopping the tears rolling down my cheeks.

If only I had a girl friend!

Yours, Anne

Thursday, 6 January, 1944

Dear Kitty,

My longing to talk to someone became so intense that somehow or other I took it into my head to choose Peter.

Sometimes if I've been upstairs into Peter's room during the day, it always struck me as very snug, but because Peter is so retiring and would never turn anyone out who became a nuisance, I never dared stay long, because I was afraid he might think me a bore. I tried to think of an excuse to stay in his room and get him talking, without it being too noticeable, and my chance came yesterday. Peter has a mania for crossword puzzles at the moment and hardly does anything else. I helped him with them and we soon sat opposite each other at his little table, he on the chair and me on the divan.

It gave me a queer feeling each time I looked into his deep blue eyes, and he sat there with that mysterious laugh playing round his lips. I was able to read his inward thoughts. I could see on his face that look of helplessness and uncertainty as to how to behave, and, at the same time, a trace of his sense of manhood. I noticed his shy manner and it made me feel very gentle; I couldn't refrain from meeting those dark eyes again and again, and with my whole heart I almost beseeched him: oh, tell me, what is going on inside you, oh, can't you look beyond this ridiculous chatter?

But the evening passed and nothing happened, except that I told him about blushing—naturally not what I have written, but just so that he would become more sure of himself as he grew older.

When I lay in bed and thought over the whole situation, I found it far from encouraging, and the idea that I should beg for Peter's patronage was simply repellent. One can do a lot to satisfy one's longings, which certainly sticks out in my case, for I have made up my mind to go and sit with Peter more often and to get him talking somehow or other.

Whatever you do, don't think I'm in love with Peter—not a bit of it! If the Van Daans had had a daughter instead of a son, I should have tried to make friends with her too.

I woke at about five to seven this morning and knew at once, quite positively, what I had dreamed. I sat on a chair and opposite me sat Peter . . . Wessel. We were looking together at a book of drawings by Mary Bos. The dream was so vivid that I can still partly remember the drawings. But that was not all—the dream went on. Suddenly Peter's eyes met mine and I looked into those fine, velvet brown eyes for a long time. Then Peter said very softly, "If I had only known, I would have come to you long before!" I turned around brusquely because the emotion was too much for me. And after that I felt a soft, and oh, such a cool kind cheek against mine and it felt so good, so good. . . .

I awoke at this point, while I could still feel his cheek

against mine and felt his brown eyes looking deep into my
heart, so deep, that there he read how much I had loved him
and how much I still love him. Tears sprang into my eyes once
more, and I was very sad that I had lost him again, but at the
same time glad because it made me feel quite certain that
Peter was still the chosen one.

It is strange that I should often see such vivid images in
my dreams here. First I saw Grandma[1] so clearly one night
that I could even distinguish her thick, soft, wrinkled velvety
skin. Then Granny appeared as a guardian angel; then followed Lies, who seems to be a symbol to me of the sufferings
of all my girl friends and all Jews. When I pray for her, I pray
for all Jews and all those in need. And now Peter, my darling
Peter—never before have I had such a clear picture of him in
my mind. I don't need a photo of him, I can see him before
my eyes, and oh, so well!

Yours, Anne

Friday, 7 January, 1944

Dear Kitty,

What a silly ass I am! I am quite forgetting that I have
never told you the history of myself and all my boy friends.

When I was quite small—I was even still at a kindergarten
—I became attached to Karel Samson. He had lost his father,
and he and his mother lived with an aunt. One of Karel's
cousins, Robby, was a slender, good-looking dark boy, who
aroused more admiration than the little, humorous fellow,
Karel. But looks did not count with me and I was very fond of
Karel for years.

We used to be together a lot for quite a long time, but for
the rest, my love was unreturned.

Then Peter crossed my path, and in my childish way I really fell in love. He liked me very much, too, and we were inseparable for one whole summer. I can still remember us walking hand in hand through the streets together, he in a white

[1]Grandma is grandmother on Father's side, Granny on Mother's side.

cotton suit and me in a short summer dress. At the end of the summer holidays he went into the first form of the high school and I into the sixth form of the lower school. He used to meet me from school and, vice versa, I would meet him. Peter was a very good-looking boy, tall, handsome, and slim, with an earnest, calm, intelligent face. He had dark hair, and wonderful brown eyes, ruddy cheeks, and a pointed nose. I was mad about his laugh, above all, when he looked so mischievous and naughty!

I went to the country for the holidays; when I returned, Peter had in the meantime moved, and a much older boy lived in the same house. He apparently drew Peter's attention to the fact that I was a childish little imp, and Peter gave me up. I adored him so that I didn't want to face the truth. I tried to hold on to him until it dawned on me that if I went on running after him I should soon get the name of being boy-mad. The years passed. Peter went around with girls of his own age and didn't even think of saying "Hello" to me any more; but I couldn't forget him.

I went to the Jewish Secondary School. Lots of boys in our class were keen on me—I thought it was fun, felt honored, but was otherwise quite untouched. Then later on, Harry was mad about me, but, as I've already told you, I never fell in love again.

There is a saying "Time heals all wounds," and so it was with me. I imagined that I had forgotten Peter and that I didn't like him a bit any more. The memory of him, however, lived so strongly in my subconscious mind that I admitted to myself sometimes I was jealous of the other girls, and that was why I didn't like him any more. This morning I knew that nothing has changed; on the contrary, as I grew older and more mature my love grew with me. I can quite understand now that Peter thought me childish, and yet it still hurt that he had so completely forgotten me. His face was shown so clearly to me, and now I know that no one else could remain with me like he does.

I am completely upset by the dream. When Daddy kissed me this morning, I could have cried out: "Oh, if only you were

Peter!" I think of him all the time and I keep repeating to my-self the whole day, "Oh, Petel, darling, darling Petel . . . !"

Who can help me now? I must live on and pray to God that He will let Peter cross my path when I come out of here, and that when he reads the love in my eyes he will say, "Oh, Anne, if I had only known, I would have come to you long before!"

I saw my face in the mirror and it looks quite different. My eyes look so clear and deep, my cheeks are pink—which they haven't been for weeks—my mouth is much softer; I look as if I am happy, and yet there is something so sad in my expres-sion and my smile slips away from my lips as soon as it has come. I'm not happy, because I might know that Peter's thoughts are not with me, and yet I still feel his wonderful eyes upon me and his cool soft cheek against mine.

Oh, Petel, Petel, how will I ever free myself of your image? Wouldn't any other in your place be a miserable substitute? I love you, and with such a great love that it can't grow in my heart any more but has to leap out into the open and sud-denly manifest itself in such a devastating way!

A week ago, even yesterday, if anyone had asked me, "Which of your friends do you consider would be the most suitable to marry?" I would have answered, "I don't know"; but now I would cry, "Petel, because I love him with all my heart and soul. I give myself completely!" But one thing, he may touch my face, but no more.

Once, when we spoke about sex, Daddy told me that I couldn't possibly understand the longing yet; I always knew that I did understand it and now I understand it fully. Noth-ing is so beloved to me now as he, my Petel.

                                                          Yours, Anne

                                        Wednesday, 12 January, 1944

Dear Kitty,

Elli has been back a fortnight. Miep and Henk were away from their work for two days—they both had tummy upsets.

I have a craze for dancing and ballet at the moment, and

practice dance steps every evening diligently. I have made a supermodern dance frock from a light blue petticoat edged with lace belonging to Mansa. A ribbon is threaded through round the top and ties in a bow in the center, and a pink corded ribbon completes the creation. I tried in vain to convert my gym shoes into real ballet shoes. My stiff limbs are well on the way to becoming supple again like they used to be. One terrific exercise is to sit on the floor, hold a heel in each hand, and then lift both legs up in the air. I have to have a cushion under me, otherwise my poor little behind has a rough time.

Everyone here is reading the book *Cloudless Morn*. Mummy thought it exceptionally good; there are a lot of youth problems in it. I thought to myself rather ironically: "Take a bit more trouble with your own young people first!"

I believe Mummy thinks there could be no better relationship between parents and their children, and that no one could take a greater interest in their children's lives than she. But quite definitely she only looks at Margot, who I don't think ever had such problems and thoughts as I do. Still, I wouldn't dream of pointing out to Mummy that, in the case of her daughters, it isn't at all as she imagines, because she would be utterly amazed and wouldn't know how to change anyway; I want to save her the unhappiness it would cause her, especially as I know that for me everything would remain the same anyway.

Mummy certainly feels that Margot loves her much more than I do, but she thinks that this just goes in phases! Margot has grown so sweet; she seems quite different from what she used to be, isn't nearly so catty these days and is becoming a real friend. Nor does she any longer regard me as a little kid who counts for nothing.

I have an odd way of sometimes, as it were, being able to see myself through someone else's eyes. Then I view the affairs of a certain "Anne" at my ease, and browse through the pages of her life as if she were a stranger. Before we came here, when I didn't think about things as much as I do now, I used at times to have the feeling that I didn't belong to Mansa,

Pim, and Margot, and that I would always be a bit of an outsider. Sometimes I used to pretend I was an orphan, until I reproached and punished myself, telling myself it was all my own fault that I played this self-pitying role, when I was really so fortunate. Then came the time that I used to force myself to be friendly. Every morning, as soon as someone came downstairs I hoped that it would be Mummy who would say good morning to me; I greeted her warmly, because I really longed for her to look lovingly at me. Then she made some remark or other that seemed unfriendly, and I would go off to school again feeling thoroughly disheartened. On the way home I would make excuses for her because she had so many worries, arrive home very cheerful, chatter nineteen to the dozen, until I began repeating myself, and left the room wearing a pensive expression, my satchel under my arm. Sometimes I decided to remain cross, but when I came home from school I always had so much news that my resolutions were gone with the wind and Mummy, whatever she might be doing, had to lend an ear to all my adventures. Then the time came once more when I didn't listen for footsteps on the staircase any longer, and at night my pillow was wet with tears.

Everything grew much worse at that point; *enfin*, you know all about it.

Now God has sent me a helper—Peter . . . I just clasp my pendant, kiss it, and think to myself, "What do I care about the lot of them! Peter belongs to me and no one knows anything about it." This way I can get over all the snubs I receive. Who would ever think that so much can go on in the soul of a young girl?

Yours, Anne

Saturday, 15 January, 1944

Dear Kitty,

There is no point in telling you every time the exact details of our rows and arguments. Let it suffice to tell you that we have divided up a great many things, such as butter and meat, and that we fry our own potatoes. For some time now we've been eating whole-meal bread between meals as an extra, because by four o'clock in the afternoon we are longing for our supper so much that we hardly know how to control our rumbling tummies.

Mummy's birthday is rapidly approaching. She got some extra sugar from Kraler, which made the Van Daans jealous as Mrs. Van Daan had not been favored in this way for her birthday. But what's the use of annoying each other with yet more unkind words, tears, and angry outbursts. You can be sure of one thing, Kitty, that we are even more fed up with them than ever! Mummy has expressed the wish—one which cannot come true just now—not to see the Van Daans for a fortnight.

I keep asking myself, whether one would have trouble in the long run, whoever one shared a house with. Or did we strike it extra unlucky? Are most people so selfish and stingy then? I think it's all to the good to have learned a bit about human beings, but now I think I've learned enough. The war goes on just the same, whether or not we choose to quarrel, or long for freedom and fresh air, and so we should try to make the best of our stay here. Now I'm preaching, but I also believe that if I stay here for very long I shall grow into a dried-up old beanstalk. And I did so want to grow into a real young woman!

                                                        Yours, Anne

                                        Saturday, 22 January, 1944

Dear Kitty,

I wonder whether you can tell me why it is that people always try so hard to hide their real feelings? How is it that I always behave quite differently from what I should in other people's company?

Why do we trust one another so little? I know there must be a reason, but still I sometimes think it's horrible that you find you can never really confide in people, even in those who are nearest to you.

It seems as if I've grown up a lot since my dream the other night. I'm much more of an "independent being." You'll certainly be amazed when I tell you that even my attitude towards the Van Daans has changed. I suddenly see all the arguments and the rest of it in a different light, and am not as prejudiced as I was.

How can I have changed so much? Yes, you see it suddenly struck me that if Mummy had been different, a real Mumsie, the relationship might have been quite, quite different. It's true that Mrs. Van Daan is by no means a nice person, but still I do think that half the quarrels could be avoided if it weren't for the fact that when the conversation gets tricky Mummy is a bit difficult too.

Mrs. Van Daan has one good side, and that is that you can talk to her. Despite all her selfishness, stinginess, and underhandedness, you can make her give in easily, as long as you don't irritate her and get on the wrong side of her. This way doesn't work every time, but if you have patience you can try again and see how far you get.

All the problems of our "upbringing," of our being spoiled, the food—it could have been quite different if we'd remain perfectly open and friendly, and not always only on the lookout for something to seize on.

I know exactly what you'll say, Kitty: "But, Anne, do these words really come from *your* lips? From you, who have had to listen to so many harsh words from the people upstairs, from you, the girl who has suffered so many injustices?" And yet they come from me.

I want to start afresh and try to get to the bottom of it all, not be like the saying "the young always follow a bad example." I want to examine the whole matter carefully myself and find out what is true and what is exaggerated. Then if I myself am disappointed in them, I can adopt the same line as Mummy and Daddy; if not, I shall try first of all to make them alter their ideas and if I don't succeed I shall stick to my own opinions and judgment. I shall seize every opportunity to discuss openly all our points of argument with Mrs. Van Daan and not be afraid of declaring myself neutral, even at the cost of being called a "know-all." It is not that I shall be going against my own family, but from today there will be no more unkind gossip on my part.

Until now I was immovable! I always thought the Van Daans were in the wrong, but we too are partly to blame. We have certainly been right over the subject matter; but handling of others from intelligent people (which we consider ourselves to be!) one expects more insight. I hope that I have acquired a bit of insight and will use it well when the occasion arises.

Yours, Anne

Monday, 24 January, 1944

Dear Kitty,

Something has happened to me; or rather, I can hardly describe it as an event, except that I think it is pretty crazy. Whenever anyone used to speak of sexual problems at home or at school, it was something either mysterious or revolting. Words which had any bearing on the subject were whispered, and often if someone didn't understand he was laughed at. It struck me as very odd and I thought, "Why are people so secretive and tiresome when they talk about these things?" But as I didn't think that I could change things, I kept my mouth shut as much as possible, or sometimes asked girl friends for information. When I had learned quite a lot and had also spoken about it with my parents, Mummy said one day, "Anne, let me give you some good advice; never speak about this subject to boys and don't reply if they begin about it." I remember exactly what my answer was: I said, "No, of course not! The very idea!" And there it remained.

When we first came here, Daddy often told me about things that I would really have preferred to hear from Mummy, and I found out the rest from books and things I picked up from conversations. Peter Van Daan was never as tiresome over this as the boys at school—once or twice at first perhaps—but he never tried to get me talking.

Mrs. Van Daan told us that she had never talked about these things to Peter, and for all she knew neither had her husband. Apparently she didn't even know how much he knew.

Yesterday, when Margot, Peter, and I were peeling potatoes, somehow the conversation turned to Boche. "We still don't know what sex Boche is, do we?" I asked.

"Yes, certainly," Peter answered. "He's a tom."

I began to laugh. "A tomcat that's expecting, that's marvelous!"

Peter and Margot laughed too over this silly mistake. You see, two months ago, Peter had stated that Boche would soon be having a family, her tummy was growing visibly. However, the fatness appeared to come from the many stolen bones, because the children didn't seem to grow fast, let alone make their appearance!

Peter just had to defend himself. "No," he said, "you can go with me yourself to look at him. Once when I was playing around with him, I noticed quite clearly that he's a tom."

I couldn't control my curiosity, and went with him to the warehouse. Boche, however, was not receiving visitors, and was nowhere to be seen. We waited for a while, began to get cold, and went upstairs again. Later in the afternoon I heard Peter go downstairs for the second time. I mustered up all my courage to walk through the silent house alone, and reached the warehouse. Boche stood on the packing table playing with Peter, who had just put him on the scales to weigh him.

"Hello, do you want to see him?" He didn't make any lengthy preparations, but picked up the animal, turned him over on to his back, deftly held his head and paws together, and the lesson began. "These are the male organs, these are just a few stray hairs, and that is his bottom." The cat did another half turn and was standing on his white socks once more.

If any other boy had shown me "the male organs," I would never have looked at him again. But Peter went on talking quite normally on what is otherwise such a painful subject, without meaning anything unpleasant, and finally put me sufficiently at my ease for me to be normal too. We played with Boche, amused ourselves, chattered together, and then sauntered through the large warehouse towards the door.

"Usually, when I want to know something, I find it in some book or other, don't you?" I asked.

"Why on earth? I just ask upstairs. My father knows more than me and has had more experience in such things."

We were already on the stair, so I kept my mouth shut after that.

"Things may alter," as Brer Rabbit said. Yes. Really I shouldn't have discussed these things in such a normal way with a girl. I know too definitely that Mummy didn't mean it that way when she warned me not to discuss the subject with boys. I wasn't quite my usual self for the rest of the day though, in spite of everything. When I thought over our talk, it still seemed rather odd. But at least I'm wiser about one thing, that there really are young people—and of the opposite sex too—who can discuss these things naturally without making fun of them.

I wonder if Peter really does ask his parents much. Would he honestly behave with them as he did with me yesterday? Ah, what would I know about it!

Yours, Anne

Thursday, 27 January, 1944

Dear Kitty,

Lately I have developed a great love for family trees and genealogical tables of the royal families, and have come to the conclusion that, once you begin, you want to delve still deeper into the past, and can keep on making fresh and interesting discoveries. Although I am extraordinarily industrious over my lessons, and can already follow the English Home Service quite well on the wireless, I still devote many Sundays to sorting and looking over my large collection of film stars, which is quite a respectable size by now.

I am awfully pleased whenever Mr. Kraler brings the

Cinema and Theater with him on Mondays. Although this little gift is often called a waste of money by the less worldly members of the household, they are amazed each time at how accurately I can state who is in a certain film, even after a year. Elli, who, on her days off, often goes to the movies with her boy friend, tells me the titles of the new films each week; and in one breath I rattle off the names of the stars who appear in them, together with what the reviews say. Not so long ago, Mum said that I wouldn't need to go to a cinema later on because I knew the plots, the names of the stars, and the opinions of the reviews all by heart.

If ever I come sailing in with a new hair style, they all look disapprovingly at me, and I can be quite sure that someone will ask which glamorous star I'm supposed to be imitating. They only half believe me if I reply that it's my own invention.

But to continue about the hair style—it doesn't stay put for more than half an hour; then I'm so tired of the remarks people pass that I quickly hasten to the bathroom and restore my ordinary house-garden-kitchen hair style.

Yours, Anne

Friday, 28 January, 1944

Dear Kitty,

I asked myself this morning whether you don't sometimes feel rather like a cow who has had to chew over all the old pieces of news again and again, and who finally yawns loudly and silently wishes that Anne would occasionally dig up something new.

Alas, I know it's dull for you, but try to put yourself in my place, and imagine how sick I am of the old cows who keep having to be pulled out of the ditch again. If the conversation at mealtimes isn't over politics or a delicious meal, then Mummy or Mrs. Van Daan trot out one of the old stories of their youth, which we've heard so many times before; or Dussel twaddles on about his wife's extensive wardrobe, beautiful race horses, leaking rowboats, boys who can swim at the age of four, muscular pains and nervous patients. What it all boils down to is this—that if one of the eight of us opens his mouth, the other seven can finish the story for him! We all know the point of every joke from the start, and the storyteller is alone in laughing at his witticisms. The various milkmen, grocers, and butchers of the two ex-housewives have already grown beards in our minds, so often have they been praised to the skies or pulled to pieces; it is impossible for anything in the conversation here to be fresh or new.

Still, all this would be bearable if the grownups didn't have their little way of telling the stories, with which Koophuis, Henk, or Miep oblige the company, ten times over and adding their own little frills and furbelows, so that I often have to pinch my arm under the table to prevent myself from putting them right. Little children such as Anne must never, under any circumstances, know better than the grownups, however many blunders they make, and to whatever extent they allow their imaginations to run away with them.

One favorite subject of Koophuis's and Henk's is that of people in hiding and in the underground movement. They know very well that anything to do with other people in hiding interests us tremendously, and how deeply we can sympathize with the sufferings of people who get taken away, and rejoice with the liberated prisoner.

We are quite as used to the idea of going into hiding, or "underground," as in bygone days one was used to Daddy's bedroom slippers warming in front of the fire.

There are a great number of organizations, such as "The Free Netherlands," which forge identity cards, supply money to people "underground," find hiding places for people, and work for young men in hiding, and it is amazing how much noble, unselfish work these people are doing, risking their own lives to help and save others. Our helpers are a very good example. They have pulled us through up till now and we hope they will bring us safely to dry land. Otherwise, they will have to share the same fate as the many others who are being searched for. Never have we heard *one* word of the burden which we certainly must be to them, never has one of them complained of all the trouble we give.

They all come upstairs every day, talk to the men about business and politics, to the women about food and wartime difficulties, and about newspapers and books with the children. They put on the brightest possible faces, bring flowers and presents for birthdays and bank holidays, are always ready to help and do all they can. That is something we must never forget; although others may show heroism in the war or against the Germans, our helpers display heroism in their cheerfulness and affection.

The wildest tales are going around, but still they are usually founded on fact. For instance, Koophuis told us this week that in Gelderland two football elevens met, and one side consisted solely of members of the "underground" and the other was made up of members of the police. New ration books are being handed out in Hilversum. In order that the many people in hiding may also draw rations, the officials have given instructions to those of them in the district to come at a certain time, so that they can collect their documents from a separate little table. Still, they'll have to be careful that such impudent tricks do not reach the ears of the Germans.

Yours, Anne

Thursday, 3 February, 1944

Dear Kitty,

Invasion fever in the country is mounting daily. If you were here, on the one hand, you would probably feel the effect of all these preparations just as I do and, on the other, you would laugh at us for making such a fuss—who knows—perhaps for nothing.

All the newspapers are full of the invasion and are driving people mad by saying that "In the event of the English landing in Holland, the Germans will do all they can to defend the country; if necessary they will resort to flooding." With this, maps have been published, on which the parts of Holland that will be under water are marked. As this applies to large parts of Amsterdam, the first question was, what shall we do if the water in the streets rises to one meter? The answers given by different people vary considerably.

"As walking or cycling is out of the question, we shall have to wade through the stagnant water."

"Of course not, one will have to try and swim. We shall all put on our bathing suits and caps and swim under water as much as possible, then no one will see that we are Jews."

"Oh, what nonsense! I'd like to see the ladies swimming, if the rats started biting their legs!" (That was naturally a man: just see who screams the loudest!)

"We shan't be able to get out of the house anyway; the warehouse will definitely collapse if there is a flood, it is so wobbly already."

"Listen, folks, all joking apart, we shall try and get a boat."

"Why bother? I know something much better. We each get hold of a wooden packing case from the attic and row with a soup ladle!"

"I shall walk on stilts: I used to be an expert at it in my youth."

"Henk Van Santen won't need to, he's sure to take his wife on his back, then she'll be on stilts."

This gives you a rough idea, doesn't it, Kit?

This chatter is all very amusing, but the truth may be otherwise. A second question about the invasion was bound to arise: what do we do if the Germans evacuate Amsterdam?

"Leave the city too, and disguise ourselves as best we can."

"Don't go, whatever happens, stay put! The only thing to do is to remain here! The Germans are quite capable of driving the whole population right into Germany, where they will all die."

"Yes, naturally, we shall stay here, since this is the safest place. We'll try and fetch Koophuis and his family over here to come and live with us. We'll try and get hold of a sack of wood wool, then we can sleep on the floor. Let's ask Miep and Koophuis to start bringing blankets here."

"We'll order some extra corn in addition to our sixty

pounds. Let's get Henk to try and obtain more peas and beans; we have about sixty pounds of beans and ten pounds of peas in the house at present. Don't forget that we've got fifty tins of vegetables."

"Mummy, just count up how much we've got of other food, will you?"

"Ten tins of fish, forty tins of milk, ten kilos of milk powder, three bottles of salad oil, four preserving jars of butter, four ditto of meat, two wicker-covered bottles of strawberries, two bottles of raspberries, twenty bottles of tomatoes, ten pounds of rolled oats, eight pounds of rice; and that's all.

"Our stock's not too bad, but if you think that we may be having visitors as well and drawing from reserves each week, then it seems more than it actually is. We have sufficient coal and firewood in the house, also candles. Let's all make little moneybags, which could easily be hidden in our clothing, in case we want to take money with us.

"We'll make lists of the most important things to take, should we have to run for it, and pack rucksacks now in readiness. If it gets that far, we'll put two people on watch, one in the front and one in the back loft. I say, what's the use of collecting such stocks of food, if we haven't any water, gas, or electricity?"

"Then we must cook on the stove. Filter and boil our water. We'll clean out some large wicker bottles and store water in them."

I hear nothing but this sort of talk the whole day long, invasion and nothing but invasion, arguments about suffering from hunger, dying, bombs, fire extinguishers, sleeping bags, Jewish vouchers, poisonous gases, etc., etc. None of it is exactly cheering. The gentlemen in the "Secret Annexe" give pretty straightforward warnings; an example is the following conversation with Henk:

"Secret Annexe": "We are afraid that if the Germans withdraw, they will take the whole population with them."

Henk: "That is impossible, they haven't the trains at their disposal."

"S.A.": "Trains? Do you really think they'd put civilians in carriages? Out of the question. They could use 'shank's mare.'" *(Per pedes apostolorum,* Dussel always says.)

H.: "I don't believe a word of it, you look on the black side of everything. What would be their object in driving all the civilians along with them?"

"S.A.": "Didn't you know that Goebbels said, 'If we have to withdraw, we shall slam the doors of all the occupied countries behind us'?"

H.: "They have said so much already."

"S.A.": "Do you think the Germans are above doing such a thing or too humane? What they think is this: 'If we have got to go down, then everybody in our clutches will go down with us.'"

H.: "Tell that to the Marines; I just don't believe it!"

"S.A.": "It's always the same song; no one will see danger approaching until it is actually on top of him."

H.: "But you know nothing definite; you just simply suppose."

"S.A.": "We have all been through it ourselves, first in Germany, and then here. And what is going on in Russia?"

H.: "You mustn't include the Jews. I don't think anyone knows what is going on in Russia. The English and the Russians are sure to exaggerate things for propaganda purposes, just like the Germans."

"S.A.": "Out of the question, the English have always told the truth over the wireless. And suppose they do exaggerate the news, the facts are bad enough anyway, because you can't deny that many millions of peace-loving people were just simply murdered or gassed in Poland and Russia."

I will spare you further examples of these conversations; I myself keep very quiet and don't take any notice of all the fuss and excitement. I have now reached the stage that I don't care much whether I live or die. The world will still keep on turning without me; what is going to happen, will happen, and anyway it's no good trying to resist.

I trust to luck and do nothing but work, hoping that all will end well.

Yours, Anne

Saturday, 12 February, 1944

Dear Kitty,

The sun is shining, the sky is a deep blue, there is a lovely breeze and I'm longing—so longing—for everything. To talk, for freedom, for friends, to be alone. And I do so long . . . to cry! I feel as if I'm going to burst, and I know that it would get better with crying; but I can't, I'm restless, I go from one room to the other, breathe through the crack of a closed window, feel my heart beating, as if it is saying, "Can't you satisfy my longings at last?"

I believe that it's spring within me, I feel that spring is awakening, I feel it in my whole body and soul. It is an effort to behave normally, I feel utterly confused, don't know what to read, what to write, what to do, I only know that I am longing . . . !

Yours, Anne

Sunday, 13 February, 1944

Dear Kitty,

Since Saturday a lot has changed for me. It came about like this. I longed—and am still longing—but . . . now something has happened, which has made it a little, just a little, less.

To my great joy—I will be quite honest about it—already this morning I noticed that Peter kept looking at me all the time. Not in the ordinary way, I don't know how, I just can't explain.

I used to think that Peter was in love with Margot, but yesterday I suddenly had the feeling that it is not so. I made a special effort not to look at him too much, because whenever I did, he kept on looking too and then—yes, then—it gave me a lovely feeling inside, but which I mustn't feel too often.

I desperately want to be alone. Daddy has noticed that I'm not quite my usual self, but I really can't tell him everything. "Leave me in peace, leave me alone," that's what I'd like to

keep crying out all the time. Who knows, the day may come
when I'm left alone more than I would wish!

Yours, Anne

Monday, 14 February, 1944

Dear Kitty,

On Sunday evening everyone except Pim and me was sitting beside the wireless in order to listen to the "Immortal
Music of the German Masters." Dussel fiddled with the knobs
continually. This annoyed Peter, and the others too. After re-
straining himself for half an hour, Peter asked somewhat irri-
tably if the twisting and turning might stop. Dussel answered
in his most hoity-toity manner, "I'm getting it all right." Peter
became angry, was rude, Mr. Van Daan took his side, and
Dussel had to give in. That was all.

The reason in itself was very unimportant, but Peter seems
to have taken it very much to heart. In any case, when I was
rummaging about in the bookcase in the attic, he came up to
me and began telling me the whole story. I didn't know anything about it, but Peter soon saw that he had found an attentive ear and got fairly into his stride.

"Yes, and you see," he said, "I don't easily say anything,
because I know beforehand that I'll only become tongue-tied.
I begin to stutter, blush, and twist around what I want to say,
until I have to break off because I simply can't find the words.
That's what happened yesterday, I wanted to say something
quite different, but once I had started, I got in a hopeless
muddle and that's frightful. I used to have a bad habit; I wish
I still had it now. If I was angry with anyone, rather than
argue it out I would get to work on him with my fists. I quite
realize that this method doesn't get me anywhere; and that is
why I admire you. You are never at a loss for a word, you say
exactly what you want to say to people and are never the least
bit shy."

"I can tell you, you're making a big mistake," I answered.
"I usually say things quite differently from the way I meant to

say them, and then I talk too much and far too long, and that's just as bad."

I couldn't help laughing to myself over this last sentence. However, I wanted to let him go on talking about himself, so I kept my amusement to myself, went and sat on a cushion on the floor, put my arms around my bent knees, and looked at him attentively.

I am very glad that there is someone else in the house who can get into the same fits of rage as I get into. I could see it did Peter good to pull Dussel to pieces to his heart's content, without fear of my telling tales. And as for me, I was very pleased, because I sensed a real feeling of fellowship, such as I can only remember having had with my girl friends.

Yours, Anne

Wednesday, 16 February, 1944

Dear Kitty,

It's Margot's birthday. Peter came at half past twelve to look at the presents and stayed talking much longer than was strictly necessary—a thing he'd have never done otherwise. In the afternoon I went to get some coffee and, after that, potatoes, because I wanted to spoil Margot for just that one day in the year. I went through Peter's room; he took all his papers off the stairs at once and I asked whether I should close the trap door to the attic. "Yes," he replied, "knock when you come back, then I'll open it for you."

I thanked him, went upstairs, and searched at least ten minutes in the large barrel for the smallest potatoes. Then my back began to ache and I got cold. Naturally I didn't knock, but opened the trap door myself, but still he came to meet me most obligingly, and took the pan from me.

"I've looked for a long time, these are the smallest I could find," I said.

"Did you look in the big barrel?"

"Yes, I've been over them all."

By this time I was standing at the bottom of the stairs and

he looked searchingly in the pan which he was still holding. "Oh, but these are first-rate," he said, and added when I took the pan from him, "I congratulate you!" At the same time he gave me such a gentle warm look which made a tender glow within me. I could really see that he wanted to please me, and because he couldn't make a long complimentary speech he spoke with his eyes. I understood him, oh, so well, and was very grateful. It gives me pleasure even now when I recall those words and that look he gave me.

When I went downstairs, Mummy said that I must get some more potatoes, this time for supper. I willingly offered to go upstairs again.

When I came into Peter's room, I apologized at having to disturb him again. When I was already on the stairs he got up, and went and stood between the door and the wall, firmly took hold of my arm, and wanted to hold me back by force.

"I'll go," he said. I replied that it really wasn't necessary and that I didn't have to get particularly small ones this time. Then he was convinced and let my arm go. On the way down, he came and opened the trap door and took the pan again. When I reached the door, I asked, "What are you doing?" "French," he replied. I asked if I might glance through the exercises, washed my hands, and went and sat on the divan opposite him.

We soon began talking, after I'd explained some of the French to him. He told me that he wanted to go to the Dutch East Indies and live on a plantation later on. He talked about his home life, about the black market, and then he said that he felt so useless. I told him that he certainly had a very strong inferiority complex. He talked about the Jews. He would have found it much easier if he'd been a Christian and if he could be one after the war. I asked if he wanted to be baptized, but that wasn't the case either. Who was to know whether he was a Jew when the war was over? he said.

This gave me rather a pang; it seems such a pity that there's always just a tinge of dishonesty about him. For the rest we chatted very pleasantly about Daddy, and about judging people's characters and all kinds of things, I can't remember exactly what now.

It was half past four by the time I left.

In the evening he said something else that I thought was nice. We were talking about a picture of a film star that I'd given him once, which has now been hanging in his room for at least a year and a half. He liked it very much and I offered to give him a few more sometime. "No," he replied, "I'd rather leave it like this. I look at these every day and they have grown to be my friends."

Now I understand more why he always hugs Mouschi. He needs some affection, too, of course.

I'd forgotten something else that he talked about. He said, "I don't know what fear is, except when I think of my own shortcomings. But I'm getting over that too."

Peter has a terrible inferiority complex. For instance, he always thinks that he is so stupid, and we are so clever. If I help him with his French, he thanks me a thousand times. One day I shall turn around and say: "Oh, shut up, you're much better at English and geography!"

Yours, Anne

Friday, 18 February, 1944

Dear Kitty,

Whenever I go upstairs now I keep on hoping that I shall see "him." Because my life now has an object, and I have something to look forward to, everything has become more pleasant.

At least the object of my feelings is always there, and I needn't be afraid of rivals, except Margot. Don't think I'm in love, because I'm not, but I do have the feeling all the time that something fine can grow up between us, something that gives confidence and friendship. If I get half a chance, I go up to him now. It's not like it used to be when he didn't know how to begin. It's just the opposite—he's still talking when I'm half out of the room.

Mummy doesn't like it much, and always says I'll be a nuisance and that I must leave him in peace. Honestly, doesn't she realize that I've got some intuition? She looks at me so queerly every time I go into Peter's little room. If I come downstairs from there, she asks me where I've been. I simply can't bear it, and think it's horrible.

Yours, Anne

Saturday, 19 February, 1944

Dear Kitty,

It is Saturday again and that really speaks for itself.

The morning was quiet. I helped a bit upstairs, but I didn't have more than a few fleeting words with "him." At half past two, when everyone had gone to their own rooms, either to sleep or to read, I went to the private office, with my blanket and everything, to sit at the desk and read or write. It was not long before it all became too much for me, my head drooped on to my arm, and I sobbed my heart out. The tears streamed down my cheeks and I felt desperately unhappy. Oh, if only "he" had come to comfort me. It was four o'clock by the time I went upstairs again. I went for some potatoes, with fresh hope in my heart of a meeting, but while I was still smartening up my hair in the bathroom he went down to see Boche in the warehouse.

Suddenly I felt the tears coming back and I hurried to the lavatory, quickly grabbing a pocket mirror as I passed. There I sat then, fully dressed, while the tears made dark spots on the red of my apron, and I felt very wretched.

This is what was going through my mind. Oh, I'll never reach Peter like this. Who knows, perhaps he doesn't like me at all and doesn't need anyone to confide in. Perhaps he only thinks about me in a casual sort of way. I shall have to go on alone once more, without friendship and without Peter. Perhaps soon I'll be without hope, without comfort, or anything to look forward to again. Oh, if I could nestle my head against his shoulder and not feel so hopelessly alone and deserted!

Who knows, perhaps he doesn't care about me at all and
looks at the others in just the same way. Perhaps I only
imagined that it was especially for me? Oh, Peter, if only you
could see or hear me. If the truth were to prove as bad as that,
it would be more than I could bear.

However, a little later fresh hope and anticipation seemed
to return, even though the tears were still streaming down
my cheeks.

                                                    Yours, Anne

Wednesday, 23 February, 1944

Dear Kitty,

It's lovely weather outside and I've quite perked up since
yesterday. Nearly every morning I go to the attic where Peter
works to blow the stuffy air out of my lungs. From my favorite spot on the floor I look up at the blue sky and the bare
chestnut tree, on whose branches little raindrops shine, appearing like silver, and at the seagulls and the other birds as
they glide on the wind .

He stood with his head against a thick beam, and I sat
down. We breathed the fresh air, looked outside, and both
felt that the spell should not be broken by words. We remained like this for a long time, and when he had to go up to
the loft to chop wood, I knew that he was a nice fellow. He
climbed the ladder, and I followed; then he chopped wood
for about a quarter of an hour, during which time we still
remained silent. I watched him from where I stood, he was
obviously doing his best to show off his strength. But I looked
out of the open window too, over a large area of Amsterdam,
over all the roofs and on to the horizon, which was such a
pale blue that it was hard to see the dividing line. "As long as
this exists," I thought, "and I may live to see it, this sunshine,
the cloudless skies, while this lasts, I cannot be unhappy."

The best remedy for those who are afraid, lonely, or unhappy is to go outside, somewhere where they can be quite
alone with the heavens, nature, and God. Because only then

does one feel that all is as it should be and that God wishes to see people happy, amidst the simple beauty of nature. As long as this exists, and it certainly always will, I know that then there will always be comfort for every sorrow, whatever the circumstances may be. And I firmly believe that nature brings solace in all troubles.

Oh, who knows, perhaps it won't be long before I can share this overwhelming feeling of bliss with someone who feels the way I do about it.

Yours, Anne

A thought:

We miss so much here, so very much and for so long now: I miss it too, just as you do. I'm not talking of outward things, for we are looked after in that way; no, I mean the inward things. Like you, I long for freedom and fresh air, but I believe now that we have ample compensation for our privations. I realized this quite suddenly when I sat in front of the window this morning. I mean inward compensation.

When I looked outside right into the depth of Nature and God, then I was happy, really happy. And Peter, so long as I have that happiness here, the joy in nature, health and a lot more besides, all the while one has that, one can always recapture happiness.

Riches can all be lost, but that happiness in your own heart can only be veiled, and it will still bring you happiness again, as long as you live. As long as you can look fearlessly up into the heavens, as long as you know that you are pure within and that you will still find happiness.

Sunday, 27 February, 1944

Dearest Kitty,

From early in the morning till late at night, I really do hardly anything else but think of Peter. I sleep with his image before my eyes, dream about him and he is still looking at me when I awake.

I have a strong feeling that Peter and I are really not so different as we would appear to be, and I will tell you why. We both lack a mother. His is too superficial, loves flirting and doesn't trouble much about what he thinks. Mine does bother about me, but lacks sensitiveness, real motherliness.

Peter and I both wrestle with our inner feelings, we are still uncertain and are really too sensitive to be roughly treated. If we are, then my reaction is to "get away from it all." But as that is impossible, I hide my feelings, throw my weight about the place, am noisy and boisterous, so that everyone wishes that I was out of the way.

He, on the contrary, shuts himself up, hardly talks at all, is quiet, day-dreams and in his way carefully conceals his true self.

But how and when will we finally reach each other? I don't know quite how long my common sense will keep this longing under control.

                                                    Yours, Anne

                                    Monday, 28 February, 1944

Dearest Kitty,

It is becoming a bad dream—in daytime as well as at night. I see him nearly all the time and can't get at him, I mustn't show anything, must remain gay while I'm really in despair.

Peter Wessel and Peter Van Daan have grown into one Peter, who is beloved and good, and for whom I long desperately.

Mummy is tiresome, Daddy sweet and therefore all the more tiresome, Margot the most tiresome because she expects me to wear a pleasant expression; and all I want is to be left in peace.

Peter didn't come to me in the attic. He went up to the loft instead and did some carpentry. At every creak and every knock some of my courage seemed to seep away and I grew more unhappy. In the distance a bell was playing "Pure in

body, pure in soul."[1] I'm sentimental—I know. I'm desperate
and silly—I know that too. Oh, help me!

Yours, Anne

Wednesday, 1 March, 1944

Dear Kitty,

My own affairs have been pushed into the background by
—a burglary. I'm becoming boring with all my burglars, but
what can I do, they seem to take such a delight in honoring
Kolen & Co. with their visits. This burglary is much more
complicated than the one in July 1943.

When Mr. Van Daan went to Kraler's office at half past
seven, as usual, he saw that the communicating glass doors
and the office door were open. Surprised at this, he walked
through and was even more amazed to see that the doors of
the little dark room were open too, and that there was a terrible mess in the main office. "There has been a burglar," he
thought to himself at once, and to satisfy himself he went
straight downstairs to look at the front door, felt the Yale
lock, and found everything closed. "Oh, then both Peter and
Elli must have been very slack this evening," he decided. He
remained in Kraler's room for a while, then switched off the
lamp, and went upstairs, without worrying much about either
the open doors or the untidy office.

This morning Peter knocked at our door early and came
with the not so pleasant news that the front door was wide
open. He also told us that the projector and Kraler's new
portfolio had both disappeared from the cupboard. Peter was
told to close the door. Van Daan told us of his discoveries
the previous evening and we were all awfully worried.

What must have happened is that the thief had a skeleton
key, because the lock was quite undamaged. He must have
crept into the house quite early and closed the door behind
him, hidden himself when disturbed by Mr. Van Daan, and

[1]The bells in old clock towers play tunes.

when he departed fled with his spoils, leaving the door open in his haste. Who can have our key? Why didn't the thief go to the warehouse? Might it be one of our own warehouse-men, and would he perhaps betray us, since he certainly heard Van Daan and perhaps even saw him?

It is all very creepy, because we don't know whether this same burglar may not take it into his head to visit us again. Or perhaps it gave him a shock to find that there was some-one walking about in the house?

Yours, Anne

Thursday, 2 March, 1944

Dear Kitty,

Margot and I were both up in the attic today; although we were not able to enjoy it together as I had imagined, still I do know that she shares my feelings over most things.

During dish washing Elli began telling Mummy and Mrs. Van Daan that she felt very discouraged at times. And what help do you think they gave her? Do you know what Mummy's advice was? She should try to think of all the other people who are in trouble! What is the good of think-ing of misery when one is already miserable oneself? I said this too and was told, "You keep out of this sort of con-versation."

Aren't the grownups idiotic and stupid? Just as if Peter, Margot, Elli, and I don't all feel the same about things, and only a mother's love or that of a very, very good friend can help us. These mothers here just don't understand us at all. Perhaps Mrs. Van Daan does a little more than Mummy. Oh, I would have so liked to say something to poor Elli, some-thing that I know from experience would have helped her. But Daddy came between us and pushed me aside.

Aren't they all stupid! We aren't allowed to have any opinions. People can tell you to keep your mouth shut, but it doesn't stop you having your own opinion. Even if people are still very young, they shouldn't be prevented from saying what they think.

Only great love and devotion can help Elli, Margot, Peter, and me, and none of us gets it. And no one, especially the stupid "know-alls" here, can understand us, because we are much more sensitive and much more advanced in our thoughts than anyone here would ever imagine in their wildest dreams.

Mummy is grumbling again at the moment—she is obviously jealous because I talk more to Mrs. Van Daan than to her nowadays.

I managed to get hold of Peter this afternoon and we talked for at least three quarters of an hour. Peter had the greatest difficulty in saying anything about himself; it took a long time to draw him out. He told me how often his parents quarrel over politics, cigarettes, and all kinds of things. He was very shy.

Then I talked to him about my parents. He defended Daddy: he thought him a "first-rate chap." Then we talked about "upstairs" and "downstairs" again; he was really rather amazed that we don't always like his parents. "Peter," I said, "you know I'm always honest, so why shouldn't I tell you that we can see their faults too." And among other things I also said, "I would so like to help you, Peter; can't I? You are in such an awkward position and, although you don't say anything, it doesn't mean that you don't care."

"Oh, I would always welcome your help."

"Perhaps you would do better to go to Daddy, he wouldn't let anything go any further, take it from me; you can easily tell him!"

"Yes, he is a real pal."

"You're very fond of him, aren't you?" Peter nodded and I went on: "And he is of you too!"

He looked up quickly and blushed, it was really moving to see how these few words pleased him.

"Do you think so?" he asked.

"Yes," I said, "you can easily tell by little things that slip out now and then!"

Peter is a first-rate chap, too, just like Daddy!

Yours, Anne

Friday, 3 March, 1944

Dear Kitty,

When I looked into the candle this evening[1] I felt calm and happy. Oma seems to be in the candle and it is Oma too who shelters and protects me and who always makes me feel happy again.

But . . . there is someone else who governs all my moods and that is . . . Peter. When I went up to get potatoes today and was still standing on the stepladder with the pan, he at once asked, "What have you been doing since lunch?" I went and sat on the steps and we started talking. At a quarter past five (an hour later) the potatoes, which had been sitting on the floor in the meantime, finally reached their destinations.

Peter didn't say another word about his parents; we just talked about books and about the past. The boy has such warmth in his eyes; I believe I'm pretty near to being in love with him. He talked about that this evening. I went into his room, after peeling the potatoes, and said that I felt so hot.

"You can tell what the temperature is by Margot and me; if it's cold we are white, and if it is hot we are red in the face," I said.

"In love?" he asked.

"Why should I be in love?" My answer was rather silly.

"Why not?" he said, and then we had to go for supper.

Would he have meant anything by that question? I finally managed to ask him today whether he didn't find my chatter a nuisance; he only said: "It's okay, I like it!"

To what extent this answer was just shyness, I am not able to judge.

Kitty, I'm just like someone in love, who can only talk about her darling. And Peter really is a darling. When shall I be able to tell him so? Naturally, only if he thinks I'm a darling too. But I'm quite capable of looking after myself, and he knows that very well. And he likes his tranquillity, so I have no idea how much he likes me. In any case, we are

[1]In Jewish homes candles are lit on the Sabbath eve.

getting to know each other a bit. I wish we dared to tell each other much more already. Who knows, the time may come sooner than I think! I get an understanding look from him about twice a day, I wink back, and we both feel happy.

I certainly seem quite mad to be talking about him being happy, and yet I feel pretty sure that he thinks just the same as I do.

Yours, Anne

Saturday, 4 March, 1944

Dear Kitty,

This is the first Saturday for months and months that hasn't been boring, dreary, and dull. And Peter is the cause.

This morning I went to the attic to hang up my apron, when Daddy asked whether I'd like to stay and talk some French. I agreed. First we talked French, and I explained something to Peter; then we did some English. Daddy read out loud to us from Dickens and I was in the seventh heaven, because I sat on Daddy's chair very close to Peter.

I went downstairs at eleven o'clock. When I came upstairs again at half past eleven, he was already waiting for me on the stairs. We talked until a quarter to one. If, as I leave the room, he gets a chance after a meal, for instance, and if no one can hear, he says: "Good-by, Anne, see you soon."

Oh, I am so pleased! I wonder if he is going to fall in love with me after all? Anyway, he is a very nice fellow and no one knows what lovely talks I have with him!

Mrs. Van Daan quite approves when I go and talk to him, but she asked today teasingly, "Can I really trust you two up there together?"

"Of course," I protested, "really you quite insult me!"

From morn till night I look forward to seeing Peter.

Yours, Anne

Monday, 6 March, 1944

Dear Kitty,

I can tell by Peter's face that he thinks just as much as I do, and when Mrs. Van Daan yesterday evening said scoffingly: "The thinker!" I was irritated. Peter flushed and looked very embarrassed, and I was about to explode.

Why can't these people keep their mouths shut?

You can't imagine how horrible it is to stand by and see how lonely he is and yet not be able to do anything. I can so well imagine, just as if I were in his place, how desperate he must feel sometimes in quarrels and in love. Poor Peter, he needs love very much!

When he said he didn't need any friends how harsh the words sounded to my ears. Oh, how mistaken he is! I don't believe he meant it a bit.

He clings to his solitude, to his affected indifference and his grown-up ways, but it's just an act, so as never, never to show his real feelings. Poor Peter, how long will he be able to go on playing this role? Surely a terrible outburst must follow as the result of this superhuman effort?

Oh, Peter, if only I could help you, if only you would let me! Together we could drive away your loneliness and mine!

I think a lot, but I don't say much. I am happy if I see him and if the sun shines when I'm with him. I was very excited yesterday; while I was washing my hair, I knew that he was sitting in the room next to ours. I couldn't do anything about it; the more quiet and serious I feel inside, the more noisy I become outwardly.

Who will be the first to discover and break through this armor? I'm glad after all that the Van Daans have a son and not a daughter, my conquest could never have been so difficult, so beautiful, so good, if I had not happened to hit on someone of the opposite sex.

Yours, Anne

P.S. You know that I'm always honest with you, so I must tell you that I actually live from one meeting to the next.

I keep hoping to discover that he too is waiting for me all the time and I'm thrilled if I notice a small shy advance from his side. I believe he'd like to say a lot just like I would; little does he know that it's just his clumsiness that attracts me.

Yours, Anne

Tuesday, 7 March, 1944

Dear Kitty,

If I think now of my life in 1942, it all seems so unreal. It was quite a different Anne who enjoyed that heavenly existence from the Anne who has grown wise within these walls. Yes, it was a heavenly life. Boy friends at every turn, about twenty friends and acquaintances of my own age, the darling of nearly all the teachers, spoiled from top to toe by Mummy and Daddy, lots of sweets, enough pocket money, what more could one want?

You will certainly wonder by what means I got around all these people. Peter's word "attractiveness" is not altogether true. All the teachers were entertained by my cute answers, my amusing remarks, my smiling face, and my questioning looks. That is all I was—a terrible flirt, coquettish and amusing. I had one or two advantages, which kept me rather in favor. I was industrious, honest, and frank. I would never have dreamed of cribbing from anyone else. I shared my sweets generously, and I wasn't conceited.

Wouldn't I have become rather forward with so much admiration? It was a good thing that in the midst of, at the height of, all this gaiety, I suddenly had to face reality, and it took me at least a year to get used to the fact that there was no more admiration forthcoming.

How did I appear at school? The one who thought of new jokes and pranks, always "king of the castle," never in a bad mood, never a crybaby. No wonder everyone liked to cycle with me, and I got their attentions.

Now I look back at that Anne as an amusing, but very

superficial girl, who has nothing to do with the Anne of today. Peter said quite rightly about me: "If ever I saw you, you were always surrounded by two or more boys and a whole troupe of girls. You were always laughing and always the center of everything!"

What is left of this girl? Oh, don't worry, I haven't forgotten how to laugh or to answer back readily. I'm just as good, if not better, at criticizing people, and I can still flirt if . . . I wish. That's not it though, I'd like that sort of life again for an evening, a few days, or even a week; the life which seems so carefree and gay But at the end of that week, I should be dead beat and would be only too thankful to listen to anyone who began to talk about something sensible. I don't want followers, but friends, admirers who fall not for a flattering smile but for what one does and for one's character.

I know quite well that the circle around me would be much smaller. But what does that matter, as long as one still keeps a few sincere friends?

Yet I wasn't entirely happy in 1942 in spite of everything; I often felt deserted, but because I was on the go the whole day long, I didn't think about it and enjoyed myself as much as I could. Consciously or unconsciously, I tried to drive away the emptiness I felt with jokes and pranks. Now I think seriously about life and what I have to do. One period of my life is over forever. The carefree schooldays are gone, never to return.

I don't even long for them any more; I have outgrown them, I can't just only enjoy myself as my serious side is always there.

I look upon my life up till the New Year, as it were, through a powerful magnifying glass. The sunny life at home, then coming here in 1942, the sudden change, the quarrels, the bickerings. I couldn't understand it, I was taken by surprise, and the only way I could keep up some bearing was by being impertinent.

The first half of 1943: my fits of crying, the loneliness, how I slowly began to see all my faults and shortcomings, which are so great and which seemed much greater then. During the day I deliberately talked about anything and everything that was farthest from my thoughts, tried to draw Pim to me; but couldn't. Alone I had to face the difficult task of changing myself, to stop the everlasting reproaches, which were so oppressive and which reduced me to such terrible despondency.

Things improved slightly in the second half of the year, I became a young woman and was treated more like a grownup. I started to think, and write stories, and came to the conclusion that the others no longer had the right to throw me about like an india-rubber ball. I wanted to change in accordance with my own desires. But *one* thing that struck me even more was when I realized that even Daddy would never become my confidant over everything. I didn't want to trust anyone but myself any more.

At the beginning of the New Year: the second great change, my dream. . . . And with it I discovered my longing, not for a girl friend, but for a boy friend. I also discovered my inward happiness and my defensive armor of superficiality and gaiety. In due time I quieted down and discovered my boundless desire for all that is beautiful and good.

And in the evening, when I lie in bed and end my prayers with the words, "I thank you, God, for all that is good and dear and beautiful," I am filled with joy. Then I think about "the good" of going into hiding, of my health and with my whole being of the "dearness" of Peter, of that which is still embryonic and impressionable and which we neither of us dare to name or touch, of that which will come sometime; love, the future, happiness and of "the beauty" which exists in the world; the world, nature, beauty and all, all that is exquisite and fine.

I don't think then of all the misery, but of the beauty that still remains. This is one of the things that Mummy and I are so entirely different about. Her counsel when one feels melancholy is: "Think of all the misery in the world and be thankful that you are not sharing in it!" My advice is: "Go outside, to the fields, enjoy nature and the sunshine, go out and try to recapture happiness in yourself and in God. Think of all the beauty that's still left in and around you and be happy!"

I don't see how Mummy's idea can be right, because then how are you supposed to behave if you go through the misery yourself? Then you are lost. On the contrary, I've found that there is always some beauty left—in nature, sunshine, freedom, in yourself; these can all help you. Look at these things, then you find yourself again, and God, and then you regain your balance.

And whoever is happy will make others happy too. He who has courage and faith will never perish in misery!

Yours, Anne

Sunday, 12 March, 1944

Dear Kitty,

I can't seem to sit still lately; I run upstairs and down and then back again. I love talking to Peter, but I'm always afraid of being a nuisance. He has told me a bit about the past, about his parents and about himself. It's not half enough though and I ask myself why it is that I always long for more. He used to think I was unbearable; and I returned the compliment; now I have changed my opinion, has he changed his too?

I think so; still it doesn't necessarily mean that we shall become great friends, although as far as I am concerned it would make the time here much more bearable. But still, I won't get myself upset about it—I see quite a lot of him and there's no need to make you unhappy about it too, Kitty, just because I feel so miserable.

On Saturday afternoon I felt in such a whirl, after hearing a whole lot of sad news, that I went and lay on my divan for a sleep. I only wanted to sleep to stop myself thinking. I slept till four o'clock, then I had to go into the living room. I found it difficult to answer all Mummy's questions and think of some little excuse to tell Daddy, as an explanation for my long sleep. I resorted to a "headache," which wasn't a lie, as I had one . . . but inside!

Ordinary people, ordinary girls, teen-agers like myself, will think I'm a bit cracked with all my self-pity. Yes, that's what it is, but I pour out my heart to you, then for the rest of the day I'm as impudent, gay, and self-confident as I can be, in order to avoid questions and getting on my own nerves.

Margot is very sweet and would like me to trust her, but still, I can't tell her everything. She's a darling, she's good and pretty, but she lacks the nonchalance for conducting deep discussions; she takes me so seriously, much too seriously, and then thinks about her queer little sister for a long time afterwards, looks searchingly at me, at every word I say, and keeps on thinking: "Is this just a joke or does she really mean it?" I think that's because we are together the whole day long, and that if I trusted someone completely, then I shouldn't want them hanging around me all the time.

When shall I finally untangle my thoughts, when shall I find peace and rest within myself again?

Yours, Anne

Tuesday, 14 March, 1944

Dear Kitty,

Perhaps it would be entertaining for you—though not in the least for me—to hear what we are going to eat today. As the charwoman is at work downstairs, I'm sitting on the Van Daans' table at the moment. I have a handkerchief soaked in some good scent (bought before we came here) over my mouth and held against my nose. You won't gather much from this, so let's "begin at the beginning."

The people from whom we obtained food coupons have been caught, so we just have our five ration cards and no extra coupons, and no fats. As both Miep and Koophuis are ill, Elli hasn't time to do any shopping, so the atmosphere is dreary and dejected, and so is the food. From tomorrow we shall not have a scrap of fat, butter, or margarine left. We can't have fried potatoes (to save bread) for breakfast any longer, so we have porridge instead, and as Mrs. Van Daan thinks we're starving, we have bought some full cream milk "under the counter." Our supper today consists of a hash made from kale which has been preserved in a barrel. Hence the precautionary measure with the handkerchief! It's incredible how kale can stink when it's a year old! The smell in the room is a mixture of bad plums, strong preservatives, and rotten eggs. Ugh! the mere thought of eating that muck makes me feel sick.

Added to this, our potatoes are suffering from such peculiar diseases that out of two buckets of *pommes de terre,* one whole one ends up on the stove. We amuse ourselves by searching for all the different kinds of diseases, and have come to the conclusion that they range from cancer and smallpox to measles! Oh, no, it's no joke to be in hiding during the fourth year of the war. If only the whole rotten business was over!

Quite honestly, I wouldn't care so much about the food, if only it were more pleasant here in other ways. There's the rub: this tedious existence is beginning to make us all touchy.

The following are the views of the five grownups on the present situation:

Mrs. Van Daan: "The job as queen of the kitchen lost its attraction a long time ago. It's dull to sit and do nothing, so I go back to my cooking again. Still, I have to complain that it's impossible to cook without any fats, and all these nasty smells make me feel sick. Nothing but ingratitude and rude remarks do I get in return for my services. I am always the black sheep, always the guilty one. Moreover, according to me, very little progress is being made in the war; in the end the Germans will still win. I'm afraid we're going to starve, and if I'm in a bad mood I scold everyone."

Mr. Van Daan: "I must smoke and smoke and smoke, and then the food, the political situation, and Kerli's moods don't seem so bad. Kerli is a darling wife."

But if he hasn't anything to smoke, then nothing is right,

and this is what one hears: "I'm getting ill, we don't live well enough, I must have meat. Frightfully stupid person, my Kerli!" After this a terrific quarrel is sure to follow.

Mrs. Frank: "Food is not very important, but I would love a slice of rye bread now, I feel so terribly hungry. If I were Mrs. Van Daan I would have put a stop to Mr. Van Daan's everlasting smoking a long time ago. But now I must definitely have a cigarette, because my nerves are getting the better of me. The English make a lot of mistakes, but still the war is progressing. I must have a chat and be thankful I'm not in Poland."

Mr. Frank: "Everything's all right. I don't require anything. Take it easy, we've ample time. Give me my potatoes and then I will keep my mouth shut. Put some of my rations on one side for Elli. The political situation is very promising, I'm extremely optimistic!"

Mr. Dussel: "I must get my task for today, everything must be finished on time. Political situation 'outschtänding' and it is 'eempossible' that we'll be caught.
"I, I, I . . . !"

Yours, Anne

Wednesday, 15 March, 1944

Dear Kitty,

Phew! Oh dear, oh dear—released from the somber scenes for a moment! Today I hear nothing but "if this or that should happen, then we are going to be in difficulties . . . if he or she should become ill, then we'll be completely isolated, and then if . . ." *Enfin,* I expect you know the rest, at least I presume you know the "Secret Annexers" well enough by this time to be able to guess the trend of their conversations.

The reason for all this "if, if" is that Mr. Kraler has been called up to go digging. Elli has a streaming cold and will probably have to stay at home tomorrow. Miep hasn't fully recovered from her flu yet, and Koophuis has had such bad hemorrhage of the stomach that he lost consciousness. What a tale of woe!

The warehouse people are getting a free day tomorrow; Elli can stay at home, then the door will remain locked and we shall have to be as quiet as mice, so that the neighbors don't hear us. Henk is coming to visit the deserted ones at one o'clock—playing the role of zoo-keeper, as it were. For the first time in ages he told us something about the great wide world this afternoon. You should have seen the eight of us sitting around him; it looked exactly like a picture of grandmother telling a story. He talked nineteen to the dozen to his grateful audience about food, of course, and then Miep's doctor, and everything that we asked about. "Doctor," he said, "don't talk to me about the doctor! I rang him up this morning, had his assistant on the phone and asked for a prescription for flu. The reply was that I could come and get the prescription any time between eight and nine in the morning. If you have a very bad attack of flu, the doctor comes to the telephone himself and says 'Put out your tongue, say Aah, I can hear all right that your throat is inflamed. I'll write out a prescription for you to order from the chemist. Good-by.' And that's that." A fine practice that, run by telephone only.

But I don't want to criticize the doctors; after all, a person has but two hands, and in these days there's an abundance of patients and very few doctors to cope with them. Still, we couldn't help laughing when Henk repeated the telephone conversation to us.

I can just imagine what a doctor's waiting room must look like nowadays. One doesn't look down on panel patients any more, but on the people with minor ailments, and thinks: "Hi, you, what are you doing here, end of the line, please; urgent cases have priority!"

Yours, Anne

Thursday, 16 March, 1944

Dear Kitty,

The weather is lovely, superb, I can't describe it; I'm going up to the attic in a minute.

Now I know why I'm so much more restless than Peter. He has his own room where he can work, dream, think, and sleep. I am shoved about from one corner to another. I hardly spend any time in my "double" room and yet it's something I long for so much. That is the reason too why I so frequently escape to the attic. There, and with you, I can be myself for a while, just a little while. Still, I don't want to moan about myself, on the contrary, I want to be brave. Thank goodness the others can't tell what my inward feelings are, except that I'm growing cooler towards Mummy daily, I'm not so affectionate to Daddy and don't tell Margot a single thing. I'm completely closed up. Above all, I must maintain my outward reserve, no one must know that war still reigns incessantly within. War between desire and common sense. The latter has won up till now; yet will the former prove to be the stronger of the two? Sometimes I fear that it will and sometimes I long for it to be!

Oh, it is so terribly difficult never to say anything to Peter, but I know that the first to begin must be he; there's so much I want to say and do, I've lived it all in my dreams, it is so hard to find that yet another day has gone by, and none of it comes true! Yes, Kitty, Anne is a crazy child, but I do live in crazy times and under still crazier circumstances.

But, still, the brightest spot of all is that at least I can write down my thoughts and feelings, otherwise I would be absolutely stifled! I wonder what Peter thinks about all these things? I keep hoping that I can talk about it to him one day. There must be something he has guessed about me, because he certainly can't love the outer Anne, which is the one he knows so far.

How can he, who loves peace and quiet, have any liking for all my bustle and din? Can he possibly be the first and only one to have looked through my concrete armor? And will it take him long to get there? Isn't there an old saying that love often springs from pity, or that the two go hand in hand? Is that the case with me too? Because I'm often just as sorry for him as I am for myself.

I really don't honestly know how to begin, and however would he be able to, when he finds talking so much more difficult than I do? If only I could write to him, then at least I would know that he would grasp what I want to say, because it's so terribly difficult to put it into words!

Yours, Anne

Friday, 17 March, 1944

Dear Kitty,

A sigh of relief has gone through the "Secret Annexe." Kraler has been exempted from digging by the Court. Elli has given her nose a talking to and strictly forbidden it to be a nuisance to her today. So everything is all right again, except that Margot and I are getting a bit tired of our parents. Don't misunderstand me, I can't get on well with Mummy at the moment, as you know. I still love Daddy just as much, and Margot loves Daddy and Mummy, but when you are as old as we are, you do want to decide just a few things for yourself, you want to be independent sometimes.

If I go upstairs, then I'm asked what I'm going to do, I'm not allowed salt with my food, every evening regularly at a quarter past eight Mummy asks whether I ought not to start undressing, every book I read must be inspected. I must admit that they are not at all strict, and I'm allowed to read nearly everything, and yet we are both sick of all the remarks plus all the questioning that go on the whole day long.

Something else, especially about me, that doesn't please them: I don't feel like giving lots of kisses any more and I think fancy nicknames are terribly affected. In short, I'd really like to be rid of them for a while. Margot said last evening, "I think it's awfully annoying, the way they ask if you've got a headache, or whether you don't feel well, if you happen to give a sigh and put your hand to your head!"

It is a great blow to us both, suddenly to realize how little remains of the confidence and harmony that we used to have at home. And it's largely due to the fact that we're all "skew-wiff" here. By this I mean that we are treated as children over outward things, and we are much older than most girls of our age inwardly.

Although I'm only fourteen, I know quite well what I want, I know who is right and who is wrong, I have my opinions, my own ideas and principles, and although it may sound pretty mad from an adolescent, I feel more of a person than a child, I feel quite independent of anyone.

I know that I can discuss things and argue better than Mummy, I know I'm not so prejudiced, I don't exaggerate so much, I am more precise and adroit and because of this—you may laugh—I feel superior to her over a great many things. If I love anyone, above all I must have admiration for them, admiration and respect. Everything would be all right if only I had Peter, for I do admire him in many ways. He is such a nice, good-looking boy!

                                                        Yours, Anne

                                              Sunday, 19 March, 1944

Dear Kitty,

Yesterday was a great day for me. I had decided to talk things out with Peter. Just as we were going to sit down to supper I whispered to him, "Are you going to do shorthand this evening, Peter?" "No," was his reply. "Then I'd just like to talk to you later!" He agreed. After the dishes were done, I stood by the window in his parents' room awhile for the look of things, but it wasn't long before I went to Peter. He was standing on the left side of the open window, I went and stood on the right side, and we talked. It was much easier to talk beside the open window in semidarkness than in bright light, and I believe Peter felt the same.

We told each other so much, so very very much, that I can't repeat it all, but it was lovely; the most wonderful evening I

have ever had in the "Secret Annexe." I will just tell you briefly the various things we talked about. First we talked about
the quarrels and how I regard them quite differently now, and
then about the estrangement between us and our parents.

I told Peter about Mummy and Daddy, and Margot, and
about myself.

At one moment he asked, "I suppose you always give each
other a good night kiss, don't you?"

"*One*, dozens, why, don't you?"

"No, I have hardly ever kissed anyone."

"Not even on your birthday?"

"Yes, I have then."

We talked about how we neither of us confide in our parents, and how his parents would have loved to have his confidence, but that he didn't wish it. How I cry my heart out in
bed, and he goes up into the loft and swears. How Margot and
I really only know each other well for a little while, but that,
even so, we don't tell each other everything, because we are
always together. Over every imaginable thing—oh, he was just
as I thought!

Then we talked about 1942, how different we were then.
We just don't recognize ourselves as the same people any
more. How we simply couldn't bear each other in the beginning. He thought I was much too talkative and unruly, and I
soon came to the conclusion that I'd no time for him. I couldn't
understand why he didn't flirt with me, but now I'm glad. He
also mentioned how much he isolated himself from us all. I
said that there was not much difference between my noise and
his silence. That I love peace and quiet too, and have nothing
for myself alone, except my diary. How glad he is that my
parents have children here, and that I'm glad he is here. That
I understand his reserve now and his relationship with his
parents, and how I would love to be able to help him.

"You always do help me," he said. "How?" I asked, very
surprised. "By your cheerfulness." That was certainly the
loveliest thing he said. It was wonderful, he must have grown
to love me as a friend, and that is enough for the time being.

I am so grateful and happy, I just can't find the words. I must apologize, Kitty, that my style is not up to standard today.

I have just written down what came into my head. I have the feeling now that Peter and I share a secret. If he looks at me with those eyes that laugh and wink, then it's just as if a little light goes on inside me. I hope it will remain like this and that we may have many, many more glorious times together!

Your grateful, happy Anne

Monday, 20 March, 1944

Dear Kitty,

This morning Peter asked me if I would come again one evening, and said that I really didn't disturb him, and if there's room for one there's room for two. I said that I couldn't come every evening, because they wouldn't like it downstairs, but he thought that I needn't let that bother me. Then I said that I would love to come one Saturday evening and especially asked him to warn me when there was a moon. "Then we'll go downstairs," he answered, "and look at the moon from there."

In the meantime a little shadow has fallen on my happiness. I've thought for a long time that Margot liked Peter quite a lot too. How much she loves him I don't know, but I think it's wretched. I must cause her terrible pain each time I'm with Peter, and the funny part of it is that she hardly shows it.

I know quite well that I'd be desperately jealous, but Margot only says that I needn't pity her.

"I think it's so rotten that you should be the odd one out," I added. "I'm used to that," she answered, somewhat bitterly.

I don't dare tell Peter this yet, perhaps later on, but we've got to talk about so many other things first.

I had a little ticking off yesterday evening from Mummy, which I certainly deserved. I mustn't overdo my indifference towards her. So in spite of everything, I must try once again to be friendly and keep my observations to myself.

Even Pim is different lately. He is trying not to treat me as such a child, and it makes him much too cool. See what comes of it!

Enough for now, I'm full to the brim with Peter and can do nothing but look at him!

Evidence of Margot's goodness: I received this today,

March 20th, 1944

Anne, when I said yesterday that I was not jealous of you I was only fifty per cent honest. It is like this; I'm jealous of neither you nor Peter. I only feel a bit sorry that I haven't found anyone yet, and am not likely to for the time being, with whom I can discuss my thoughts and feelings. But I should not grudge it to you for that reason. One misses enough here anyway, things that other people just take for granted.

On the other hand, I know for certain that I would never have got so far with Peter, anyway, because I have the feeling that if I wished to discuss a lot with anyone, I should want to be on rather intimate terms with him. I would want to have the feeling that he understood me through and through without my having to say much. But for that reason it would have to be someone whom I felt was my superior intellectually, and that is not the case with Peter. But I can imagine it being so with you and Peter.

You are not doing me out of anything which is my due; do not reproach yourself in the least on my account. You and Peter can only gain by the friendship.

My reply:

Dear Margot,

I thought your letter was exceptionally sweet, but I still don't feel quite happy about it and nor do I think that I shall.

At present there is no question of such confidence as you have in mind between Peter and myself, but in the twilight beside an open window you can say more to each other than in brilliant sunshine. Also it's easier to whisper your feelings than to trumpet them forth out loud. I believe that you are beginning to feel a kind of sisterly affection for Peter, and that you would love to help him, just as much as I. Perhaps you will still be able to do that sometime, although that is not the kind of confidence we have in mind. I think it must come from both sides, and I believe that's the reason why Daddy and I have never got so far.

Let's not talk about it any more; but if you still want anything

*please write to me about it, because I can say what I mean much
better on paper.*

*You don't know how much I admire you, and I only hope that I
may yet acquire some of the goodness that you and Daddy have,
because now I don't see much difference between you and Daddy
in that sense.*

Yours, Anne

Wednesday, 22 March, 1944

Dear Kitty,

I received this from Margot last evening:

Dear Anne,

*After your letter yesterday I have the unpleasant feeling that you
will have prickings of conscience when you visit Peter; but really
there is no reason for this. In my heart of hearts I feel that I have
the right to share mutual confidence with someone, but I could not
bear Peter in that role yet.*

*However, I do feel just as you say, that Peter is a bit like a
brother, but—a younger brother; we have put out feelers towards
each other, the affection of a brother and sister might grow if they
touched, perhaps they will later—perhaps never; however, it has
certainly not reached that stage yet.*

*Therefore you really needn't pity me. Now that you've found
companionship, enjoy it as much as you can.*

In the meantime it is getting more and more wonderful
here. I believe, Kitty, that we may have a real great love in
the "Secret Annexe." Don't worry, I'm not thinking of marry-
ing him. I don't know what he will be like when he grows up,
nor do I know whether we should ever love each other enough
to marry. I know now that Peter loves me, but just how I myself don't know yet.

Whether he only wants a great friend, or whether I attract
him as a girl or as a sister, I can't yet discover.

When he said that I always helped him over his parents'
quarrels, I was awfully glad; it was one step towards making
me believe in his friendship. I asked him yesterday what he
would do if there were a dozen Annes here who always kept

coming to him. His reply was, "If they were all like you, it certainly wouldn't be too bad!" He's tremendously hospitable towards me and I really believe he likes to see me. Meanwhile he is working diligently at his French, even when he's in bed, going on until a quarter past ten. Oh, when I think about Saturday evening and recall it all, word for word, then for the first time I don't feel discontented about myself; I mean that I would still say exactly the same and wouldn't wish to change anything, as is usually the case.

He is so handsome, both when he laughs and when he looks quietly in front of him; he is such a darling and so good. I believe what surprised him most about me was when he discovered that I'm not a bit the superficial worldly Anne that I appear, but just as dreamy a specimen, with just as many difficulties as he himself.

Yours, Anne

Reply:

Dear Margot,

I think the best thing we can do is simply to wait and see what happens. It can't be very long before Peter and I come to a definite decision, either to go on as before or be different. Just which way it will go I don't know myself, and I don't bother to look beyond my own nose. But I shall certainly do one thing, if Peter and I decide to be friends, I shall tell him that you are very fond of him too and would always be prepared to help him should the need arise. The latter may not be what you wish, but I don't care now; I don't know what Peter thinks about you, but I shall ask him then.

I'm sure it's not bad—the opposite! You are always welcome to join us in the attic, or wherever we are; you honestly won't disturb us because I feel we have a silent agreement to talk only in the evenings when it's dark.

Keep your courage up! Like I do. Although it's not always easy; your time may come sooner than you think.

Yours, Anne

Thursday, 23 March, 1944

Dear Kitty,

Things are running more or less normally again now. Our coupon men are out of prison again, thank goodness!

Miep returned yesterday. Elli is better, although she still has a cough; Koophuis will have to stay at home for a long time still.

A plane crashed near here yesterday; the occupants were able to jump out in time by parachute. The machine crashed onto a school, but there were no children there at the time. The result was a small fire and two people killed. The Germans shot at the airmen terribly as they were coming down. The Amsterdammers who saw it nearly exploded with rage and indignation at the cowardliness of such a deed. We—I'm speaking of the ladies—nearly jumped out of our skins, I loathe the blasted shooting.

I often go upstairs after supper nowadays and take a breath of the fresh evening air. I like it up there, sitting on a chair beside him and looking outside.

Van Daan and Dussel make very feeble remarks when I disappear into his room; "Anne's second home," they call it, or "Is it suitable for young gentlemen to receive young girls in semidarkness?" Peter shows amazing wit in his replies to these so-called humorous sallies. For that matter, Mummy too is somewhat curious and would love to ask what we talk about, if she wasn't secretly afraid of being snubbed. Peter says it's nothing but envy on the part of the grownups, because we are young and we don't pay much attention to their spitefulness. Sometimes he comes and gets me from downstairs, but he turns simply scarlet in spite of all precautions, and can hardly get the words out of his mouth. How thankful I am that I don't blush, it must be a highly unpleasant sensation. Daddy always says I'm prudish and vain but that's not true, I'm just simply vain! I have not often had anyone tell me I was pretty. Except a boy at school, who said I looked so attractive when I laughed. Yesterday I received a genuine compliment from

Peter, and just for fun I will tell you roughly how the conversation went:

Peter so often used to say, "Do laugh, Anne!" This struck me as odd, and I asked, "Why must I always laugh?"

"Because I like it; you get such dimples in your cheeks when you laugh; how do they come, actually?"

"I was born with them. I've got one in my chin too. That's my only beauty!"

"Of course not, that's not true."

"Yes, it is, I know quite well that I'm not a beauty; I never have been and never shall be."

"I don't agree at all, I think you're pretty."

"That's not true."

"If I say so, then you can take it from me it is!"

Then I naturally said the same of him.

I hear a lot from all sides about the sudden friendship. We don't take much notice of all this parental chatter, their remarks are so feeble. Have the two sets of parents forgotten their own youth? It seems like it, at least they seem to take us seriously, if we make a joke, and laugh at us when we are serious.

Yours, Anne

Monday, 27 March, 1944

Dear Kitty,

One very big chapter of our history in hiding should really be about politics, but as this subject doesn't interest me personally very much, I've rather let it go. So for once I will devote my whole letter to politics today.

It goes without saying that there are very many different opinions on this topic, and it's even more logical that it should be a favorite subject for discussion in such critical times, but—it's just simply stupid that there should be so many quarrels over it.

They may speculate, laugh, abuse, and grumble, let them do what they will, as long as they stew in their own juice and don't quarrel, because the consequences are usually unpleasant.

The people from outside bring with them a lot of news that is not true; however, up till now our radio set hasn't lied to us. Henk, Miep, Koophuis, Elli, and Kraler all show ups and downs in their political moods, Henk least of all.

Political feeling here in the "Secret Annexe" is always about the same. During the countless arguments over invasion, air raids, speeches, etc., etc., one also always hears the countless cries of "impossible," or *"Um Gottes Willen,* if they are going to start now however long is it going to last?" "It's going splendidly, first class, good!" Optimists and pessimists, and, above all, don't let's forget the realists who give their opinions with untiring energy and, just as with everything else, each one thinking he is right. It annoys a certain lady that her spouse has such unparalleled faith in the British, and a certain gentleman attacks his lady because of her teasing and disparaging remarks about his beloved nation.

They never seem to tire of it. I have discovered something —the effects are stupendous, just like pricking someone with a pin and waiting to see how they jump. This is what I do: begin on politics. One question, one word, one sentence, and at once they're off!

Just as if the German Wehrmacht news bulletins and the English B.B.C. were not enough, they have now introduced "Special Air-Raid Announcements." In one word, magnificent; but on the other hand often disappointing too. The British are making a non-stop business of their air attacks, with the same zest as the Germans make a business of lying. The radio therefore goes on early in the morning and is listened to at all hours of the day, until nine, ten, and often eleven o'clock in the evening.

This is certainly a sign that the grownups have infinite patience, but it also means the power of absorption of their brains is pretty limited, with exceptions, of course—I don't want to hurt anyone's feelings. One or two news bulletins would be ample per day! But the old geese, well—I've said my piece!

Arbeiter-Programm, Radio "Oranje," Frank Phillips or Her Majesty Queen Wilhelmina, they each get their turn, and an ever attentive ear. And if they are not eating or sleeping, then they're sitting around the radio and discussing food, sleep, and politics.

Ugh! It gets so boring, and it's quite a job not to become a dull old stick oneself. Politics can't do much more harm to the parents!

I must mention one shining exception—a speech by our beloved Winston Churchill is quite perfect.

Nine o'clock on Sunday evening. The teapot stands, with the cozy over it, on the table, and the guests come in. Dussel next to the radio on the left, Mr. Van Daan in front of it, with Peter beside him. Mummy next to Mr. Van Daan and Mrs. Van Daan behind him, and Pim at the table, Margot and I beside. I see I haven't described very clearly how we sit. The gentlemen puff away at their pipes, Peter's eyes are popping out of his head with the strain of listening, Mummy wearing a long dark negligée, and Mrs. Van Daan trembling because of the planes, which take no notice of the speech but fly blithely on towards Essen, Daddy sipping tea, Margot and I united in a sisterly fashion by the sleeping Mouschi, who is monopolizing both our knees. Margot's hair is in curlers, I am wearing a nightdress, which is much too small, too narrow, and too short.

It all looks so intimate, snug, peaceful, and this time it is too; yet I await the consequences with horror. They can hardly wait till the end of the speech, stamping their feet, so impatient are they to get down to discussing it. Brr, brr, brr—they egg each other on until the arguments lead to discord and quarrels.

Yours, Anne

Tuesday, 28 March, 1944

Dearest Kitty,

I could write a lot more about politics, but I have heaps of

other things to tell you today. First, Mummy has more or less
forbidden me to go upstairs so often, because, according to
her, Mrs. Van Daan is jealous. Secondly, Peter has invited
Margot to join us upstairs; I don't know whether it's just out
of politeness or whether he really means it. Thirdly, I went
and asked Daddy if he thought I need pay any regard to Mrs.
Van Daan's jealousy, and he didn't think so. What next? Mummy is cross, perhaps jealous too. Daddy doesn't grudge us
these times together, and thinks it's nice that we get on so
well. Margot is fond of Peter too, but feels that two's company
and three's a crowd.

Mummy thinks that Peter is in love with me; quite frankly,
I only wish he were, then we'd be quits and really be able to
get to know each other. She also says that he keeps on looking
at me. Now, I suppose that's true, but still I can't help it if
he looks at my dimples and we wink at each other occasionally, can I?

I'm in a very difficult position. Mummy is against me and
I'm against her, Daddy closes his eyes and tries not to see the
silent battle between us. Mummy is sad, because she does
really love me, while I'm not in the least bit sad, because I
don't think she understands. And Peter—I don't want to give
Peter up, he's such a darling. I admire him so; it can grow into
something beautiful between us; why do the "old 'uns" have
to poke their noses in all the time? Luckily I'm quite used to
hiding my feelings and I manage extremely well not to let
them see how mad I am about him. Will he ever say anything?
Will I ever feel his cheek against mine, like I felt Petel's cheek
in my dream? Oh, Peter and Petel, you are one and the same!
They don't understand us; won't they ever grasp that we are
happy, just sitting together and not saying a word. They don't
understand what has driven us together like this. Oh, when
will all these difficulties be overcome? And yet it is good to
overcome them, because then the end will be all the more
wonderful. When he lies with his head on his arm with his
eyes closed, then he is still a child; when he plays with Boche,
he is loving; when he carries potatoes or anything heavy, then
he is strong; when he goes and watches the shooting, or looks

for burglars in the darkness, then he is brave; and when he is so awkward and clumsy, then he is just a pet.

I like it much better if he explains something to me than when I have to teach him; I would really adore him to be my superior in almost everything.

What do we care about the two mothers? Oh, but if only he would speak!

Yours, Anne

Wednesday, 29 March, 1944

Dear Kitty,

Bolkestein, an M.P., was speaking on the Dutch News from London, and he said that they ought to make a collection of diaries and letters after the war. Of course, they all made a rush at my diary immediately. Just imagine how interesting it would be if I were to publish a romance of the "Secret Annexe." The title[1] alone would be enough to make people think it was a detective story.

But, seriously, it would seem quite funny ten years after the war if we Jews were to tell how we lived and what we ate and talked about here. Although I tell you a lot, still, even so, you only know very little of our lives.

How scared the ladies are during the air raids. For instance, on Sunday, when 350 British planes dropped half a million kilos of bombs on Ijmuiden, how the houses trembled like a wisp of grass in the wind, and who knows how many epidemics now rage. You don't know anything about all these things, and I would need to keep on writing the whole day if I were to tell you everything in detail. People have to line up for vegetables and all kinds of other things; doctors are unable to visit the sick, because if they turn their backs on their cars for a moment, they are stolen; burglaries and thefts abound, so much so that you wonder what has taken hold of the Dutch for them suddenly to have become such thieves. Little children of

---

[1] The original title of this diary was *Het Achterhuis*. There is no exact translation into English, the nearest being *The Secret Annexe*.

eight and eleven years break the windows of people's homes and steal whatever they can lay their hands on. No one dares to leave his house unoccupied for five minutes, because if you go, your things go too. Every day there are announcements in the newspapers offering rewards for the return of lost property, typewriters, Persian rugs, electric clocks, cloth, etc., etc. Electric clocks in the streets are dismantled, public telephones are pulled to pieces—down to the last thread. Morale among the population can't be good, the weekly rations are not enough to last for two days except the coffee substitute. The invasion is a long time coming, and the men have to go to Germany. The children are ill or undernourished, everyone is wearing old clothes and old shoes. A new sole costs 7.50 florins in the black market; moreover, hardly any of the shoemakers will accept shoe repairs or, if they do, you have to wait months, during which time the shoes often disappear.

There's one good thing in the midst of it all, which is that as the food gets worse and the measures against the people more severe, so sabotage against the authorities steadily increases. The people in the food offices, the police, officials, they all either work with their fellow citizens and help them or they tell tales on them and have them sent to prison. Fortunately, only a small percentage of Dutch people are on the wrong side.

Yours, Anne

Friday, 31 March, 1944

Dear Kitty,

Think of it, it's still pretty cold, but most people have been without coal for about a month—pleasant, eh! In general public feeling over the Russian front is optimistic again, because that is terrific! You know I don't write much about politics, but I must just tell you where they are now; they are right by the Polish border and have reached the Pruth near Rumania. They are close to Odessa. Every evening here they expect an extra communiqué from Stalin.

They fire off so many salvos in Moscow to celebrate their victories that the city must rumble and shake just about every day—whether they think it's fun to pretend that the war is close at hand again or that they know of no other way of expressing their joy, I don't know!

Hungary is occupied by German troops. There are still a million Jews there, so they too will have had it now.

The chatter about Peter and me has calmed down a bit now. We are very good friends, are together a lot and discuss every imaginable subject. It is awfully nice never to have to keep a check on myself as I would have to with other boys, whenever we get on to precarious ground. We were talking, for instance, about blood and via that subject we began talking about menstruation. He thinks we women are pretty tough. Why on earth? My life here has improved, greatly improved. God has not left me alone and will not leave me alone.

Yours, Anne

Saturday, 1 April, 1944

Dear Kitty,

And yet everything is still so difficult; I expect you can guess what I mean, can't you? I am so longing for a kiss, the kiss that is so long in coming. I wonder if all the time he still regards me as a friend? Am I nothing more?

You know and I know that I am strong, that I can carry most of my burdens alone. I have never been used to sharing my troubles with anyone, I have never clung to my mother, but now I would so love to lay my head on "his" shoulder just once and remain still.

I can't, I simply can't ever forget that dream of Peter's cheek, when it was all, all so good! Wouldn't he long for it too? Is it that he is just too shy to acknowledge his love? Why does he want me with him so often? Oh, why doesn't he speak?

I'd better stop, I must be quiet, I shall remain strong and with a bit of patience the other will come too, but—and that is the worst of it—it looks just as if I'm running after him; *I* am always the one who goes upstairs, *he* doesn't come to me.

But that is just because of the rooms, and he is sure to understand the difficulty.

Oh, yes, and there's more he'll understand.

Yours, Anne

Monday, 3 April, 1944

Dear Kitty,

Contrary to my usual custom, I will for once write more fully about food because it has become a very difficult and important matter, not only here in the "Secret Annexe" but in the whole of Holland, all Europe, and even beyond.

In the twenty-one months that we've spent here we have been through a good many "food cycles"—you'll understand what that means in a minute. When I talk of "food cycles" I mean periods in which one has nothing else to eat but one particular dish or kind of vegetable. We had nothing but endive for a long time, day in, day out, endive with sand, endive without sand, stew with endive, boiled or *en casserole;* then it was spinach, and after that followed kohlrabi, salsify, cucumbers, tomatoes, sauerkraut, etc., etc.

For instance, it's really disagreeable to eat a lot of sauerkraut for lunch and supper every day, but you do it if you're hungry. However, we have the most delightful period of all now, because we don't get any fresh vegetables at all. Our weekly menu for supper consists of kidney beans, pea soup, potatoes with dumplings, potato-chalet and, by the grace of God, occasionally turnip tops or rotten carrots, and then the kidney beans once again. We eat potatoes at every meal, beginning with breakfast, because of the bread shortage. We make our soup from kidney or haricot beans, potatoes, Julienne soup in packets, French beans in packets, kidney beans in packets. Everything contains beans, not to mention the bread!

In the evening we always have potatoes with gravy substitute and—thank goodness we've still got it—beetroot salad. I must still tell you about the dumplings, which we make out of government flour, water, and yeast. They are so sticky and tough, they lie like stones in one's stomach—ah, well!

The great attraction each week is a slice of liver sausage, and jam on dry bread. But we're still alive, and quite often we even enjoy our poor meals.

Yours, Anne

Tuesday, 4 April, 1944

Dear Kitty,

For a long time I haven't had any idea of what I was working for any more; the end of the war is so terribly far away, so unreal, like a fairy tale. If the war isn't over by September I shan't go to school any more, because I don't want to be two years behind. Peter filled my days—nothing but Peter, dreams and thoughts until Saturday, when I felt so utterly miserable; oh, it was terrible. I was holding back my tears all the while I was with Peter, then laughed with Van Daan over lemon punch, was cheerful and excited, but the moment I was alone I knew that I would have to cry my heart out. So, clad in my nightdress, I let myself go and slipped down onto the floor. First I said my long prayer very earnestly, then I cried with my head on my arms, my knees bent up, on the bare floor, completely folded up. One large sob brought me back to earth again, and I quelled my tears because I didn't want them to hear anything in the next room. Then I began trying to talk some courage into myself. I could only say: "I must, I must, I must . . ." Completely stiff from the unnatural position, I fell against the side of the bed and fought on, until I climbed into bed again just before half past ten. It was over!

And now it's all over. I must work, so as not to be a fool, to get on, to become a journalist, because that's what I want! I know that I can write, a couple of my stories are good, my descriptions of the "Secret Annexe" are humorous, there's a lot in my diary that speaks, but—whether I have real talent remains to be seen.

"Eva's Dream" is my best fairy tale, and the queer thing about it is that I don't know where it comes from. Quite a lot of "Cady's Life" is good too, but, on the whole, it's nothing.

I am the best and sharpest critic of my own work. I know myself what is and what is not well written. Anyone who doesn't write doesn't know how wonderful it is; I used to bemoan the fact that I couldn't draw at all, but now I am more than happy that I can at least write. And if I haven't any talent for writing books or newspaper articles, well, then I can always write for myself.

I want to get on; I can't imagine that I would have to lead the same sort of life as Mummy and Mrs. Van Daan and all the women who do their work and are then forgotten. I must have something besides a husband and children, something that I can devote myself to!

I want to go on living even after my death! And therefore I am grateful to God for giving me this gift, this possibility of developing myself and of writing, of expressing all that is in me.

I can shake off everything if I write; my sorrows disappear, my courage is reborn. But, and that is the great question, will I ever be able to write anything great, will I ever become a journalist or a writer? I hope so, oh, I hope so very much, for I can recapture everything when I write, my thoughts, my ideals and my fantasies.

I haven't done anything more to "Cady's Life" for ages; in my mind I know exactly how to go on, but somehow it doesn't flow from my pen. Perhaps I never shall finish it, it may land up in the wastepaper basket, or the fire . . . that's a horrible idea, but then I think to myself, "At the age of fourteen and with so little experience, how can you write about philosophy?"

So I go on again with fresh courage; I think I shall succeed, because I want to write!

                                        Yours, Anne

Thursday, 6 April, 1944

Dear Kitty,

You asked me what my hobbies and interests were, so I
want to reply. I warn you, however, that there are heaps of
them, so don't get a shock!

First of all: writing, but that hardly counts as a hobby.

Number two: family trees. I've been searching for family
trees of the French, German, Spanish, English, Austrian, Russian, Norwegian, and Dutch royal families in all the newspapers, books, and pamphlets I can find. I've made great
progress with a lot of them, as, for a long time already, I've
been taking down notes from all the biographies and history
books that I read; I even copy out many passages of history.

My third hobby then is history, on which Daddy has already bought me a lot of books. I can hardly wait for the day
that I shall be able to comb through the books in a public
library.

Number four is Greek and Roman mythology. I have various books about this too.

Other hobbies are film stars and family photos. Mad on
books and reading. Have a great liking for history of art, poets
and painters. I may go in for music later on. I have a great
loathing for algebra, geometry, and figures.

I enjoy all the other school subjects, but history above all!

Yours, Anne

Tuesday, 11 April, 1944

Dear Kitty,

My head throbs, I honestly don't know where to begin.

On Friday (Good Friday) we played Monopoly, Saturday
afternoon too. These days passed quickly and uneventfully.
On Sunday afternoon, on my invitation, Peter came to my
room at half past four; at a quarter past five we went to the
front attic, where we remained until six o'clock. There was a
beautiful Mozart concert on the radio from six o'clock until a

quarter past seven. I enjoyed it all very much, but especially the "Kleine Nachtmusik." I can hardly listen in the room because I'm always so inwardly stirred when I hear lovely music.

On Sunday evening Peter and I went to the front attic together and, in order to sit comfortably, we took with us a few divan cushions that we were able to lay our hands on. We seated ourselves on one packing case. Both the case and the cushions were very narrow, so we sat absolutely squashed together, leaning against other cases. Mouschi kept us company too, so we weren't unchaperoned.

Suddenly, at a quarter to nine, Mr. Van Daan whistled and asked if we had one of Dussel's cushions. We both jumped up and went downstairs with cushion, cat, and Van Daan.

A lot of trouble arose out of this cushion, because Dussel was annoyed that we had one of his cushions, one that he used as a pillow. He was afraid that there might be fleas in it and made a great commotion about his beloved cushion! Peter and I put two hard brushes in his bed as a revenge. We had a good laugh over this little interlude!

Our fun didn't last long. At half past nine Peter knocked softly on the door and asked Daddy if he would just help him upstairs over a difficult English sentence. "That's a blind," I said to Margot, "anyone could see through that one!" I was right. They were in the act of breaking into the warehouse. Daddy, Van Daan, Dussel, and Peter were downstairs in a flash. Margot, Mummy, Mrs. Van Daan, and I stayed upstairs and waited.

Four frightened women just have to talk, so talk we did, until we heard a bang downstairs. After that all was quiet, the clock struck a quarter to ten. The color had vanished from our faces, we were still quiet, although we were afraid. Where could the men be? What was that bang? Would they be fighting the burglars? Ten o'clock, footsteps on the stairs: Daddy, white and nervous, entered, followed by Mr. Van Daan. "Lights out, creep upstairs, we expect the police in the house!"

There was no time to be frightened: the lights went out, I quickly grabbed a jacket, and we were upstairs. "What has happened? Tell us quickly!" There was no one to tell us, the men having disappeared downstairs again. Only at ten past ten did they reappear; two kept watch at Peter's open window, the door to the landing was closed, the swinging cupboard shut. We hung a jersey round the night light, and after that they told us:

Peter heard two loud bangs on the landing, ran downstairs, and saw there was a large plank out of the left half of the door. He dashed upstairs, warned the "Home Guard" of the family, and the four of them proceeded downstairs. When they entered the warehouse, the burglars were in the act of enlarging the hole. Without further thought Van Daan shouted: "Police!"

A few hurried steps outside, and the burglars had fled. In order to avoid the hole being noticed by the police, a plank was put against it, but a good hard kick from outside sent it flying to the ground. The men were perplexed at such impudence, and both Van Daan and Peter felt murder welling up within them; Van Daan beat on the ground with a chopper, and all was quiet again. Once more they wanted to put the plank in front of the hole. Disturbance! A married couple outside shone a torch through the opening, lighting up the whole warehouse. "Hell!" muttered one of the men, and now they switched over from their role of police to that of burglars. The four of them sneaked upstairs, Peter quickly opened the doors and windows of the kitchen and private office, flung the telephone onto the floor, and finally the four of them landed behind the swinging cupboard.

END OF PART ONE

The married couple with the torch would probably have warned the police: it was Sunday evening, Easter Sunday, no one at the office on Easter Monday, so none of us could budge until Tuesday morning. Think of it, waiting in such fear for two nights and a day! No one had anything to suggest, so we simply sat there in pitch-darkness, because Mrs. Van Daan in

her fright had unintentionally turned the lamp right out;
talked in whispers, and at every creak one heard "Sh! sh!"

It turned half past ten, eleven, but not a sound; Daddy and
Van Daan joined us in turns. Then a quarter past eleven, a
bustle and noise downstairs. Everyone's breath was audible,
otherwise no one moved. Footsteps in the house, in the private
office, kitchen, then . . . on our staircase. No one breathed
audibly now, footsteps on our staircase, then a rattling of the
swinging cupboard. This moment is indescribable. "Now we
are lost!" I said, and could see us all being taken away by the
Gestapo that very night. Twice they rattled at the cupboard,
then there was nothing, the footsteps withdrew, we were
saved so far. A shiver seemed to pass from one to another, I
heard someone's teeth chattering, no one said a word.

There was not another sound in the house, but a light was
burning on our landing, right in front of the cupboard. Could
that be because it was a secret cupboard? Perhaps the police
had forgotten the light? Would someone come back to put it
out? Tongues loosened, there was no one in the house any
longer, perhaps there was someone on guard outside.

Next we did three things: we went over again what we supposed had happened, we trembled with fear, and we had to
go to the lavatory. The buckets were in the attic, so all we had
was Peter's tin wastepaper basket. Van Daan went first, then
Daddy, but Mummy was too shy to face it. Daddy brought
the wastepaper basket into the room, where Margot, Mrs.
Van Daan, and I gladly made use of it. Finally Mummy decided to do so too. People kept on asking for paper—fortunately I had some in my pocket!

The tin smelled ghastly, everything went on in a whisper,
we were tired, it was twelve o'clock. "Lie down on the floor
then and sleep." Margot and I were each given a pillow and
one blanket; Margot lying just near the store cupboard and I
between the table legs. The smell wasn't quite so bad when
one was on the floor, but still Mrs. Van Daan quietly brought
some chlorine, a tea towel over the pot serving as a second
expedient.

Talk, whispers, fear, stink, flatulation, and always someone

on the pot; then try to go to sleep! However, by half past two
I was so tired that I knew no more until half past three. I
awoke when Mrs. Van Daan laid her head on my foot.

"For heaven's sake, give me something to put on!" I asked.
I was given something, but don't ask what—a pair of woolen
knickers over my pajamas, a red jumper, and a black skirt,
white oversocks and a pair of sports stockings full of holes.
Then Mrs. Van Daan sat in the chair and her husband came
and lay on my feet. I lay thinking till half past three, shivering the whole time, which prevented Van Daan from sleeping.
I prepared myself for the return of the police, then we'd have
to say that we were in hiding; they would either be good
Dutch people, then we'd be saved, or N.S.B.-ers,[1] then we'd
have to bribe them!

"In that case, destroy the radio," sighed Mrs. Van Daan.
"Yes, in the stove!" replied her husband. "If they find us, then
let them find the radio as well!"

"Then they will find Anne's diary," added Daddy. "Burn it
then," suggested the most terrified member of the party. This,
and when the police rattled the cupboard door, were my
worst moments. "Not my diary; if my diary goes, I go with it!"
But luckily Daddy didn't answer.

There is no object in recounting all the conversations that I
can still remember; so much was said. I comforted Mrs. Van
Daan, who was very scared. We talked about escaping and
being questioned by the Gestapo, about ringing up, and being
brave.

"We must behave like soldiers, Mrs. Van Daan. If all is up
now, then let's go for Queen and Country, for freedom, truth,
and the right, as they always say on the Dutch News from
England. The only thing that is really rotten is that we get a
lot of other people into trouble too."

Mr. Van Daan changed places again with his wife after an
hour, and Daddy came and sat beside me. The men smoked
non-stop, now and then there was a deep sigh, then someone
went on the pot and everything began all over again.

Four o'clock, five o'clock, half past five. Then I went and

[1] The Dutch National Socialist Movement.

sat with Peter by his window and listened, so close together that we could feel each other's bodies quivering; we spoke a word or two now and then, and listened attentively. In the room next door they took down the blackout. They wanted to call up Koophuis at seven o'clock and get him to send someone around. Then they wrote down everything they wanted to tell Koophuis over the phone. The risk that the police on guard at the door, or in the warehouse, might hear the telephone was very great, but the danger of the police returning was even greater.

The points were these:

Burglars broken in: police have been in the house, as far as the swinging cupboard, but no further.

Burglars apparently disturbed, forced open the door in the warehouse and escaped through the garden.

Main entrance bolted, Kraler must have used the second door when he left. The typewriters and adding machine are safe in the black case in the private office.

Try to warn Henk and fetch the key from Elli, then go and look round the office—on the pretext of feeding the cat.

Everything went according to plan. Koophuis was phoned, the typewriters which we had upstairs were put in the case. Then we sat around the table again and waited for Henk or the police.

Peter had fallen asleep and Van Daan and I were lying on the floor, when we heard loud footsteps downstairs. I got up quietly: "That's Henk."

"No, no, it's the police," some of the others said.

Someone knocked at the door, Miep whistled. This was too much for Mrs. Van Daan, she turned as white as a sheet and sank limply into a chair; had the tension lasted one minute longer she would have fainted.

Our room was a perfect picture when Miep and Henk entered, the table alone would have been worth photographing! A copy of *Cinema and Theater*, covered with jam and a remedy for diarrhea, opened at a page of dancing girls, two jam pots, two started loaves of bread, a mirror, comb, matches, ash, cigarettes, tobacco, ash tray, books, a pair of pants, a torch, toilet paper, etc., etc., lay jumbled together in variegated splendor.

Of course Henk and Miep were greeted with shouts and tears. Henk mended the hole in the door with some planks, and soon went off again to inform the police of the burglary. Miep had also found a letter under the warehouse door from the night watchman Slagter, who had noticed the hole and warned the police, whom he would also visit.

So we had half an hour to tidy ourselves. I've never seen such a change take place in half an hour. Margot and I took the bedclothes downstairs, went to the W.C., washed, and did our teeth and hair. After that I tidied the room a bit and went upstairs again. The table there was already cleared, so we ran off some water and made coffee and tea, boiled the milk, and laid the table for lunch. Daddy and Peter emptied the potties and cleaned them with warm water and chlorine.

At eleven o'clock we sat round the table with Henk, who was back by that time, and slowly things began to be more normal and cozy again. Henk's story was as follows:

Mr. Slagter was asleep, but his wife told Henk that her husband had found the hole in our door when he was doing his tour round the canals, and that he had called a policeman, who had gone through the building with him. He would be coming to see Kraler on Tuesday and would tell him more then. At the police station they knew nothing of the burglary yet, but the policeman had made a note of it at once and would come and look round on Tuesday. On the way back Henk happened to meet our greengrocer at the corner, and told him that the house had been broken into. "I know that," he said quite coolly. "I was passing last evening with my wife and saw the hole in the door. My wife wanted to walk on, but I just had a look in with my torch; then the thieves cleared at once. To be on the safe side, I didn't ring up the police, as with you I didn't think it was the thing to do. I don't know anything, but I guess a lot."

Henk thanked him and went on. The man obviously guesses

that we're here, because he always brings the potatoes during the lunch hour. Such a nice man!

It was one by the time Henk had gone and we'd finished doing the dishes. We all went for a sleep. I awoke at a quarter to three and saw that Mr. Dussel had already disappeared. Quite by chance, and with my sleepy eyes, I ran into Peter in the bathroom; he had just come down. We arranged to meet downstairs.

I tidied myself and went down. "Do you still dare to go to the front attic?" he asked. I nodded, fetched my pillow, and we went up to the attic. It was glorious weather, and soon the sirens were wailing; we stayed where we were. Peter put his arm around my shoulder, and I put mine around his and so we remained, our arms around each other, quietly waiting until Margot came to fetch us for coffee at four o'clock.

We finished our bread, drank lemonade and joked (we were able to again), otherwise everything went normally. In the evening I thanked Peter because he was the bravest of us all.

None of us has ever been in such danger as that night. God truly protected us; just think of it—the police at our secret cupboard, the light on right in front of it, and still we remained undiscovered.

If the invasion comes, and bombs with it, then it is each man for himself, but in this case the fear was also for our good, innocent protectors. "We are saved, go on saving us!" That is all we can say.

This affair has brought quite a number of changes with it. Mr. Dussel no longer sits downstairs in Kraler's office in the evenings, but in the bathroom instead. Peter goes round the house for a checkup at half past eight and half past nine. Peter isn't allowed to have his window open at nights any more. No one is allowed to pull the plug after half past nine. This evening there's a carpenter coming to make the warehouse doors even stronger.

Now there are debates going on all the time in the "Secret Annexe." Kraler reproached us for our carelessness. Henk, too, said that in a case like that we must never go downstairs. We have been pointedly reminded that we are in hiding, that we are Jews in chains, chained to one spot, without any rights, but with a thousand duties. We Jews mustn't show our feelings, must be brave and strong, must accept all inconveniences and not grumble, must do what is within our power and trust in God. Sometime this terrible war will be over. Surely the time will come when we are people again, and not just Jews.

Who has inflicted this upon us? Who has made us Jews different from all other people? Who has allowed us to suffer so terribly up till now? It is God that has made us as we are, but it will be God, too, who will raise us up again. If we bear all this suffering and if there are still Jews left, when it is over, then Jews, instead of being doomed, will be held up as an example. Who knows, it might even be our religion from which the world and all peoples learn good, and for that reason and that reason only do we have to suffer now. We can never become just Netherlanders, or just English, or representatives of any country for that matter, we will always remain Jews, but we want to, too.

Be brave! Let us remain aware of our task and not grumble, a solution will come, God has never deserted our people. Right through the ages there have been Jews, through all the ages they have had to suffer, but it has made them strong too; the weak fall, but the strong will remain and never go under!

During that night I really felt that I had to die, I waited for the police, I was prepared, as the soldier is on the battlefield. I was eager to lay down my life for the country, but now, now I've been saved again, now my first wish after the war is that I may become Dutch! I love the Dutch, I love this country, I love the language and want to work here. And even if I have to write to the Queen myself, I will not give up until I have reached my goal.

I am becoming still more independent of my parents, young as I am, I face life with more courage than Mummy; my feeling for justice is immovable, and truer than hers. I know what I want, I have a goal, an opinion, I have a religion and love. Let me be myself and then I am satisfied. I know that I'm a woman, a woman with inward strength and plenty of courage.

If God lets me live, I shall attain more than Mummy ever has done, I shall not remain insignificant, I shall work in the world and for mankind!

And now I know that first and foremost I shall require courage and cheerfulness!

Yours, Anne

Friday, 14 April, 1944

Dear Kitty,

The atmosphere here is still extremely strained. Pim has just about reached boiling point. Mrs. Van Daan is in bed with a cold and trumpeting away. Mr. Van Daan grows pale without his fags, Dussel, who is giving up a lot of his comfort, is full of observations, etc., etc.

There is no doubt that our luck's not in at the moment. The lavatory leaks and the washer of the tap has gone, but, thanks to our many connections, we shall soon be able to get these things put right.

I am sentimental sometimes, I know that, but there is occasion to be sentimental here at times, when Peter and I are sitting somewhere together on a hard, wooden crate in the midst of masses of rubbish and dust, our arms around each other's shoulders, and very close, he with one of my curls in his hand; when the birds sing outside and you see the trees changing to green, the sun invites one to be out in the open air, when the sky is so blue, then—oh, then, I wish for so much!

One sees nothing but dissatisfied, grumpy faces here, nothing but sighs and suppressed complaints; it really would seem as if suddenly we were very badly off here. If the truth is told, things are just as bad as you yourself care to make them. There's no one here that sets a good example; everyone should see that he gets the better of his own moods. Every day you hear, "If only it was all over."

My work, my hope, my love, my courage, all these things keep my head above water and keep me from complaining.

I really believe, Kits, that I'm slightly bats today, and yet I don't know why. Everything here is so mixed up, nothing's connected any more, and sometimes I very much doubt whether in the future anyone will be interested in all my tosh.

"The unbosomings of an ugly duckling" will be the title of all this nonsense. My diary really won't be much use to Messrs. Bolkestein or Gerbrandy.[1]

Yours, Anne

Saturday, 15 April, 1944

Dear Kitty,

"Shock upon shock. Will there ever be an end?" We honestly can ask ourselves that question now. Guess what's the latest. Peter forgot to unbolt the front door (which is bolted on the inside at night) and the lock of the other door doesn't work. The result was that Kraler and the men could not get into the house, so he went to the neighbors, forced open the kitchen window, and entered the building from the back. He is livid at us for being so stupid.

I can tell you, it's upset Peter frightfully. At one meal, when Mummy said she felt more sorry for Peter than anyone else, he almost started to cry. We're all just as much to blame as he is, because nearly every day the men ask whether the door's been unbolted and, just today, no one did.

Perhaps I shall be able to console him a bit later on; I would so love to help him.

Yours, Anne

Sunday morning, just before eleven o'clock,
16 April, 1944

Darlingest Kitty,

Remember yesterday's date, for it is a very important day in my life. Surely it is a great day for every girl when she re-

[1]Two members of the wartime Dutch Cabinet-in-Exile in London.

ceives her first kiss? Well, then, it is just as important for me too! Bram's kiss on my right cheek doesn't count any more, likewise the one from Mr. Walker on my right hand.

How did I suddenly come by this kiss? Well, I will tell you.

Yesterday evening at eight o'clock I was sitting with Peter on his divan, it wasn't long before his arm went round me. "Let's move up a bit," I said, "then I don't bump my head against the cupboard." He moved up, almost into the corner, I laid my arm under his and across his back, and he just about buried me, because his arm was hanging on my shoulder.

Now we've sat like this on other occasions, but never so close together as yesterday. He held me firmly against him, my left shoulder against his chest; already my heart began to beat faster, but we had not finished yet. He didn't rest until my head was on his shoulder and his against it. When I sat upright again after about five minutes, he soon took my head in his hands and laid it against him once more. Oh, it was so lovely, I couldn't talk much, the joy was too great. He stroked my cheek and arm a bit awkwardly, played with my curls and our heads lay touching most of the time. I can't tell you, Kitty, the feeling that ran through me all the while. I was too happy for words, and I believe he was as well.

We got up at half past eight. Peter put on his gym shoes, so that when he toured the house he wouldn't make a noise, and I stood beside him. How it came about so suddenly, I don't know, but before we went downstairs he kissed me, through my hair, half on my left cheek, half on my ear; I tore downstairs without looking round, and am simply longing for today!

Yours, Anne

Monday, 17 April, 1944

Dear Kitty,

Do you think that Daddy and Mummy would approve of my sitting and kissing a boy on a divan—a boy of seventeen and a half and a girl of just under fifteen? I don't really think they would, but I must rely on myself over this. It is so quiet and peaceful to lie in his arms and to dream, it is so thrilling to feel his cheek against mine, it is so lovely to know that there is someone waiting for me. But there is indeed a big "but," because will Peter be content to leave it at this? I haven't forgotten his promise already, but . . . he *is* a boy!

I know myself that I'm starting very soon, not even fifteen, and so independent already! It's certainly hard for other people to understand, I know almost for certain that Margot would never kiss a boy unless there had been some talk of an engagement or marriage, but neither Peter nor I have anything like that in mind. I'm sure too that Mummy never touched a man before Daddy. What would my girl friends say about it if they knew that I lay in Peter's arms, my heart against his chest, my head on his shoulder and with his head against mine!

Oh, Anne, how scandalous! But honestly, I don't think it is; we are shut up here, shut away from the world, in fear and anxiety, especially just lately. Why, then, should we who love each other remain apart? Why should we wait until we've reached a suitable age? Why should we bother?

I have taken it upon myself to look after myself; he would never want to cause me sorrow or pain. Why shouldn't I follow the way my heart leads me, if it makes us both happy? All the same, Kitty, I believe you can sense that I'm in doubt, I think it must be my honesty which rebels against doing anything on the sly! Do you think it's my duty to tell Daddy what I'm doing? Do you think we should share our secret with a third person? A lot of the beauty would be lost, but would my conscience feel happier? I will discuss it with "him."

Oh, yes, there's still so much I want to talk to him about, for I don't see the use of only just cuddling each other. To exchange our thoughts, that shows confidence and faith in each other, we would both be sure to profit by it!

                                                    Yours, Anne

Tuesday, 18 April, 1944

Dear Kitty,

Everything goes well here. Daddy's just said that he definitely expects large-scale operations to take place before the twentieth of May, both in Russia and Italy, and also in the West; I find it more and more difficult to imagine our liberation from here.

Yesterday Peter and I finally got down to our talk, which had already been put off for at least ten days. I explained everything about girls to him and didn't hesitate to discuss the most intimate things. The evening ended by each giving the other a kiss, just about beside my mouth, it's really a lovely feeling.

Perhaps I'll take my diary up there sometime, to go more deeply into things for once. I don't get any satisfaction out of lying in each other's arms day in, day out, and would so like to feel that he's the same.

We are having a superb spring after our long, lingering winter; April is really glorious, not too hot and not too cold, with little showers now and then. Our chestnut tree is already quite greenish and you can even see little blooms here and there.

Elli gave us a treat on Saturday, by bringing four bunches of flowers, three bunches of narcissus and one of grape hyacinths, the latter being for me.

I must do some algebra, Kitty—good-by.

Yours, Anne

Wednesday, 19 April, 1944

My darling,

Is there anything more beautiful in the world than to sit before an open window and enjoy nature, to listen to the birds singing, feel the sun on your cheeks and have a darling boy in your arms? It is so soothing and peaceful to feel his arms around me, to know that he is close by and yet to re-

main silent, it can't be bad, for this tranquillity is good. Oh,
never to be disturbed again, not even by Mouschi.

Yours, Anne

Friday, 21 April, 1944

Dear Kitty,
  Yesterday afternoon I was lying in bed with a sore throat,
but since I was already bored on the first day and did not
have a temperature, I got up again today. It's the eighteenth
birthday of Her Royal Highness Princess Elizabeth of York.
The B.B.C. has said that she will not be declared of age yet,
though it's usually the case with royal children. We have been
asking ourselves what prince this beauty is going to marry, but
cannot think of anyone suitable. Perhaps her sister, Princess
Margaret Rose, can have Prince Baudouin of Belgium one
day.
  Here we are having one misfortune after another. Scarcely
had the outside doors been strengthened than the warehouse
man appeared again. In all probability it was he who stole
the potato meal and wants to put the blame on to Elli's
shoulders. The whole "Secret Annexe" is understandably het
up again. Elli is beside herself with anger.
  I want to send in to some paper or other to see if they will
take one of my stories, under a pseudonym, of course.
  Till next time, darling!

Yours, Anne

Tuesday, 25 April, 1944

Dear Kitty,
  Dussel has not been on speaking terms with Van Daan for
ten days and just because, ever since the burglary, a whole lot
of fresh security measures have been made that don't suit
him. He maintains that Van Daan has been shouting at him.
  "Everything here happens upside down," he told me. "I

am going to speak to your father about it." He is not supposed to sit in the office downstairs on Saturday afternoons
and Sundays any more, but he goes on doing it just the same.
Van Daan was furious and Father went downstairs to talk to
him. Naturally, he kept on inventing excuses, but this time he
could not get around even Father. Father now talks to him
as little as possible, as Dussel has insulted him. None of us
know in what way, but it must have been very bad.

I have written a lovely story called "Blurr, the Explorer,"
which pleased the three to whom I read it very much.

Yours, Anne

Thursday, 27 April, 1944

Dear Kitty,

Mrs. Van Daan was in such a bad mood this morning,
nothing but complaints! First, there's her cold, and she can't
get any lozenges, and so much nose-blowing is unendurable.
Next, it's that the sun's not shining, that the invasion doesn't
come, that we can't look out of the windows, etc., etc. We all
had to laugh at her; and she was sporting enough to join in.
At the moment I'm reading *The Emperor Charles V*, written
by a professor at Göttingen University; he worked at the book
for forty years. I read fifty pages in five days; it's impossible
to do more. The book has 598 pages, so now you can work
out how long it will take me—and there is a second volume to
follow. But very interesting.

What doesn't a schoolgirl get to know in a single day! Take
me, for example. First, I translated a piece from Dutch into
English, about Nelson's last battle. After that, I went through
some more of Peter the Great's war against Norway (1700-
1721), Charles XII, Augustus the Strong, Stanislavs Leczin-
sky, Mazeppa, Von Görz, Brandenburg, Pomerania and Denmark, plus the usual dates.

After that I landed up in Brazil, read about Bahia tobacco,
the abundance of coffee and the one and a half million in-

habitants of Rio de Janeiro, of Pernambuco and Sao Paulo,
not forgetting the river Amazon; about Negroes, Mulattos,
Mestizos, Whites, more than fifty per cent of the population
being illiterate, and the malaria. As there was still some time
left, I quickly ran through a family tree. Jan the Elder,
Willem Lodewijk, Ernst Casimir I, Hendrik Casimir I, right
up to the little Margriet Franciska (born in 1943 in Ottawa).

Twelve o'clock: In the attic, I continued my program with
the history of the Church—Phew! Till one o'clock.

Just after two, the poor child sat working ('hm, 'hm!)
again, this time studying narrow- and broad-nosed monkeys.
Kitty, tell me quickly how many toes a hippopotamus has! !
Then followed the Bible, Noah and the Ark, Shem, Ham,
and Japheth. After that Charles V. Then with Peter: *The
Colonel*, in English by Thackeray. Heard my French verbs
and then compared the Mississippi with the Missouri.

I've still got a cold and have given it to Margot as well as
to Mummy and Daddy. As long as Peter doesn't get it! He
called me his "Eldorado" and wanted a kiss. Of course, I
couldn't! Funny boy! But still, he's a darling.

Enough for today, good-by!

Yours, Anne

Friday, 28 April, 1944

Dear Kitty,

I have never forgotten my dream about Peter Wessel (see
beginning of January). If I think of it, I can still feel his
cheek against mine now, and recall that lovely feeling that
made everything good.

Sometimes I have had the same feeling here with Peter, but
never to such an extent, until yesterday, when we were, as
usual, sitting on the divan, our arms around each other's
waists. Then suddenly the ordinary Anne slipped away and
a second Anne took her place, a second Anne who is not reckless and jocular, but one who just wants to love and be gentle.

I sat pressed closely against him and felt a wave of emotion come over me, tears sprang into my eyes, the left one trickled onto his dungarees, the right one ran down my nose and also fell onto his dungarees. Did he notice? He made no move or sign to show that he did. I wonder if he feels the same as I do? He hardly said a word. Does he know that he has two Annes before him? These questions must remain unanswered.

At half past eight I stood up and went to the window, where we always say good-by. I was still trembling, I was still Anne number two. He came towards me, I flung my arms around his neck and gave him a kiss on his left cheek, and was about to kiss the other cheek, when my lips met his and we pressed them together. In a whirl we were clasped in each other's arms, again and again, never to leave off. Oh, Peter does so need tenderness. For the first time in his life he has discovered a girl, has seen for the first time that even the most irritating girls have another side to them, that they have hearts and can be different when you are alone with them. For the first time in his life he has given of himself and, having never had a boy or girl friend in his life before, shown his real self. Now we have found each other. For that matter, I didn't know him either, like him having never had a trusted friend, and this is what it has come to. . . .

Once more there is a question which gives me no peace: "Is it right? Is it right that I should have yielded so soon, that I am so ardent, just as ardent and eager as Peter himself? May I, a girl, let myself go to this extent?" There is but *one* answer: "I have longed so much and for so long—I am so lonely—and now I have found consolation."

In the mornings we just behave in an ordinary way, in the afternoons more or less so (except just occasionally); but in the evenings the suppressed longings of the whole day, the happiness and the blissful memories of all the previous occasions come to the surface and we only think of each other. Every evening, after the last kiss, I would like to dash away, not to look into his eyes any more—away, away, alone in the darkness.

And what do I have to face, when I reach the bottom of the staircase? Bright lights, questions, and laughter; I have to swallow it all and not show a thing. My heart still feels too much; I can't get over a shock such as I received yesterday all at once. The Anne who is gentle shows herself too little anyway and, therefore, will not allow herself to be suddenly driven into the background. Peter has touched my emotions more deeply than anyone has ever done before—except in my dreams. Peter has taken possession of me and turned me inside out; surely it goes without saying that anyone would require a rest and a little while to recover from such an upheaval?

Oh Peter, what have you done to me? What do you want of me? Where will this lead us? Oh, now I understand Elli; now, now that I am going through this myself, now I understand her doubt; if I were older and he should ask me to marry him, what should I answer? Anne, be honest! You would not be able to marry him, but yet, it would be hard to let him go. Peter hasn't enough character yet, not enough will power, too little courage and strength. He is still a child in his heart of hearts, he is no older than I am; he is only searching for tranquillity and happiness.

Am I only fourteen? Am I really still a silly little schoolgirl? Am I really so inexperienced about everything? I have more experience than most; I have been through things that hardly anyone of my age has undergone. I am afraid of myself, I am afraid that in my longing I am giving myself too quickly. How, later on, can it ever go right with other boys? Oh, it is so difficult, always battling with one's heart and reason; in its own time, each will speak, but do I know for certain that I have chosen the right time?

Yours, Anne

Tuesday, 2 May, 1944

Dear Kitty,

On Saturday evening I asked Peter whether he thought that I ought to tell Daddy a bit about us; when we'd discussed it a little, he came to the conclusion that I should. I was glad, for it shows that he's an honest boy. As soon as I got downstairs I went off with Daddy to get some water; and while we were on the stairs I said, "Daddy, I expect you've gathered that when we're together Peter and I don't sit miles apart. Do you think it's wrong?" Daddy didn't reply immediately, then said, "No, I don't think it's wrong, but you must be careful, Anne, you're in such a confined space here." When we went upstairs, he said something else on the same lines. On Sunday morning he called me to him and said, "Anne, I have thought more about what you said." I felt scared already. "It's not really very right—here in this house; I thought that you were just pals. Is Peter in love?"

"Oh, of course not," I replied.

"You know that I understand both of you, but you must be the one to hold back. Don't go upstairs so often, don't encourage him more than you can help. It is the man who is always the active one in these things; the woman can hold him back. It is quite different under normal circumstances, when you are free, you see other boys and girls, you can get away sometimes, play games and do all kinds of other things; but here, if you're together a lot, and you want to get away, you can't; you see each other every hour of the day—in fact, all the time. Be careful, Anne, and don't take it too seriously!"

"I don't, Daddy, but Peter is a decent boy, really a nice boy!"

"Yes, but he is not a strong character; he can be easily influenced, for good, but also for bad; I hope for his sake that his good side will remain uppermost, because, by nature, that is how he is."

We talked on for a bit and agreed that Daddy should talk to him too.

On Sunday morning in the attic he asked, "And have you talked to your father, Anne?"

"Yes," I replied, "I'll tell you about it. Daddy doesn't think it's bad, but he says that here, where we're so close together all the time, clashes may easily arise."

"But we agreed, didn't we, never to quarrel; and I'm determined to stick to it!"

"So will I, Peter, but Daddy didn't think that it was like

this, he just thought we were pals; do you think that we still can be?"

"I can—what about you?"

"Me too, I told Daddy that I trusted you. I do trust you, Peter, just as much as I trust Daddy, and I believe you to be worthy of it. You are, aren't you, Peter?"

"I hope so." (He was very shy and rather red in the face.)

"I believe in you, Peter," I went on, "I believe that you have good qualities, and that you'll get on in the world."

After that, we talked about other things. Later I said, "If we come out of here, I know quite well that you won't bother about me any more!"

He flared right up. "That's not true, Anne, oh no, I won't let you think that of me!"

Then I was called away.

Daddy has talked to him; he told me about it today. "Your father thought that the friendship might develop into love sooner or later," he said. But I replied that we would keep a check on ourselves.

Daddy doesn't want me to go upstairs so much in the evenings now, but I don't want that. Not only because I like being with Peter; I have told him that I trust him. I do trust him and I want to show him that I do, which can't happen if I stay downstairs through lack of trust.

No, I'm going!

In the meantime the Dussel drama has righted itself again. At supper on Saturday evening he apologized in beautiful Dutch. Van Daan was nice about it straight away; it must have taken Dussel a whole day to learn that little lesson off by heart.

Sunday, his birthday, passed peacefully. We gave him a bottle of good 1919 wine, from the Van Daans (who could give their presents now after all), a bottle of piccalilli and a packet of razor blades, a jar of lemon jam from Kraler, a book, *Little Martin*, from Miep, and a plant from Elli. He treated each one of us to an egg.

Yours, Anne

Wednesday, 3 May, 1944

Dear Kitty,

First, just the news of the week. We're having a holiday from politics; there is nothing, absolutely nothing to announce. I too am gradually beginning to believe that the invasion will come. After all, they can't let the Russians clear up everything; for that matter, they're not doing anything either at the moment.

Mr. Koophuis comes to the office every morning again now. He's got a new spring for Peter's divan, so Peter will have to do some upholstering, about which, quite understandably, he doesn't feel a bit happy.

Have I told you that Boche has disappeared? Simply vanished—we haven't seen a sign of her since Thursday of last week. I expect she's already in the cats' heaven, while some animal lover is enjoying a succulent meal from her. Perhaps some little girl will be given a fur cap out of her skin. Peter is very sad about it.

Since Saturday we've changed over, and have lunch at half past eleven in the mornings, so we have to last out with one cupful of porridge; this saves us a meal. Vegetables are still very difficult to obtain: we had rotten boiled lettuce this afternoon. Ordinary lettuce, spinach, and boiled lettuce, there's nothing else. With these we eat rotten potatoes, so it's a delicious combination!

As you can easily imagine we often ask ourselves here despairingly: "What, oh, what is the use of the war? Why can't people live peacefully together? Why all this destruction?"

The question is very understandable, but no one has found a satisfactory answer to it so far. Yes, why do they make still more gigantic planes, still heavier bombs and, at the same time, prefabricated houses for reconstruction? Why should millions be spent daily on the war and yet there's not a penny available for medical services, artists, or for poor people?

Why do some people have to starve, while there are surpluses rotting in other parts of the world? Oh, why are people so crazy?

I don't believe that the big men, the politicians and the capitalists alone, are guilty of the war. Oh no, the little man is just as guilty, otherwise the peoples of the world would have risen in revolt long ago! There's in people simply an urge to destroy, an urge to kill, to murder and rage, and until all mankind, without exception, undergoes a great change, wars will be waged, everything that has been built up, cultivated, and grown will be destroyed and disfigured, after which mankind will have to begin all over again.

I have often been downcast, but never in despair; I regard our hiding as a dangerous adventure, romantic and interesting at the same time. In my diary I treat all the privations as amusing. I have made up my mind now to lead a different life from other girls and, later on, different from ordinary housewives. My start has been so very full of interest, and that is the sole reason why I have to laugh at the humorous side of the most dangerous moments.

I am young and I possess many buried qualities; I am young and strong and am living a great adventure; I am still in the midst of it and can't grumble the whole day long. I have been given a lot, a happy nature, a great deal of cheerfulness and strength. Every day I feel that I am developing inwardly, that the liberation is drawing nearer and how beautiful nature is, how good the people are about me, how interesting this adventure is! Why, then, should I be in despair?

Yours, Anne

Friday, 5 May, 1944

Dear Kitty,

Daddy is not pleased with me; he thought that after our talk on Sunday I automatically wouldn't go upstairs every evening. He doesn't want any "necking," a word I can't bear. It was bad enough talking about it, why must he make it so unpleasant now? I shall talk to him today. Margot has given

me some good advice, so listen; this is roughly what I want
to say:

"I believe, Daddy, that you expect a declaration from me,
so I will give it you. You are disappointed in me, as you had
expected more reserve from me, and I suppose you want me to
be just as a fourteen-year-old should be. But that's where
you're mistaken!

"Since we've been here, from July 1942 until a few weeks
ago, I can assure you that I haven't had an easy time. If
you only knew how I cried in the evening, how unhappy I
was, how lonely I felt, then you would understand that I
want to go upstairs!

"I have now reached the stage that I can live entirely on
my own, without Mummy's support or anyone else's for that
matter. But it hasn't just happened in a night; it's been a
bitter, hard struggle and I've shed many a tear, before I became as independent as I am now. You can laugh at me and
not believe me, but that can't harm me. I know that I'm a
separate individual and I don't feel in the least bit responsible
to any of you. I am only telling you this because I thought
that otherwise you might think that I was underhand, but I
don't have to give an account of my deeds to anyone but myself.

"When I was in difficulties you all closed your eyes and
stopped up your ears and didn't help me; on the contrary, I
received nothing but warnings not to be so boisterous. I was
only boisterous so as not to be miserable all the time. I was
reckless so as not to hear that persistent voice within me
continually. I played a comedy for a year and a half, day in,
day out, I never grumbled, never lost my cue, nothing like
that—and now, now the battle is over. I have won! I am independent both in mind and body. I don't need a mother any
more, for all this conflict has made me strong.

"And now, now that I'm on top of it, now that I know
that I've fought the battle, now I want to be able to go on in
my own way too, the way that I think is right. You can't and
mustn't regard me as fourteen, for all these troubles have
made me older; I shall not be sorry for what I have done, but

shall act as I think I can. You can't coax me into not going upstairs; *either* you forbid it, *or* you trust me through thick and thin, but then leave me in peace as well!"

Yours, Anne

Saturday, 6 May, 1944

Dear Kitty,

I put a letter, in which I wrote what I explained to you yesterday, in Daddy's pocket before supper yesterday. After reading it, he was, according to Margot, very upset for the rest of the evening. (I was upstairs doing the dishes.) Poor Pim, I might have known what the effect of such an epistle would be. He is so sensitive! I immediately told Peter not to ask or say anything more. Pim hasn't said any more about it to me. Is that yet in store, I wonder?

Here everything is going on more or less normally again. What they tell us about the prices and the people outside is almost unbelievable, half a pound of tea costs 350 florins,[1] a pound of coffee 80 florins, butter 35 florins per pound, an egg 1.45 florin. People pay 14 florins for an ounce of Bulgarian tobacco! Everyone deals in the black market, every errand boy has something to offer. Our baker's boy got hold of some sewing silk, 0.9 florin for a thin little skein, the milkman manages to get clandestine ration cards, the undertaker delivers the cheese. Burglaries, murders, and theft go on daily. The police and night watchmen join in just as strenuously as the professionals, everyone wants something in their empty stomachs and because wage increases are forbidden the people simply have to swindle. The police are continually on the go, tracing girls of fifteen, sixteen, seventeen and older, who are reported missing every day.

Yours, Anne

[1] A florin is equal to approximately twenty-eight cents.

Sunday morning, 7 May, 1944

Dear Kitty,

Daddy and I had a long talk yesterday afternoon, I cried terribly and he joined in. Do you know what he said to me, Kitty? "I have received many letters in my life, but this is certainly the most unpleasant! You, Anne, who have received such love from your parents, you, who have parents who are always ready to help you, who have always defended you whatever it might be, can you talk of feeling no responsibility towards us? You feel wronged and deserted; no, Anne, you have done us a great injustice!

"Perhaps you didn't mean it like that, but it is what you wrote; no, Anne, we haven't deserved such a reproach as this!"

Oh, I have failed miserably; this is certainly the worst thing I've ever done in my life. I was only trying to show off with my crying and my tears, just trying to appear big, so that he would respect me. Certainly, I have had a lot of unhappiness, but to accuse the good Pim, who has done and still does everything for me—no, that was too low for words.

It's right that for once I've been taken down from my inaccessible pedestal, that my pride has been shaken a bit, for I was becoming much too taken up with myself again. What Miss Anne does is by no means always right! Anyone who can cause such unhappiness to someone else, someone he professes to love, and on purpose, too, is low, very low!

And the way Daddy has forgiven me makes me feel more than ever ashamed of myself, he is going to throw the letter in the fire and is so sweet to me now, just as if he had done something wrong. No, Anne, you still have a tremendous lot to learn, begin by doing that first, instead of looking down on others and accusing them!

I have had a lot of sorrow, but who hasn't at my age? I have played the clown a lot too, but I was hardly conscious of it; I felt lonely, but hardly ever in despair! I ought to be deeply ashamed of myself, and indeed I am.

What is done cannot be undone, but one can prevent it

happening again. I want to start from the beginning again
and it can't be difficult, now that I have Peter. With him to
support me, I can and will!

I'm not alone any more; he loves me. I love him, I have my
books, my storybook and my diary, I'm not so frightfully ugly,
not utterly stupid, have a cheerful temperament and want to
have a good character!

Yes, Anne, you've felt deeply that your letter was too hard
and that it was untrue. To think that you were even proud
of it! I will take Daddy as my example, and I *will* improve.

Yours, Anne

Monday, 8 May, 1944

Dear Kitty,

Have I ever really told you anything about our family?

I don't think I have, so I will begin now. My father's
parents were very rich. His father had worked himself right
up and his mother came from a prominent family, who were
also rich. So in his youth Daddy had a real little rich boy's
upbringing, parties every week, balls, festivities, beautiful
girls, dinners, a large home, etc., etc.

After Grandpa's death all the money was lost during the
World War and the inflation that followed. Daddy was
therefore extremely well brought up and he laughed very
much yesterday when, for the first time in his fifty-five years,
he scraped out the frying pan at table.

Mummy's parents were rich too and we often listen open-
mouthed to stories of engagement parties of two hundred and
fifty people, private balls and dinners. One certainly could
not call us rich now, but all my hopes are pinned on after the
war.

I can assure you I'm not at all keen on a narrow, cramped
existence like Mummy and Margot. I'd adore to go to Paris
for a year and London for a year to learn the languages and
study the history of art. Compare that with Margot, who

wants to be a midwife in Palestine! I always long to see beautiful dresses and interesting people.

I want to see something of the world and do all kinds of exciting things. I've already told you this before. And a little money as well won't do any harm.

Miep told us this morning about a party she went to, to celebrate an engagement. Both the future bride and bridegroom came from rich families and everything was very grand. Miep made our mouths water telling us about the food they had: vegetable soup with minced meat balls in it, cheese, rolls, hors d'oeuvre with eggs and roast beef, fancy cakes, wine and cigarettes, as much as you wanted of everything (black market). Miep had ten drinks—can that be the woman who calls herself a teetotaler? If Miep had all those, I wonder however many her spouse managed to knock back? Naturally, everyone at the party was a bit tipsy. There were two policemen from the fighting squad, who tooks photos of the engaged couple. It seems as if we are never far from Miep's thoughts, because she took down the addresses of these men at once, in case anything should happen at some time or other, and good Dutchmen might come in useful.

She made our mouths water. We, who get nothing but two spoonfuls of porridge for our breakfast and whose tummies were so empty that they were positively rattling, we, who get nothing but half-cooked spinach (to preserve the vitamins) and rotten potatoes day after day, we, who get nothing but lettuce, cooked or raw, spinach and yet again spinach in our hollow stomachs. Perhaps we may yet grow to be as strong as Popeye, although I don't see much sign of it at present!

If Miep had taken us to the party we shouldn't have left any rolls for the other guests. I can tell you, we positively drew the words from Miep's lips, we gathered round her, as if we'd never heard about delicious food or smart people in our lives before!

And these are the granddaughters of a millionaire. The world is a queer place!

Yours, Anne

Tuesday, 9 May, 1944

Dear Kitty,

I've finished my story of Ellen the fairy. I have copied it out on nice note paper. It certainly looks very attractive, but is it really enough for Daddy's birthday? I don't know. Margot and Mummy have both written poems for him.

Mr. Kraler came upstairs this afternoon with the news that Mrs. B., who used to act as demonstrator for the business, wants to eat her box lunch in the office here at two o'clock every afternoon. Think of it! No one can come upstairs any more, the potatoes cannot be delivered, Elli can't have any lunch, we can't go to the W.C., we mustn't move, etc., etc. We thought up the wildest and most varied suggestions to wheedle her away. Van Daan thought that a good laxative in her coffee would be sufficient. "No," replied Koophuis, "I beg of you not, then we'd never get her off the box!" Resounding laughter. "Off the box," asked Mrs. Van Daan, "what does that mean?" An explanation followed. "Can I always use it?" she then asked stupidly. "Imagine it," Elli giggled, "if one asked for the box in Bijenkorf's¹ they wouldn't even understand what you mean!"

Oh, Kit, it's such wonderful weather, if only I could go outdoors!

Yours, Anne

Wednesday, 10 May, 1944

Dear Kitty,

We were sitting in the attic doing some French yesterday afternoon when I suddenly heard water pattering down behind me. I asked Peter what it could be, but he didn't even reply, simply tore up to the loft, where the source of the disaster was, and pushed Mouschi, who, because of the wet earth box, had sat down beside it, harshly back to the right

¹"Bijenkorf" is a large store in Amsterdam.

place. A great din and disturbance followed, and Mouschi, who had finished by that time, dashed downstairs.

Mouschi, seeking the convenience of something similar to his box, had chosen some wood shavings. The pool had trickled down from the loft into the attic immediately and, unfortunately, landed just beside and in the barrel of potatoes. The ceiling was dripping, and as the attic floor is not free from holes either, several yellow drips came through the ceiling into the dining room between a pile of stockings and some books, which were lying on the table. I was doubled up with laughter, it really was a scream. There was Mouschi crouching under a chair, Peter with water, bleaching powder, and floor cloth, and Van Daan trying to soothe everyone. The calamity was soon over, but it's a well-known fact that cats' puddles positively stink. The potatoes proved this only too clearly and also the wood shavings that Daddy collected in a bucket to be burned. Poor Mouschi! How were you to know that peat is unobtainable?

Yours, Anne

P.S. Our beloved Queen spoke to us yesterday and this evening. She is taking a holiday in order to be strong for her return to Holland. She used words like "soon, when I am back, speedy liberation, heroism, and heavy burdens."

A speech by Gerbrandy followed. A clergyman concluded with a prayer to God to take care of the Jews, the people in concentration camps, in prisons, and in Germany.

Yours, Anne

Thursday, 11 May, 1944

Dear Kitty,

I'm frightfully busy at the moment, and although it sounds mad, I haven't time to get through my pile of work. Shall I tell you briefly what I have got to do? Well, then, by tomorrow I must finish reading the first part of *Galileo Galilei*, as it has to be returned to the library. I only started it yesterday, but I shall manage it.

Next week I have got to read *Palestine at the Crossroads*

and the second part of *Galilei*. Next I finished reading the first part of the biography of *The Emperor Charles V* yesterday, and it's essential that I work out all the diagrams and family trees that I have collected from it. After that I have three pages of foreign words gathered from various books, which have all got to be recited, written down, and learned. Number four is that my film stars are all mixed up together and are simply gasping to be tidied up; however, as such a clearance would take several days, and since Professor Anne, as she's already said, is choked with work, the chaos will have to remain a chaos.

Next Theseus, Oedipus, Peleus, Orpheus, Jason, and Hercules are all awaiting their turn to be arranged, as their different deeds lie crisscross in my mind like fancy threads in a dress; it's also high time Myron and Phidias had some treatment, if they wish to remain at all coherent. Likewise it's the same with the seven and nine years' war; I'm mixing everything up together at this rate. Yes, but what can one do with such a memory! Think how forgetful I shall be when I'm eighty!

Oh, something else, the Bible; how long is it still going to take before I meet the bathing Suzanna? And what do they mean by the guilt of Sodom and Gomorrah? Oh, there is still such a terrible lot to find out and to learn. And in the meantime I've left Lisolette of the Pfalz completely in the lurch.

Kitty, can you see that I'm just about bursting?

Now, about something else: you've known for a long time that my greatest wish is to become a journalist someday and later on a famous writer. Whether these leanings towards greatness (or insanity?) will ever materialize remains to be seen, but I certainly have the subjects in my mind. In any case, I want to publish a book entitled *Het Achterhuis* after the war. Whether I shall succeed or not, I cannot say, but my diary will be a great help. I have other ideas as well, besides *Het Achterhuis*. But I will write more fully about them some other time, when they have taken a clearer form in my mind.

Yours, Anne

Saturday, 13 May, 1944

Dearest Kitty,

It was Daddy's birthday yesterday. Mummy and Daddy have been married nineteen years. The charwoman wasn't below and the sun shone as it has never shone before in 1944. Our horse chestnut is in full bloom, thickly covered with leaves and much more beautiful than last year.

Daddy received a biography of the life of Linnaeus from Koophuis, a book on nature from Kraler, *Amsterdam by the Water* from Dussel, a gigantic box from Van Daan, beautifully done up and almost professionally decorated, containing three eggs, a bottle of beer, a bottle of yoghourt, and a green tie. It made our pot of syrup seem rather small. My roses smelled lovely compared with Miep's and Elli's carnations, which had no smell, but were very pretty too. He was certainly spoiled. Fifty fancy pastries have arrived, heavenly! Daddy himself treated us to spiced gingerbread, beer for the gentlemen, and yoghourt for the ladies. Enjoyment all around!

Yours, Anne

Tuesday, 16 May, 1944

Dearest Kitty,

Just for a change, as we haven't talked about them for so long, I want to tell you a little discussion that went on between Mr. and Mrs. Van Daan yesterday.

Mrs. Van Daan: "The Germans are sure to have made the Atlantic Wall very strong indeed, they will certainly do all in their power to hold back the English. It's amazing how strong the Germans are!"

Mr. Van Daan: "Oh yes, incredibly."

Mrs. Van Daan: "Ye-es."

Mr. Van Daan: "The Germans are so strong they're sure to win the war in the end, in spite of everything!"

Mrs. Van Daan: "It's quite possible, I'm not convinced of the opposite yet."

Mr. Van Daan: "I won't bother to reply any more."

Mrs. Van Daan: "Still you always do answer me, you can't resist capping me every time."

Mr. Van Daan: "Of course not, but my replies are the bare minimum."

Mrs. Van Daan: "But still you do reply, and you always have to be in the right! Your prophecies don't always come true by a long shot."

Mr. Van Daan: "They have up till now."

Mrs. Van Daan: "That's not true. The invasion was to have come last year, and the Finns were to have been out of the war by now. Italy was finished in the winter, but the Russians would already have Lemberg; oh, no, I don't think much of your prophecies."

Mr. Van Daan (standing up): "It's about time you shut your mouth. One day I'll show you that I'm right; sooner or later you'll get enough of it. I can't bear any more of your grousing. You're so infuriating but you'll stew in your own juice one day."

End of Part I.

I really couldn't help laughing. Mummy too, while Peter sat biting his lip. Oh, those stupid grownups, they'd do better to start learning themselves, before they have so much to say to the younger generation!

Yours, Anne

Friday, 19 May, 1944

Dear Kitty,

I felt rotten yesterday, really out of sorts (unusual for Anne!), with tummy-ache and every other imaginable misery. I'm much better again today, feel very hungry, but I'd better not touch the kidney beans we're having today.

All goes well with Peter and me. The poor boy seems to need a little love even more than I do. He blushes every evening when he gets his good-night kiss and simply begs for another. I wonder if I'm a good substitute for Boche? I don't mind, he is so happy now that he knows that someone loves him.

After my laborious conquest I've got the situation a bit more in hand now, but I don't think my love has cooled off. He's a darling, but I soon closed up my inner self from him. If he wants to force the lock again he'll have to work a good deal harder than before!

Yours, Anne

Saturday, 20 May, 1944

Dear Kitty,

Last evening I came downstairs from the attic and as I entered the room saw at once the lovely vase of carnations lying on the floor, Mummy down on hands and knees mopping up and Margot fishing up some papers from the floor.

"What's happened here?" I asked, full of misgivings and, not even waiting for their answer, tried to sum up the damage from a distance. My whole portfolio of family trees, writing books, textbooks, everything was soaked. I nearly wept and was so worked up that I can hardly remember what I said, but Margot said that I let fly something about "incalculable loss, frightful, terrible, can never be repaired," and still more. Daddy burst out laughing, Mummy and Margot joined in, but I could have cried over all the toil that was wasted, and the diagrams I'd so carefully worked out.

On closer inspection the "incalculable loss" didn't turn out to be as bad as I'd thought. I carefully sorted out all the papers that were stuck together and separated them in the attic. After that I hung them all up on the clothes lines to dry. It was a funny sight and I couldn't help laughing myself. Maria de Medici beside Charles V, William of Orange and Marie Antoinette; it's a "racial outrage," was Mr. Van Daan's joke on the subject. After I'd entrusted my papers into Peter's care I went downstairs again.

"Which books are spoiled?" I asked Margot, who was checking up on them. "Algebra," she said. I hurried to her side, but unfortunately not even the algebra book was spoiled. I wish it had fallen right in the vase; I've never loathed *any* other book so much as that one. There are the names of at least twenty girls in the front, all previous owners; it is old, yellow, full of scribbles and improvements. If I'm ever in a really very wicked mood, I'll tear the blasted thing to pieces!

Yours, Anne

Monday, 22 May, 1944

Dear Kitty,

On May 20th Daddy lost five bottles of yoghourt on a bet with Mrs. Van Daan. The invasion still hasn't come yet; it's no exaggeration to say that all Amsterdam, all Holland, yes, the whole west coast of Europe, right down to Spain, talks about the invasion day and night, debates about it, and makes bets on it and . . . hopes.

The suspense is rising to a climax. By no means everyone we had regarded as "good" Dutch have stuck to their faith in the English; by no means everyone thinks the English bluff a masterly piece of strategy, oh no, the people want to see deeds at last, great, heroic deeds. Nobody sees beyond his own nose, no one thinks that the English are fighting for their own land and their own people, everyone thinks that it's their duty to save Holland, as quickly and as well as they can.

What obligations have the English towards us? How have the Dutch earned the generous help that they seem so explicitly to expect? Oh no, the Dutch will have made a big mistake, the English, in spite of all their bluff, are certainly no more to blame than all the other countries, great and small, which are not under occupation. The English really won't offer us their apologies, for even if we do reproach them for being asleep during the years when Germany was rearming, we cannot deny that all the other countries, especially those bordering Germany, also slept. We shan't get anywhere by following an ostrich policy. England and the whole world have seen that only too well now, and that is why, one by one, England, no less than the rest, will have to make heavy sacrifices.

No country is going to sacrifice its men for nothing and certainly not in the interests of another. England is not going to do that either. The invasion, with liberation and freedom, will come sometime, but England and America will appoint the day, not all the occupied countries put together.

To our great horror and regret we hear that the attitude of a great many people towards us Jews has changed. We hear that there is anti-Semitism now in circles that never thought of it before. This news has affected us all very, very deeply. The cause of this hatred of the Jews is understandable, even human sometimes, but not good. The Christians blame the Jews for giving secrets away to the Germans, for betraying their helpers and for the fact that, through the Jews a great many Christians have gone the way of so many others before them, and suffered terrible punishments and a dreadful fate.

This is all true, but one must always look at these things from both sides. Would Christians behave differently in our place? The Germans have a means of making people talk. Can a person, entirely at their mercy, whether Jew or Christian, always remain silent? Everyone knows that is practically impossible. Why, then, should people demand the impossible of the Jews?

It's being murmured in underground circles that the German Jews who emigrated to Holland and who are now in Poland may not be allowed to return here; they once had the right of asylum in Holland, but when Hitler has gone they will have to go back to Germany again.

When one hears this one naturally wonders why we are carrying on with this long and difficult war. We always hear that we're all fighting together for freedom, truth, and right! Is discord going to show itself while we are still fighting, is the Jew once again worth less than another? Oh, it is sad, very sad, that once more, for the umpteenth time, the old truth is confirmed: "What *one* Christian does is his own responsibility, what *one* Jew does is thrown back at all Jews."

Quite honestly, I can't understand that the Dutch, who are such a good, honest, upright people, should judge us like this, we, the most oppressed, the unhappiest, perhaps the most pitiful of all peoples of the whole world.

I hope *one* thing only, and that is that this hatred of the Jews will be a passing thing, that the Dutch will show what they are after all, and that they will never totter and lose their sense of right. For anti-Semitism is unjust!

And if this terrible threat should actually come true, then the pitiful little collection of Jews that remain will have to leave Holland. We, too, shall have to move on again with our little bundles, and leave this beautiful country, which offered us such a warm welcome and which now turns its back on us.

I love Holland. I who, having no native country, had hoped that it might become my fatherland, and I still hope it will!

Yours, Anne

Thursday, 25 May, 1944

Dear Kitty,

There's something fresh every day. This morning our vegetable man was picked up for having two Jews in his house. It's a great blow to us, not only that those poor Jews are balancing on the edge of an abyss, but it's terrible for the man himself.

The world has turned topsy-turvy, respectable people are being sent off to concentration camps, prisons, and lonely cells, and the dregs that remain govern young and old, rich and poor. One person walks into the trap through the black market, a second through helping the Jews or other people who've had to go "underground"; anyone who isn't a member of the N.S.B. doesn't know what may happen to him from one day to another.

This man is a great loss to us too. The girls can't and aren't allowed to haul along our share of potatoes, so the only thing to do is to eat less. I will tell you how we shall do that; it's certainly not going to make things any pleasanter. Mummy says we shall cut out breakfast altogether, have porridge and bread for lunch, and for supper fried potatoes and possibly once or twice per week vegetables or lettuce, nothing more. We're going to be hungry, but anything is better than being discovered.

Yours, Anne

Friday, 26 May, 1944

Dear Kitty,

At last, at last I can sit quietly at my table in front of a crack of window and write you everything.

I feel so miserable, I haven't felt like this for months; even after the burglary I didn't feel so utterly broken. On the one hand, the vegetable man, the Jewish question, which is being discussed minutely over the whole house, the invasion delay, the bad food, the strain, the miserable atmosphere, my disappointment in Peter; and on the other hand, Elli's engagement, Whitsun reception, flowers, Kraler's birthday, fancy cakes, and stories about cabarets, films, and concerts. That difference, that huge difference, it's always there; one day we laugh and see the funny side of the situation, but the next we are afraid, fear, suspense, and despair staring from our faces. Miep and Kraler carry the heaviest burden of the eight in hiding, Miep in all she does, and Kraler through the enormous responsibility, which is sometimes so much for him that he can hardly talk from pent-up nerves and strain. Koophuis and Elli look after us well too, but they can forget us at times, even if it's only for a few hours, or a day, or even two days. They have their own worries, Koophuis over his health, Elli over her engagement,

which is not altogether rosy, but they also have their little out-
ings, visits to friends, and the whole life of ordinary people.
For them the suspense is sometimes lifted, even if it is only for
a short time, but for us it never lifts for a moment. We've been
here for two years now; how long have we still to put up with
this almost unbearable, ever increasing pressure?

The sewer is blocked, so we mustn't run water, or rather
only a trickle; when we go to the W.C. we have to take a lavatory brush with us, and we keep dirty water in a large Cologne
pot. We can manage for today, but what do we do if the
plumber can't do the job alone? The municipal scavenging
service doesn't come until Tuesday.

Miep sent us a currant cake, made up in the shape of a doll,
with the words "Happy Whitsun" on the note attached to it.
It's almost as if she's ridiculing us; our present frame of mind
and our uneasiness could hardly be called "happy." The affair
of the vegetable man has made us more nervous, you hear
"shh, shh" from all sides again, and we're being quieter over
everything. The police forced the door there, so they could do
it to us too! If one day we too should . . . no, I mustn't write
it, but I can't put the question out of my mind today. On the
contrary, all the fear I've already been through seems to face
me again in all its frightfulness.

This evening at eight o'clock I had to go to the downstairs
lavatory all alone; there was no one down there, as everyone
was listening to the radio; I wanted to be brave, but it was
difficult. I always feel much safer here upstairs than alone
downstairs in that large, silent house; alone with the mysterious muffled noises from upstairs and the tooting of motor
horns in the street. I have to hurry for I start to quiver if I begin thinking about the situation.

Again and again I ask myself, would it not have been better
for us all if we had not gone into hiding, and if we were dead
now and not going through all this misery, especially as we
shouldn't be running our protectors into danger any more. But
we all recoil from these thoughts too, for we still love life; we
haven't yet forgotten the voice of nature, we still hope, hope
about everything. I hope something will happen soon now,

shooting if need be—nothing can crush us *more* than this rest-
lessness. Let the end come, even if it is hard; then at least we
shall know whether we are finally going to win through or go
under.

Yours, Anne

Wednesday, 31 May, 1944

Dear Kitty,

It was so frightfully hot on Saturday, Sunday, Monday, and
Tuesday that I simply couldn't hold a fountain pen in my
hand. That's why it was impossible to write to you. The drains
went phut again on Friday, were mended again on Saturday;
Mr. Koophuis came to see us in the afternoon and told us
masses about Corry and her being in the same hockey club as
Jopie.

On Sunday Elli came to make sure no one had broken in
and stayed for breakfast, on Whit Monday Mr. Van Santen
acted as the hide-out watchman, and, finally, on Tuesday the
windows could be opened again at last.

There's seldom been such a beautiful, warm, one can even
say hot, Whitsun. The heat here in the "Secret Annexe" is terrible; I will briefly describe these warm days by giving you a
sample of the sort of complaints that arise:

Saturday: "Lovely, what perfect weather," we all said in
the morning. "If only it wasn't quite so warm," in the afternoon when the windows had to be closed.

Sunday: "It's positively unbearable, this heat. The butter's
melting, there's not a cool spot anywhere in the house, the
bread's getting so dry, the milk's going sour, windows can't
be opened, and we, wretched outcasts, sit here suffocating
while other people enjoy their Whitsun holiday."

Monday: "My feet hurt me, I haven't got any thin clothes.
I can't wash the dishes in this heat," all this from Mrs. Van
Daan. It was extremely unpleasant.

I still can't put up with heat and am glad that there's a stiff
breeze today, and yet the sun still shines.

Yours, Anne

Monday, 5 June, 1944

Dear Kitty,

Fresh "Secret Annexe" troubles, a quarrel between Dussel and the Franks over something very trivial: the sharing out of the butter. Dussel's capitulation. Mrs. Van Daan and the latter very thick, flirtations, kisses and friendly little laughs. Dussel is beginning to get longings for women. The Fifth Army has taken Rome. The city has been spared devastation by both armies and air forces, and is undamaged. Very few vegetables and potatoes. Bad weather. Heavy bombardments against the French coast and Pas de Calais continue.

Yours, Anne

Tuesday, 6 June, 1944

Dear Kitty,

"This is D-day," came the announcement over the English news and quite rightly, "this is *the* day."[1] The invasion has begun!

The English gave the news at eight o'clock this morning: Calais, Boulogne, Le Havre, and Cherbourg, also the Pas de Calais (as usual), were heavily bombarded. Moreover, as a safety measure for all occupied territories, all people who live within a radius of thirty-five kilometers from the coast are warned to be prepared for bombardments. If possible, the English will drop pamphlets one hour beforehand.

According to German news, English parachute troops have landed on the French coast, English landing craft are in battle with the German Navy, says the B.B.C.

We discussed it over the "Annexe" breakfast at nine o'clock: Is this just a trial landing like Dieppe two years ago?

English broadcast in German, Dutch, French, and other languages at ten o'clock: "The invasion has begun!"—that means the "real" invasion. English broadcast in German at eleven o'clock, speech by the Supreme Commander, General Dwight Eisenhower.

[1]Original English.

The English news at twelve o'clock in English: "This is D-day." General Eisenhower said to the French people: "Stiff fighting will come now, but after this the victory. The year 1944 is the year of complete victory; good luck."[1]

English news in English at one o'clock (translated): 11,000 planes stand ready, and are flying to and fro non-stop, landing troops and attacking behind the lines; 4000 landing boats, plus small craft, are landing troops and matériel between Cherbourg and Le Havre incessantly. English and American troops are already engaged in hard fighting. Speeches by Gerbrandy, by the Prime Minister of Belgium, King Haakon of Norway, De Gaulle of France, the King of England, and last, but not least, Churchill.

Great commotion in the "Secret Annexe"! Would the long-awaited liberation that has been talked of so much, but which still seems *too* wonderful, *too* much like a fairy tale, ever come true? Could we be granted victory this year, 1944? We don't know yet, but hope is revived within us; it gives us fresh courage, and makes us strong again. Since we must put up bravely with all the fears, privations, and sufferings, the great thing now is to remain calm and steadfast. Now more than ever we must clench our teeth and not cry out. France, Russia, Italy, and Germany, too, can all cry out and give vent to their misery, but we haven't the right to do that yet!

Oh, Kitty, the best part of the invasion is that I have the feeling that friends are approaching. We have been oppressed by those terrible Germans for so long, they have had their knives so at our throats, that the thoughts of friends and delivery fills us with confidence!

Now it doesn't concern the Jews any more; no, it concerns Holland and all occupied Europe. Perhaps, Margot says, I may yet be able to go back to school in September or October.

Yours, Anne

P.S. I'll keep you up to date with all the latest news!

[1]Original English.

Dear Kitty,

Super news of the invasion. The Allies have taken Bayeux, a small village on the French coast, and are now fighting for Caen. It's obvious that they intend to cut off the peninsular where Cherbourg lies. Every evening war correspondents give news from the battle front, telling us of the difficulties, courage, and enthusiasm of the army; they manage to get hold of the most incredible stories. Also some of the wounded who are already back in England again came to the microphone. The air force are up all the time in spite of the miserable weather. We heard over the B.B.C. that Churchill wanted to land with the troops on D-day, however, Eisenhower and the other generals managed to get him out of the idea. Just think of it, what pluck he has for such an old man—he must be seventy at least.

The excitement here has worn off a bit; still, we're hoping that the war will be over at the end of this year. It'll be about time too! Mrs. Van Daan's grizzling is absolutely unbearable; now she can't any longer drive us crazy over the invasion, she nags us the whole day long about the bad weather. It really would be nice to dump her in a bucket of cold water and put her up in the loft.

The whole of the "Secret Annexe" except Van Daan and Peter have read the trilogy *Hungarian Rhapsody*. This book deals with the life history of the composer, virtuoso, and child prodigy, Franz Liszt. It is a very interesting book, but in my opinion there is a bit too much about women in it. In his time Liszt was not only the greatest and most famous pianist, but also the greatest ladies' man—right up to the age of seventy. He lived with the Duchess Marie d'Agould, Princess Caroline Sayn-Wittgenstein, the dancer Lola Montez, the pianist Agnes Kingworth, the pianist Sophie Menter, Princess Olga Janina, Baroness Olga Meyendorff, the actress Lilla what's-her-name, etc., etc.; it is just endless. The parts of the book that deal with music and art are much more interesting. Among those mentioned are Schumann, Clara Wieck, Hector Berlioz,

Johannes Brahms, Beethoven, Joachim, Richard Wagner, Hans von Bülow, Anton Rubinstein, Frédéric Chopin, Victor Hugo, Honoré de Balzac, Hiller, Hummel, Czerny, Rossini, Cherubini, Paganini, Mendelssohn, etc., etc.

Liszt was personally a fine man, very generous, and modest about himself though exceptionally vain. He helped everyone, his art was everything to him, he was mad about cognac and about women, could not bear to see tears, was a gentleman, would never refuse to do anyone a favor, didn't care about money, loved religious liberty and world freedom.

Yours, Anne

Tuesday, 13 June, 1944

Dear Kitty,

Another birthday has gone by, so now I'm fifteen. I received quite a lot of presents.

All five parts of Sprenger's *History of Art,* a set of underwear, a handkerchief, two bottles of yoghourt, a pot of jam, a spiced gingerbread cake, and a book on botany from Mummy and Daddy, a double bracelet from Margot, a book from the Van Daans, sweet peas from Dussel, sweets and exercise books from Miep and Elli and, the high spot of all, the book *Maria Theresa* and three slices of full-cream cheese from Kraler. A lovely bunch of peonies from Peter; the poor boy took a lot of trouble to try and find something, but didn't have any luck.

There's still excellent news of the invasion, in spite of the wretched weather, countless gales, heavy rains, and high seas.

Yesterday Churchill, Smuts, Eisenhower, and Arnold visited French villages which have been conquered and liberated. The torpedo boat that Churchill was in shelled the coast. He appears, like so many men, not to know what fear is—makes me envious!

It's difficult for us to judge from our secret redoubt how people outside have reacted to the news. Undoubtedly people are pleased that the idle (?) English have rolled up their sleeves and are doing something at last. Any Dutch people who still look down on the English, scoff at England and her government of old gentlemen, call the English cowards, and yet hate the Germans deserve a good shaking. Perhaps it would put some sense into their woolly brains.

I hadn't had a period for over two months, but it finally started again on Saturday. Still, in spite of all the unpleasantness and bother, I'm glad it hasn't failed me any longer.

Yours, Anne

Wednesday, 14 June, 1944

Dear Kitty,

My head is haunted by so many wishes and thoughts, accusations and reproaches. I'm really not as conceited as so many people seem to think, I know my own faults and shortcomings better than anyone, but the difference is that I also know that I want to improve, shall improve, and have already improved a great deal.

Why is it then, I so often ask myself, that everyone still thinks I'm so terribly knowing and forward? Am I so knowing? Is it that I really am, or that maybe the others aren't? That sounds queer, I realize now, but I shan't cross out the last sentence, because it really isn't so crazy. Everyone knows that Mrs. Van Daan, one of my chief accusers, is unintelligent. I might as well put it plainly and say "stupid." Stupid people usually can't take it if others do better than they do.

Mrs. Van Daan thinks I'm stupid because I'm not quite so lacking in intelligence as she is; she thinks I'm forward because she's even more so; she thinks my dresses are too short, because hers are even shorter. And that's also the reason that she thinks I'm knowing, because she's twice as bad about joining in over subjects she knows absolutely nothing about. But one of my favorite sayings is "There's no smoke without fire," and I readily admit that I'm knowing.

Now the trying part about me is that I criticize and scold myself far more than anyone else does. Then if Mummy adds her bit of advice the pile of sermons becomes so insurmountable that in my despair I become rude and start contradicting and then, of course, the old well-known Anne watchword comes back: "No one understands me!" This phrase sticks in my mind; I know it sounds silly, yet there is some truth in it. I often accuse myself to such an extent that I simply long for a word of comfort, for someone who could give me sound advice and also draw out some of my real self; but, alas, I keep on looking, but I haven't found anyone yet.

I know that you'll immediately think of Peter, won't you, Kit? It's like this: Peter loves me not as a lover but as a friend and grows more affectionate every day. But what is the mysterious something that holds us both back? I don't understand it myself. Sometimes I think that my terrible longing for him was exaggerated, yet that's really not it, because if I don't go up to see him for two days, then I long for him more desperately than ever before. Peter is good and he's a darling, but still there's no denying that there's a lot about him that disappoints me. Especially his dislike of religion and all his talk about food and various other things don't appeal to me. Yet I feel quite convinced that we shall never quarrel now that we've made that straightforward agreement together. Pete is a peace-loving person; he's tolerant and gives in very easily. He lets me say a lot of things to him that he would never accept from his mother, he tries most persistently to keep his things in order. And yet why should he keep his innermost self to himself and why am I never allowed there? By nature he is more closed-up than I am, I agree, but I know—and from my own experience—that at some time or other even the most uncommunicative people long just as much, if not more, to find someone in whom they can confide.

Both Peter and I have spent our most meditative years in the "Secret Annexe." We often discuss the future, the past, and the present, but, as I've already said, I still seem to miss the real thing and yet I know that it's there.

Yours, Anne

Thursday, 15 June, 1944

Dear Kitty,

I wonder if it's because I haven't been able to poke my nose outdoors for so long that I've grown so crazy about everything to do with nature? I can perfectly well remember that there was a time when a deep blue sky, the song of the birds, moonlight and flowers could never have kept me spellbound. That's changed since I've been here.

At Whitsun, for instance, when it was so warm, I stayed awake on purpose until half past eleven one evening in order to have a good look at the moon for once by myself. Alas, the sacrifice was all in vain, as the moon gave far too much light and I didn't dare risk opening a window. Another time, some months ago now, I happened to be upstairs one evening when the window was open. I didn't go downstairs until the window had to be shut. The dark, rainy evening, the gale, the scudding clouds held me entirely in their power; it was the first time in a year and a half that I'd seen the night face to face. After that evening my longing to see it again was greater than my fear of burglars, rats, and raids on the house. I went downstairs all by myself and looked outside through the windows in the kitchen and the private office. A lot of people are fond of nature, many sleep outdoors occasionally, and people in prisons and hospitals long for the day when they will be free to enjoy the beauties of nature, but few are so shut away and isolated from that which can be shared alike by rich and poor. It's not imagination on my part when I say that to look up at the sky, the clouds, the moon, and the stars makes me calm and patient. It's a better medicine than either Valerian or bromine; Mother Nature makes me humble and prepared to face every blow courageously.

Alas, it has had to be that I am only able—except on a few rare occasions—to look at nature through dirty net curtains hanging before very dusty windows. And it's no pleasure looking through these any longer, because nature is just the one thing that really must be unadulterated.

Yours, Anne

Friday, 16 June, 1944

Dear Kitty,

New problems: Mrs. Van Daan is desperate, talks about a bullet through her head, prison, hanging, and suicide. She's jealous that Peter confides in me and not her. She's offended that Dussel doesn't enter into her flirtations with him, as she'd hoped, afraid that her husband is smoking all the fur-coat money away, she quarrels, uses abusive language, cries, pities herself, laughs, and then starts a fresh quarrel again. What on earth can one do with such a foolish, blubbering specimen? No one takes her seriously, she hasn't any character, and she grumbles to everyone. The worst of it is that it makes Peter rude, Mr. Van Daan irritable, and Mummy cynical. Yes, it's a frightful situation! There's *one* golden rule to keep before you: laugh about everything and don't bother yourself about the others! It sounds selfish, but it's honestly the only cure for anyone who has to seek consolation in himself.

Kraler has received another call-up to go digging for four weeks. He's trying to get out of it with a doctor's certificate and a letter from the business. Koophuis wants to have an operation on his stomach. All private telephones were cut off at eleven o'clock yesterday.

Yours, Anne

Friday, 23 June, 1944

Dear Kitty,

Nothing special going on here. The English have begun their big attack on Cherbourg; according to Pim and Van Daan, we're sure to be free by October 10. The Russians are taking part in the campaign, and yesterday began their offensive near Vitebsk; it's exactly three years to a day since the Germans attacked. We've hardly got any potatoes; from now on we're going to count them out for each person, then everyone knows what he's getting.

Yours, Anne

Tuesday, 27 June, 1944

Dearest Kitty,

The mood has changed, everything's going wonderfully. Cherbourg, Vitebsk, and Sloben fell today. Lots of prisoners and booty. Now the English can land what they want now they've got a harbor, the whole Cotentin Peninsular three weeks after the English invasion! A tremendous achievement! In the three weeks since D-day not a day has gone by without rain and gales, both here and in France, but a bit of bad luck didn't prevent the English and Americans from showing their enormous strength, and how! Certainly the "wonder weapon" is in full swing, but of what consequence are a few squibs apart from a bit of damage in England and pages full of it in the Boche newspapers? For that matter, when they really realize in "Bocheland" that the Bolshevists really are on the way, they'll get even more jittery.

All German women not in military service are being evacuated to Groningen, Friesland, and Gelderland with their children. Mussert[1] has announced that if they get as far as here with the invasion he'll put on a uniform. Does the old fatty want to do some fighting? He could have done so in Russia before now. Some time ago Finland turned down a peace offer, now the negotiations have just been broken off again, they'll be sorry for it later, the silly fools!

How far do you think we'll be on July 27?

Yours, Anne

Friday, 30 June, 1944

Dear Kitty,

Bad weather, or *bad weather at a stretch to the thirtieth of June.*[2] Isn't that well said! Oh yes, I have a smattering of English already; just to show that I can, I'm reading *An Ideal Husband* with the aid of a dictionary. War going wonderfully! Bobroisk, Mogilef, and Orsa have fallen, lots of prisoners.

[1] Mussert was the Dutch National Socialist leader.
[2] In English in the original.

Everything's all right here and tempers are improving. The superoptimists are triumphing. Elli has changed her hair style, Miep has the week off. That's the latest news.

Yours, Anne

Thursday, 6 July, 1944

Dear Kitty,

It strikes fear to my heart when Peter talks of later being a criminal, or of gambling; although it's meant as a joke, of course, it gives me the feeling that he's afraid of his own weakness. Again and again I hear from both Margot and Peter: "Yes, if I was as strong and plucky as you are, if I always stuck to what I wanted, if I had such persistent energy, yes then . . . !"

I wonder if it's really a good quality not to let myself be influenced. Is it really good to follow almost entirely my own conscience?

Quite honestly, I can't imagine how anyone can say: "I'm weak," and then remain so. After all, if you know it, why not fight against it, why not try to train your character? The answer was: "Because it's so much easier not to!" This reply rather discouraged me. Easy? Does that mean that a lazy, deceitful life is an easy life? Oh, no, that can't be true, it mustn't be true, people can so easily be tempted by slackness . . . and by money.

I thought for a long time about the best answer to give Peter, how to get him to believe in himself and, above all, to try and improve himself; I don't know whether my line of thought is right though, or not.

I've so often thought how lovely it would be to have someone's complete confidence, but now, now that I'm that far, I realize how difficult it is to think what the other person is thinking and then to find the *right* answer. More especially because the very ideas of "easy" and "money" are something entirely foreign and new to me. Peter's beginning to lean on me a bit and that mustn't happen under any circumstances.

A type like Peter finds it difficult to stand on his own feet, but it's even harder to stand on your own feet as a conscious, living being. Because if you do, then it's twice as difficult to steer a right path through the sea of problems and still remain constant through it all. I'm just drifting around, have been searching for days, searching for a good argument against that terrible word "easy," something to settle it once and for all.

How can I make it clear to him that what appears easy and attractive will drag him down into the depths, depths where there is no comfort to be found, no friends and no beauty, depths from which it is almost impossible to raise oneself?

We all live, but we don't know the why or the wherefore. We all live with the object of being happy; our lives are all different and yet the same. We three have been brought up in good circles, we have the chance to learn, the possibility of attaining something, we have all reason to hope for much happiness, but . . . we must earn it for ourselves. And that is never easy. You must work and do good, not be lazy and gamble, if you wish to earn happiness. Laziness may *appear* attractive, but work *gives* satisfaction.

I can't understand people who don't like work, yet that isn't the case with Peter; he just hasn't got a fixed goal to aim at, and he thinks he's too stupid and too inferior to achieve anything. Poor boy, he's never known what it feels like to make other people happy, and I can't teach him that either. He has no religion, scoffs at Jesus Christ, and swears, using the name of God; although I'm not orthodox either, it hurts me every time I see how deserted, how scornful, and how poor he really is.

People who have a religion should be glad, for not everyone has the gift of believing in heavenly things. You don't necessarily even have to be afraid of punishment after death; purgatory, hell, and heaven are things that a lot of people can't accept, but still a religion, it doesn't matter which, keeps a person on the right path. It isn't the fear of God but the upholding of one's own honor and conscience. How noble and good everyone could be if, every evening before falling asleep, they were to recall to their minds the events of the whole day and consider exactly what has been good and bad. Then, without realizing it, you try to improve yourself at the start of each new day; of course, you achieve quite a lot in the course of time. Anyone can do this, it costs nothing and is certainly very helpful. Whoever doesn't know it must learn and find by experience that: "A quiet conscience makes one strong!"

                                                                    Yours, Anne

                                                    Saturday, 8 July, 1944

Dear Kitty,

The chief representative of the business, Mr. B., has been in Beverwijk and managed, just like that, to get strawberries at the auction sale.[1] They arrived here dusty, covered with sand, but in large quantities. No less then twenty-four trays for the office people and us. That very same evening we bottled six jars and made eight pots of jam. The next morning Miep wanted to make jam for the office people.

At half past twelve, no strangers in the house, front door bolted, trays fetched, Peter, Daddy, Van Daan clattering on the stairs: Anne, get hot water; Margot, bring a bucket; all hands on deck! I went into the kitchen, which was chock-full, with a queer feeling in my tummy, Miep, Elli, Koophuis, Henk, Daddy, Peter: the families in hiding and their supply column, all mingling together, and in the middle of the day too!

People can't see in from outside because of the net curtains, but, even so, the loud voices and banging doors positively gave me the jitters. Are we really supposed to be in hiding? That's what flashed through my mind, and it gives me a very queer feeling to be able to appear in the world again. The pan was full, and I dashed upstairs again. The rest of the family was seated round our table in the kitchen busy stalk-picking—at least that's what they were supposed to be doing; more went into mouths than into buckets. Another bucket would

[1] It is compulsory in Holland for all growers to sell their produce at public auction.

soon be required. Peter went to the downstairs kitchen again—the bell rang twice; the bucket stayed where it was, Peter tore upstairs, locked the cupboard door! We were kicking our heels impatiently, couldn't turn on a tap, even though the strawberries were only half washed; the rule: "If anyone in the house, use no water, because of the noise," was strictly maintained.

At one o'clock Henk came and told us that it was the postman. Peter hurried downstairs again. Ting-a-ling . . . the bell, right about turn. I go and listen to see if I can hear anyone coming, first at our cupboard door and then creep to the top of the stairs. Finally Peter and I both lean over the banisters like a couple of thieves, listening to the din downstairs. No strange voices, Peter sneaks down, stops halfway, and calls out: "Elli!" No answer, one more: "Elli!" Peter's voice is drowned by the din in the kitchen. He goes right down and into the kitchen. I stand looking down tensely. "Get upstairs at once, Peter, the accountant is here, clear out!" It was Koophuis speaking. Peter comes upstairs sighing, the cupboard door closes. Finally Kraler arrives at half past one. "Oh, dearie me, I see nothing but strawberries, strawberries at breakfast, strawberries stewed by Miep, I smell strawberries, must have a rest from them and go upstairs—what is being washed up here . . . strawberries."

The remainder are being bottled. In the evening: two jars unsealed. Daddy quickly makes them into jam. The next morning: two more unsealed and four in the afternoon. Van Daan hadn't brought them to the right temperature for sterilizing. Now Daddy makes jam every evening.

We eat strawberries with our porridge, skimmed milk with strawberries, bread and butter with strawberries, strawberries for dessert, strawberries with sugar, strawberries with sand. For two whole days strawberries and nothing but strawberries, then the supply was finished or in bottles and under lock and key.

"I say, Anne," Margot calls out, "the greengrocer on the corner has let us have some green peas, nineteen pounds."

"That's nice of him," I replied. And it certainly is, but oh, the work . . . ugh!

"You've all got to help shelling peas on Saturday morning," Mummy announced when we were at table. And, sure enough, the big enamel pan duly appeared this morning, filled to the brim. Shelling peas is a boring job, but you ought to try "skinning" the pods. I don't think many people realize how soft and tasty the pod is when the skin on the inside has been removed. However, an even greater advantage is that the quantity which can be eaten is about triple the amount of when one only eats the peas. It's an exceptionally precise, finicky job, pulling out this skin; perhaps it's all right for pedantic dentists or precise office workers, but for an impatient teen-ager like me, it's frightful. We began at half past nine, I got up at half past ten, at half past eleven I sat down again. This refrain hummed in my ears: bend the top, pull the skin, remove the string, throw out the pod, etc., etc., they dance before my eyes, green, green, green maggots, strings, rotten pods, green, green, green. Just for the sake of doing something, I chatter the whole morning, any nonsense that comes into my head, make everyone laugh, and bore them stiff. But every string that I pull makes me feel more certain that I never, never want to be just a housewife only!

We finally have breakfast at twelve o'clock, but from half past twelve until quarter past one we've got to go skinning pods again. I'm just about seasick when I stop, the others a bit too. I go and sleep till four o'clock, but I'm still upset by those wretched peas.

                                                                Yours, Anne

Saturday, 15 July, 1944

Dear Kitty,

We have had a book from the library with the challenging title of: *What Do You Think of the Modern Young Girl?* I want to talk about this subject today.

The author of this book criticizes "the youth of today" from top to toe, without, however, condemning the whole of the young brigade as "incapable of anything good." On the contrary, she is rather of the opinion that if young people wished, they have it in their hands to make a bigger, more beautiful and better world, but that they occupy themselves with superficial things, without giving a thought to real beauty.

In some passages, the writer gave me very much the feeling she was directing her criticism at me, and that's why I want to lay myself completely bare to you for once and defend myself against this attack.

I have one outstanding trait in my character, which must strike anyone who knows me for any length of time, and that is my knowledge of myself. I can watch myself and my actions, just like an outsider. The Anne of every day I can face entirely without prejudice, without making excuses for her, and watch what's good and what's bad about her. This "self-consciousness" haunts me, and every time I open my mouth I know as soon as I've spoken whether "that ought to have been different" or "that was right as it was." There are so many things about myself that I condemn; I couldn't begin to name them all. I understand more and more how true Daddy's words were when he said: "All children must look after their own upbringing." Parents can only give good advice or put them on the right paths, but the final forming of a person's character lies in their own hands.

In addition to this, I have lots of courage, I always feel so strong and as if I can bear a great deal, I feel so free and so young! I was glad when I first realized it, because I don't think I shall easily bow down before the blows that inevitably come to everyone.

But I've talked about these things so often before. Now I want to come to the chapter of "Daddy and Mummy don't understand me." Daddy and Mummy have always thoroughly spoiled me, were sweet to me, defended me, and have done all that parents could do. And yet I've felt so terribly lonely for a long time, so left out, neglected, and misunderstood. Daddy tried all he could to check my rebellious spirit, but it was no use, I have cured myself, by seeing for myself what was wrong in my behavior and keeping it before my eyes.

How is it that Daddy was never any support to me in my struggle, why did he completely miss the mark when he wanted to offer me a helping hand? Daddy tried the wrong methods, he always talked to me as a child who was going through difficult phases. It sounds crazy, because Daddy's the only one who has always taken me into his confidence, and no one but Daddy has given me the feeling that I'm sensible. But there's one thing he's omitted: you see, he hasn't realized that for me the fight to get on top was more important than all else. I didn't want to hear about "symptoms of your age," or "other girls," or "it wears off by itself"; I didn't want to be treated as a girl-like-all-others, but as Anne-on-her-own-merits. Pim didn't understand that. For that matter, I can't confide in anyone, unless they tell me a lot about themselves, and as I know very little about Pim, I don't feel that I can tread upon more intimate ground with him. Pim always takes up the older, fatherly attitude, tells me that he too has had similar passing tendencies. But still he's not able to feel with me like a friend, however hard he tries. These things have made me never mention my views on life nor my well-considered theories to anyone but my diary and, occasionally, to Margot. I concealed from Daddy everything that perturbed me; I never shared my ideals with him. I was aware of the fact that I was pushing him away from me.

I couldn't do anything else. I have acted entirely according to my feelings, but I have acted in the way that was best for my peace of mind. Because I should completely lose my repose and self-confidence, which I have built up so shakily, if, at this stage, I were to accept criticisms of my half-completed task. And I can't do that even from Pim, although it sounds very hard, for not only have I not shared my secret thoughts with Pim but I have often pushed him even further from me, by my irritability.

This is a point that I think a lot about: why is it that Pim annoys me? So much so that I can hardly bear him teaching me, that his affectionate ways strike me as being put on, that

I want to be left in peace and would really prefer it if he dropped me a bit, until I felt more certain in my attitude towards him. Because I still have a gnawing feeling of guilt over that horrible letter that I dared to write him when I was so wound up. Oh, how hard it is to be really strong and brave in every way!

Yet this was not my greatest disappointment; no, I ponder far more over Peter than Daddy. I know very well that I conquered him instead of he conquering me. I created an image of him in my mind, pictured him as a quiet, sensitive, lovable boy, who needed affection and friendship. I needed a living person to whom I could pour out my heart; I wanted a friend who'd help to put me on the right road. I achieved what I wanted, and slowly but surely, I drew him towards me. Finally, when I had made him feel friendly, it automatically developed into an intimacy which, on second thought, I don't think I ought to have allowed.

We talked about the most private things, and yet up till now we have never touched on those things that filled, and still fill, my heart and soul. I still don't know quite what to make of Peter, is he superficial, or does he still feel shy, even of me? But dropping that, I committed one error in my desire to make a real friendship: I switched over and tried to get at him by developing it into a more intimate relation, whereas I should have explored all other possibilities. He longs to be loved and I can see that he's beginning to be more and more in love with me. He gets satisfaction out of our meetings, whereas they just have the effect of making me want to try it out with him again. And yet I don't seem able to touch on the subjects that I'm so longing to bring out into the daylight. I drew Peter towards me, far more than he realizes. Now he clings to me, and for the time being, I don't see any way of shaking him off and putting him on his own feet. When I realized that he could not be a friend for my understanding, I thought I would at least try to lift him up out of his narrow-mindedness and make him do something with his youth.

"For in its innermost depths youth is lonelier than old age."

I read this saying in some book and I've always remembered it, and found it to be true. Is it true then that grownups have a more difficult time here than we do? No. I know it isn't. Older people have formed their opinions about everything, and don't waver before they act. It's twice as hard for us young ones to hold our ground, and maintain our opinions, in a time when all ideals are being shattered and destroyed, when people are showing their worst side, and do not know whether to believe in truth and right and God.

Anyone who claims that the older ones have a more difficult time here certainly doesn't realize to what extent our problems weigh down on us, problems for which we are probably much too young, but which thrust themselves upon us continually, until, after a long time, we think we've found a solution, but the solution doesn't seem able to resist the facts which reduce it to nothing again. That's the difficulty in these times: ideals, dreams, and cherished hopes rise within us, only to meet the horrible truth and be shattered.

It's really a wonder that I haven't dropped all my ideals, because they seem so absurd and impossible to carry out. Yet I keep them, because in spite of everything I still believe that people are really good at heart. I simply can't build up my hopes on a foundation consisting of confusion, misery, and death. I see the world gradually being turned into a wilderness, I hear the ever approaching thunder, which will destroy us too, I can feel the sufferings of millions and yet, if I look up into the heavens, I think that it will all come right, that this cruelty too will end, and that peace and tranquillity will return again.

In the meantime, I must uphold my ideals, for perhaps the time will come when I shall be able to carry them out.

Yours, Anne

Friday, 21 July, 1944

Dear Kitty,
    Now I am getting really hopeful, now things are going well

at last. Yes, really, they're going well! Super news! An attempt has been made on Hitler's life and not even by Jewish communists or English capitalists this time, but by a proud German general, and what's more, he's a count, and still quite young. The Führer's life was saved by Divine Providence and, unfortunately, he managed to get off with just a few scratches and burns. A few officers and generals who were with him have been killed and wounded. The chief culprit was shot.

Anyway, it certainly shows that there are lots of officers and generals who are sick of the war and would like to see Hitler descend into a bottomless pit. When they've disposed of Hitler, their aim is to establish a military dictator, who will make peace with the Allies, then they intend to rearm and start another war in about twenty years' time. Perhaps the Divine Power tarried on purpose in getting him out of the way, because it would be much easier and more advantageous to the Allies if the impeccable Germans kill each other off; it'll make less work for the Russians and the English and they'll be able to begin rebuilding their own towns all the sooner.

But still, we're not that far yet, and I don't want to anticipate the glorious events too soon. Still, you must have noticed, this is all sober reality and that I'm in quite a matter-of-fact mood today; for once, I'm not jabbering about high ideals. And what's more, Hitler has even been so kind as to announce to his faithful, devoted people that from now on everyone in the armed forces must obey the Gestapo, and that any soldier who knows that one of his superiors was involved in this low, cowardly attempt upon his life may shoot the same on the spot, without court-martial.

What a perfect shambles it's going to be. Little Johnnie's feet begin hurting him during a long march, he's snapped at by his boss, the officer, Johnnie grabs his rifle and cries out: "You wanted to murder the Führer, so there's your reward." One bang and the proud chief who dared to tick off little Johnnie has passed into eternal life (or is it eternal death?). In the end, whenever an officer finds himself up against a soldier, or having to take the lead, he'll be wetting his pants from anxiety, because the soldiers will dare to say more than they do. Do you gather a bit what I mean, or have I been skipping too much from one subject to another? I can't help it; the prospect that I may be sitting on school benches next October makes me feel far too cheerful to be logical! Oh, dearie me, hadn't I just told you that I didn't want to be too hopeful? Forgive me, they haven't given me the name "little bundle of contradictions" all for nothing!

Yours, Anne

Tuesday, 1 August, 1944

Dear Kitty,

"Little bundle of contradictions." That's how I ended my last letter and that's how I'm going to begin this one. "A little bundle of contradictions," can you tell me exactly what it is? What does contradiction mean? Like so many words, it can mean two things, contradiction from without and contradiction from within.

The first is the ordinary "not giving in easily, always knowing best, getting in the last word," *enfin,* all the unpleasant qualities for which I'm renowned. The second nobody knows about, that's my own secret.

I've already told you before that I have, as it were, a dual personality. One half embodies my exuberant cheerfulness, making fun of everything, my high-spiritedness, and above all, the way I take everything light. This includes not taking offense at a flirtation, a kiss, an embrace, a dirty joke. This side is usually lying in wait and pushes away the other which is much better, deeper and purer. You must realize that no one knows Anne's better side and that's why most people find me so insufferable.

Certainly I'm a giddy clown for one afternoon, but then everyone's had enough of me for another month. Really, it's just the same as a love film is for deep-thinking people, simply a diversion, amusing just for once, something which is soon forgotten, not bad, but certainly not good. I loathe having to tell you this, but why shouldn't I, if I know it's true anyway?

My lighter superficial side will always be too quick for the deeper side of me and that's why it will always win. You can't imagine how often I've already tried to push this Anne away, to cripple her, to hide her, because after all, she's only half of what's called Anne: but it doesn't work and I know, too, why it doesn't work.

I'm awfully scared that everyone who knows me as I always am will discover that I have another side, a finer and better side. I'm afraid they'll laugh at me, think I'm ridiculous and sentimental, not take me seriously. I'm used to not being taken seriously but it's only the "lighthearted" Anne that's used to it and can bear it; the "deeper" Anne is too frail for it. Sometimes, if I really compel the good Anne to take the stage for a quarter of an hour, she simply shrivels up as soon as she has to speak, and lets Anne number one take over, and before I realize it, she has disappeared.

Therefore, the nice Anne is never present in company, has not appeared one single time so far, but almost always predominates when we're alone. I know exactly how I'd like to be, how I am too . . . inside. But, alas, I'm only like that for myself. And perhaps that's why, no, I'm sure it's the reason why I say I've got a happy nature within and why other people think I've got a happy nature without. I am guided by the pure Anne within, but outside I'm nothing but a frolicsome little goat who's broken loose.

As I've already said, I never utter my real feelings about anything and that's how I've acquired the name of chaser-after-boys, flirt, know-all, reader of love stories. The cheerful Anne laughs about it, gives cheeky answers, shrugs her shoulders indifferently, behaves as if she doesn't care, but, oh dearie me, the quiet Anne's reactions are just the opposite. If I'm to be quite honest, then I must admit that it does hurt me, that I try terribly hard to change myself, but that I'm always fighting against a more powerful enemy.

A voice sobs within me: "There you are, that's what's become of you: you're uncharitable, you look supercilious and peevish, people dislike you and all because you won't listen to the advice given you by your own better half." Oh, I would like to listen, but it doesn't work; if I'm quiet and serious, everyone thinks it's a new comedy and then I have to get out of it by turning it into a joke, not to mention my own family, who are sure to think I'm ill, make me swallow pills for headaches and nerves, feel my neck and my head to see whether I'm running a temperature, ask if I'm constipated and criticize me for being in a bad mood. I can't keep that up: if I'm watched to that extent, I start by getting snappy, then unhappy, and finally I twist my heart round again, so that the bad is on the outside and the good is on the inside and keep on trying to find a way of becoming what I would so like to be, and what I could be, if . . . there weren't any other people living in the world.

Yours, Anne

EPILOGUE

Anne's diary ends here. On August 4, 1944, the Grüne Polizei made a raid on the "Secret Annexe." All the occupants, together with Kraler and Koophuis, were arrested and sent to German and Dutch concentration camps.

The "Secret Annexe" was plundered by the Gestapo. Among a pile of old books, magazines, and newspapers which were left lying on the floor, Miep and Elli found Anne's diary. Apart from a very few passages, which are of little interest to the reader, the original text has been printed.

Of all the occupants of the "Secret Annexe," Anne's father alone returned. Kraler and Koophuis, who withstood the hardships of the Dutch camp, were able to go home to their families.

In March 1945, two months before the liberation of Holland, Anne died in the concentration camp at Bergen-Belsen.

READER'S SUPPLEMENT

For Greater Understanding and Appreciation of

ANNE FRANK: THE DIARY OF A YOUNG GIRL

THIS SUPPLEMENT has been designed with a twofold purpose in mind. As the title suggests, it should help you derive greater understanding of the author, the background of the story, its important characters, and the style in which it is written (Part I). This increased understanding should lead toward a deeper appreciation of the literary values as you read. The second purpose is to provide you with practical material to help you increase your vocabulary, spelling, writing, and discussion skills (Part II).

Accordingly, it makes sense to read Sections A, B, and C of Part I *before* you begin the first chapter. Knowing what episodes reflect events in the author's own life, being aware of the historical background of the period during which the story takes place, and being conscious of the writing style and techniques will greatly enrich your understanding and appreciation *as you read the book*. It's very much like the extra thrill you get when you recognize familiar places in a motion picture or witness a rehearsal of a stage or television production.

Section D of Part I had best be left for examination until you have gotten well into the reading. After you have covered at least a third of the book, you might pause for a while to go over in your mind what the characters are like. Then you can compare your own impressions with those presented in Section D. When you resume reading, you will be able to follow more closely what causes the characters to act and speak as they do. The study of human nature is always fascinating and can often help you understand yourself better.

Part II, of course, is best handled *after you have finished the book*. However, glance through the introductory remarks of the sections on vocabulary and spelling because there are several hints about what to do to get ready for those exercises as you read. Section A, Writing Skills, suggests how you can apply some of the author's techniques directly to your own writing skills, and Section D provides good material for group work in discussing or reporting on some of the important ideas in the book.

In general, then, use Part I to increase the enjoyment of the pleasant hours you spend meeting new people and sharing their ideas and experiences. Then get the extras out of your reading by working with Part II. As you become more familiar with *Reader's Supplements* for other books in this series, you may decide to change the order in which you handle a particular section. Feel free to do so. Whatever procedure turns out to be most rewarding for you should be the one you adopt. Good luck to you in your efforts to make of yourself a more cultured and articulate person!

NOTE: Throughout the Supplement you will come across references such as *p. 42T* or *p. 57B*. The code is easy to follow: *p.* (page number), *T* (top of page), *M* (middle), *B* (bottom).

Part I

A. BIOGRAPHICAL BACKGROUND

ORDINARILY, WHEN the events of an author's life are reviewed, the problem is to decide what to eliminate so that the telling will not be too lengthy. Here we have a writer whose total existence was tragically cut short three months before her sixteenth birthday. What there is to tell, therefore, must be pieced together from the pages of a remarkable diary found in a trash heap on the floor of an abandoned apartment on the Prinsengracht, one of the canals in Amsterdam, Holland.

Anne Frank tells us that her parents came from very wealthy stock (p. 202M). Her father had been a "real little rich boy" and her mother had known "engagement parties of two hundred and fifty people, private balls and dinners." The family fortunes of Anne's grandparents had apparently been lost in the inflationary periods that followed World War I, but when we first meet the Franks they are leading comparatively prosperous middle-class lives.

Mr. Frank was eleven years older than his wife when they were married, and their first child was Margot, born in Frankfort Am Main, Germany, in 1926. Three years later Anne came along. She was but a tiny tot of four when the family had to get out of Germany because, in 1933, Hitler's gangs had already begun to roam the streets, looking to victimize the national scapegoats, the Jews.

When Mr. Frank brought his family to Holland, he became Managing Director of an established firm and for seven years did rather well. But on May 10, 1940, on the pretext that they were protecting the Dutch from attack by France and Great Britain, the Nazi armies invaded the Netherlands. In four days all resistance was crushed and the difficult period for the Frank family began. They, among thousands of others, were prime targets for the anti-Jewish laws that followed almost before the dust of battle had settled.

For six years Anne, a carefree little girl, had been quite acceptable to the Montessori School, which she had entered as a kindergartner shortly after her arrival from Germany. Now she suddenly had to become aware that she was somehow different, could not be taught by her sixth-form teacher, and would henceforth have to attend schools reserved for the wearers of the yellow Star of David.

Although restricted on every side by racial regulations, the Franks courageously pretended to live normal lives for two more years. Each day, however, the vise closed tighter and it was only a matter of time before a decision would have to be made—submit to arrest and eventual gas chambers, or hide. Mr. Frank had long planned the "disappearance" of his family when the critical hour arrived. Early in July, 1942, when it would have been sheer suicide to wait any longer, the Franks, together with the Van Daans, went through a door above a warehouse and virtually vanished.

The rest of Anne's "biography," covering two years in the hiding place, you will be privileged to read in the fascinating pages that follow. You may laugh now and then, sigh often, and perhaps be moved to tears—but out of this emotional experience will come a realization that Anne Frank was destined to live many years more than are counted by dates and birthdays.

On this theme, George Stevens, producer of the

CinemaScope motion picture, *The Diary of Anne Frank,* wrote:

Of all the many remarkable things about Anne Frank, I believe the most important is the fact of her survival—a survival contained between the covers of a small red-checkered cloth-covered diary book.

Within this diary exists a young girl touched with a perceptive genius on one hand and an almost consuming sensitivity on the other. And combined with these is a most exquisite sense of feeling and knowledge of life at its finest. "I believe in the good of man," said Anne, with her quiet smile. "My mission is to destroy and exterminate," hoarsely shouted the leader of the great forces of Nazi Germany.

In 1943, this seemed quite a hopeless and unequal contest. All the communications machinery of a powerful nation was projecting the voice of its Fuehrer, and his words were heard around the world. At the same time, Anne was quietly penning her words in the little diary seen only by herself.

Today, the shouting voice is no longer heard, but daily more and more people of many tongues are repeating and reflecting on what Anne Frank had to say.

This destiny to survive was illustrated dramatically in a conversation I had with Mr. Otto Frank in 1957. We were sitting in a cramped attic in Amsterdam and I was holding in my hand a printed edition of *The Diary of a Young Girl.* It was in this building that Mr. Frank had sheltered his little group while they hid from the Nazis. After serious hesitation, I asked Mr. Frank a question to which I felt I must have the answer—"Can you tell me something about what occurred when the Gestapo broke into this room? Their mission was to destroy—how was it they did not find and destroy the diary?"

While Mr. Frank bravely described what happened on that fateful day, I looked at the little volume in my hand and realized that Anne's persistent belief in the triumph

of the good in human nature was best exemplified by the
very survival of her writing.

On that day in August, 1944, Sergeant Silverbauer, of
the Green Police, and four subordinates were executing
just another phase of what Hitler and Goebbels had con-
ceived as the "final solution of the Jewish problem." Their
mission was to remove the Jews from Holland. While so
doing, they were to loot and to plunder and, most im-
portantly, they were to leave no record or documentation
of this work.

While searching the attic, the sergeant picked up Mr.
Frank's brief case. He asked if there were any jewels. Mr.
Frank said there was nothing but papers. The sergeant
opened it. Disappointed, he threw the papers and the
diary to the floor and put the silverware and the Hanukkah
candlestick into the brief case. The little group which
had spent the last twenty-five months in this attic was led
away. The room was left in disarray.

However, there remained on the floor the diary of a
young girl. The Nazi soldiers had failed in their mission.
They had left behind a statement to the world. They had
left behind a comment on their work. They had left behind a story of a girl in adolescence, her troubles with her
parents, and her young love.

B. HISTORICAL BACKGROUND

THE RELATIONSHIP of Anne Frank's touching story to
the history of her time and ours was beautifully put
into words by the late Eleanor Roosevelt:

This is a remarkable book. Written by a young girl—and
the young are not afraid of telling the truth—it is one of the
wisest and most moving commentaries on war and its impact on human beings that I have ever read. Anne Frank's
account of the changes wrought upon eight people hiding
out from the Nazis for two years during the occupation of
Holland, living in constant fear and isolation, imprisoned

not only by the terrible outward circumstances of war but inwardly by themselves, made me intimately and shockingly aware of war's greatest evil—the degradation of the human spirit.

At the same time, Anne's diary makes poignantly clear the ultimate shining nobility of that spirit. Despite the horror and the humiliation of their daily lives, these people never gave up. Anne herself—and, most of all, it is her portrait which emerges so vividly and so appealingly from this book—matured very rapidly in these two years, the crucial years from thirteen to fifteen in which change is so swift and so difficult for every young girl. Sustained by her warmth and her wit, her intelligence and the rich resources of her inner life, Anne wrote and thought much of the time about things which very sensitive and talented adolescents without the threat of death will write—her relations with her parents, her developing self-awareness, the problems of growing up.

These are the thoughts and expression of a young girl living under extraordinary conditions, and for this reason her diary tells us much about ourselves and about our own children. And for this reason, too, I felt how close we all are to Anne's experience, how very much involved we are in her short life and in the entire world.

Anne's diary is an appropriate monument to her fine spirit and to the spirits of those who have worked and are working still for peace.

Mrs. Roosevelt—in her lifetime a valiant champion of peace, freedom, human dignity, and justice—was eminently qualified to comment on the events and "impacts on human beings" suggested by Anne's diary. With her husband, one of our greatest Presidents, Franklin Delano Roosevelt, she had lived through the trying years when the world stood by—amazed, horrified, but inactive—and watched a maniacal flophouse habitué hypnotize the German people into acts of incredible violence against all mankind, and against the Jews especially.

Anne Frank's story really began in 1929 when Adolf Hitler seized upon the international economic crisis to re-establish his Nazi Party, which had suffered an ignominious defeat just a few years earlier. By 1933 he had become Chancellor of Germany. This was the same year Anne's father, realizing his hopeless position in a land where storm troopers made public sport of Jews, moved his family to Amsterdam.

In the next five years, Hitler consolidated his position. He threatened Austria, took over the Saar district unopposed, sent troops into the demilitarized Rhineland, eventually annexed Austria, and began to move on Czechoslovakia. Neville Chamberlain, Britain's Prime Minister, feebly waved an umbrella, piously talked of "peace in our time," and smugly set up the Munich Treaty in September, 1938, which forced Czechoslovakia to give the Sudetenland to Germany.

Only when the Nazi hordes overran Prague and occupied Poland did the western powers realize the mistake they had made. But it was too late! In the spring and summer of 1940, Norway and then Denmark were blitzed (a term used to describe the lightning-like strike of the mechanized divisions of the German Army). And then the steel-helmeted Nazis roared into Holland on their motorcycles and in their tanks and dive bombers, bringing with them the very terrors the Frank family had sought to escape.

From this point on, Anne's diary supplies many of the details of human misery, bloodshed, and murder that told the story of Nazi brutality. Anti-Jewish decrees were imported from Berlin to Amsterdam. Anne and her people had to wear yellow stars, stay off public conveyances, observe a curfew, shop in restricted stores, keep out of places of entertainment or recreation, and avoid mingling with Christians anywhere, even in school (p. 3B). We learn of the concentration camps (p. 34), the harassment and slaughter of local citizenry (p. 35B). We take heart at the courageous words of Winston Churchill (p. 42T) and cheer the British Army in North Africa (p. 43M). We are depressed again when the house-to-house search for Jews begins (pp. 47B, 56M) and the Dutch children beg for food in the streets (p. 57T).

Conditions change from despair to hope almost daily. A ray of sunshine breaks through the gloom when a bishop tells the people of the Netherlands to resist (p. 60T), but the evil cloud descends again when the staged interviews with German wounded are broadcast (p. 64T). Anne's shock at Rauter's announcement that Jews must be "cleaned out . . . like cockroaches" is balanced by the news that Dutch patriots have sabotaged some Nazi-occupied buildings (p. 67M).

The only escape for the inhabitants of the cramped quarters of the Secret Annexe lies in the hope that someone will drive out the Nazis from Amsterdam and permit sanity to return to a civilization gone mad. Reports from the outside continue to filter through the hinged cupboard guarding the hideaway. The English begin systematic bombing of Germany (p. 70T); there is a mass strike by Dutch workers (p. 71M); students choose labor camps over signing approval of the New Order (p. 72T); the Italians become disenchanted with Mussolini and his Fascists (p. 84M) and soon surrender unconditionally (p. 97T); the story of the underground begins to unfold (p. 129B); and then comes wild hope with news that the Allies are preparing an invasion of the Continent.

But the events march on. Now hope becomes fused with fear into a frozen, shapeless mass. Miep's husband, Henk, debates Goebbels' threat to "slam the door" on the invaders (p. 132B); the ghouls of the Black Market who fed on war's carrion are mentioned (p. 154T); the British continue their round-the-clock air raids (p. 167B) and the ladies in the Annexe are happy over the retaliation but terribly frightened (p. 170M); the massive might of the Russians begins to shove the Germans back (p. 171B); and, amidst the nightmare of World War II, talk about the eighteenth birthday of the future Queen of England offers a moment of relief.

By May, 1944, the invasion by the Allies still seems remote and anti-Semitism more fashionable than ever (pp. 210B, 212B). The Fifth Army takes Rome and then, D-Day (p. 216)! The Allies gain a foothold (p. 224T), and some of his generals almost succeed in destroying Hitler (p. 234T). The faint flicker of hope for the Franks, the Van Daans, and Mr. Dussel bursts into flame. But two weeks later . . .

C. FEATURES OF THE AUTHOR'S STYLE

Any analysis of the style used in the *Diary* must take two things into account. First, we must note that the book, as we read it, is a translation from the Dutch, and some of the original flavor of Anne Frank's native language may not have come through in English. A translator cannot always substitute word for word or phrase for phrase, since no two languages have exactly the same idioms or constructions.

Secondly, we must remember that a girl in her early teens is the author. A writer's technique rarely reaches full maturity in adolescence. But, in many ways, this is what makes Anne's diary so straightforward, so intensely human and personal, so sensitive to the changes that take place both about her and within herself. Her lack of sophistication and experience in writing removed any possibility that her style would contain the artificial flourishes and studied touches that so frequently mask the true character of older authors. The *Diary is* Anne Frank; it is her personality on paper; it reveals the complete human being behind the pen.

Anne tells us how self-conscious she feels about writing (p. 2M) and then reveals her true motive in starting a diary: "paper is more patient than man." She wants to unburden herself, but she seems to sense that her words and sentences still retain the painful correctness, almost stiffness, of classroom "composition" writing.

Observe the sentences (p. 3T) beginning with "But it's the same . . ." Her concession to an easy, conversational style is found in the contractions *it's* and *don't*, but "I can never bring myself to talk of anything outside the common round" and "that is the root of the trouble" are just the kind of tight little expressions that look good on theme papers. Her teacher might not have approved of the run-on sentence "error" coming after "get any closer," yet this is a typical thirteen-year-old's slip, if we want to call it that. There are many more examples of this looseness of sentence structure: "It was at the end . . ." (p. 4M), "There is a little boat . . ." (p. 7M), "I went to the telephone . . ." (p. 8M).

However, the childish preciseness mixed with carelessness is far less pronounced than is the extraordinary maturity displayed in those passages that show keen insight, intelligent introspection, and self-analysis. Anne, like an accomplished novelist, rapidly sketches the character traits of the other inmates of the Secret Annexe (p. 22M) and gives us the first hint of things to come with Peter (p. 24T). The emotions of a young girl who feels neglected by an elder sister and her mother are remarkably presented (pp. 39–41). A delightful talent for wry humor is evident when Anne talks of "using up" her brains (p. 56T) keeping out of trouble. She recognizes and comments wisely on "growing pains" (p. 75T) and keeps returning to her favorite problem, "Mumsie" (p. 110B).

In all these journeys into herself, Anne drops her adolescent veneer and writes with the wisdom of an analyst. Her words express doubt, conviction, wonder, perplexity, understanding—and at these times we are not reading halting prose but are listening to a tape recording of a heart and brain. That Anne was aware of her strengths and shortcomings as a writer is touchingly noted when she calls herself the "best and sharpest critic of my own work" (p. 175T).

In the midst of the slowly unfolding tragedy in the Secret Annexe, one is struck by the humor Anne is able to find and express even in this impossible situation. How delightful are her stories of Mr. Keptor and his "Chatterbox" assignments (p. 6M), the opened sack of beans (p. 42B), the "Prospectus" (p. 46), the "soup-eaters" (p. 59), and the daily routine (pp. 85–91). It took natural writing talent to project the humor by inserting a little touch here and a broad scene there.

Observe how well Anne handles the technique of creating a concise summary or injecting emotional tone by the use of exclamatory expressions. See the sentences beginning with "And all because . . ." (p. 48T); "No light . . ." (p. 49M); "Therefore, I can only advise . . ." (p. 50B); "Mrs. Van Daan . . ." (p. 53B); and "If only . . ." (p. 63M). The quick thrust of the exclamation mark, used appropriately, adds spice to language.

Besides looking inwardly, Anne shows superior skill in observing the scene about her and commenting philosophically on the oddities and realities present. Witness her detached analysis of "grownups" (p. 29M), her remarks on nature and God (p. 152T), her bitter charge against the "little man" (p. 198T), and her praise of work and religion (p. 226M). In examining the last two examples, you might want to compare the style of Anne when she is fifteen to what it was two years earlier. You can sense the assurance that is improving the shape of her language: the longer, more involved sentence structure; the more colorful detail; the greater depth of understanding (p. 231T). The *Diary* offers the student of writing a fine opportunity to watch a style emerge from awkward uncertainty into grace and maturity. One grows heartsick at the thought of what this writer might have accomplished had she been granted the years to reach her full flowering as an artist.

D. CHARACTER ANALYSIS

IT HAS BEEN SAID that tension, fear, or confinement bring out the best and worst traits of a human being. Surely, as we observe the eight occupants of the Secret Annexe through Anne's eyes, we can agree that there is much truth in the statement.

It might be argued that, with the exception of Anne, the characters in the *Diary* are drawn in one-dimensional lines, since we know them only from what the author says of them. But there is ample opportunity to study some of them in fairly good depth; the careful recording of what they do and say under varying circumstances allows inferences to be drawn. Necessarily stripped as they are of all pretense in the narrow confines of a few rooms, they function much more genuinely than if they had had a broader background within which to hide the nakedness of elemental emotions. They aptly illustrate the theory: "You have to live with someone, to really get to know him."

There is Mummy, overwhelmed by events and unable to adjust to the unnatural way of life suddenly thrust upon her. At first Mrs. Frank cannot perform even the ordinary duties of a housewife (pp. 17B, 19B). It is not surprising that a literate woman (p. 26T), accustomed to the comforts of middle-class life, should fall into a temporary state of shock when she discovers her entire security threatened. She cannot understand Anne's sensitivity (p. 27B), but in this she is not unlike many mothers faced with the problem of coping with a precocious daughter. One can picture Mrs. Frank as having been a calm, serene hostess in better days (p. 30M), and her "weaknesses" probably stem more from her failure to forget that Anne is no longer a child than from any inherent failings (p. 40B). Certainly her courage and patience cannot be denied, as she gradually forces herself to participate in the routines of the day as if she were managing a perfectly normal household.

Daddy is probably an idealized portrait created by the devoted mind of a daughter who fastens upon him all the affection she would in reality love to share with Mummy, too. It is not uncommon for daughters to reject their mothers for real or fancied grievances and become overattached to their fathers. The psychologists have much to say on this point. But, parting the Oedipus veil, we can see a strong, thoughtful, loyal, incredibly brave man, fighting with all his resources to protect his brood from the relentless enemy. He plans the hideout in advance (p. 11M), and pitches right in to clean things up when the group slips away from the outer world. Mr. Frank dislikes quarrels and tries to make peace frequently as tempers flare all about him (pp. 24M, 28B, 40M). An odd insight into Daddy's meticulous nature comes when Anne describes his absorption in peeling potatoes (p. 93T), and this impression is strengthened when we see his correct behavior with Peter as young love blossoms (p. 195M). The letter that Anne sends disturbs Mr. Frank deeply and we admire his gentle but firm handling of a difficult situation.

Mrs. Van Daan is highly interesting, despite her apparent shortcomings. She quarrels constantly with her husband (pp. 22M, 100M), is jealous and suspicious (p. 23T), is lazy and careless about housework (p. 25T), tries to push her opinions onto others (pp. 28T, 30M), and scurries for cover or weeps whenever the going gets rough (pp. 61M, 84B, 180M, 191M). But she is intensely human and her constant awareness of herself as a woman, much to Anne's adolescent disgust, adds a touch of color to the drabness of the dreary life about the warehouse (p. 83B).

Three of the inmates of the Annexe are rather shadowy figures, appearing periodically in the diary pages but remaining rather unidentified beings by and large. Mr. Dussel emerges somewhat more sharply defined than the other two. He acts like a crochety bachelor (pp. 47T, 49B) much of the time, seems quite unemotional (p. 53M), and almost drives Anne mad with his strange habits (pp. 55B, 77M). Margot is every elder sister as viewed by a younger one—too delicate for hard work (p. 17B), favored by Mummy (p. 23B), useless as a companion (p. 27B), and annoying as an example (p. 58B). She comes out a little better when the girls write letters to each other because talk would be embarrassing to both (p. 162T). Mr. Van Daan is hardly more than the butt of his wife's peevishness (p. 22M), tries to be a stern father (p. 24M), and covers his inadequacies by being pigheaded and selfish (p. 89M).

Symbolizing the kindly Dutch and their efforts, at great personal risk, to save their Jewish friends from the gas chambers, are Miep and Elli, two former business associates who act as the main contacts with the outside world; Mr. Kraler and Mr. Koophuis, who are later imprisoned in Dutch camps for their help; Miep's husband Henk; and several others who appear briefly. Without these fearless sympathizers, the Franks and the Van Daans could not have survived as long as they did. Minor characters these, but in the history of the day they played heroic major roles.

Peter is exactly what one would expect him to be when described by a girl—"a rather soft, shy, gawky youth" (p. 20M.) So long as Anne remains uninterested in him, he rarely comes out of his shell, being alternately "boring" (p. 22T) and complaining (p. 22M), stubborn (p. 24B) and forward (p. 26B). Gradually he becomes more prominent as Anne discovers new aspects of his character. For a brief moment he is surprisingly funny (p. 33B), and, much later, displays an amazing knowledge of nature (p. 126M).

As Anne, somewhat bewildered by it all, realizes she enjoys Peter's company, we get a little closer and find a boy groping toward maturity, tongue-tied on occasion, withdrawn, painfully sensitive beneath an unruffled exterior (pp. 135M, 145T, 146T). His fumbling gestures of affection toward Anne are delightfully characteristic of first love and soon he is the center of her universe—for the time being. She sees him brave as a lion (p. 178T), a bold lover (p. 187M), an honest gentleman (p. 194B). Then, as soon as the conquest has been made complete, he becomes less important, less impressive, and less worth pursuing (p. 208B). Such is the portrait of a young man when he is sketched by the mature hand of a perceptive woman!

Anne, of course, is a complete study. Unlike static characters in some books who are set in a rigid mold from the first page to the last, the heroic little author of the *Diary* grows before our eyes. When she resolutely plans what to say to Daddy about his objections to her "going upstairs" (p. 199T), she is far different from the girl who dreamed of Peter Wessel. The change is gradual but quite noticeable: anger against Mummy turns into an effort to understand her (p. 114M), and even Mrs. Van Daan comes in for her share of sympathy (p. 124T); Peter is no longer a lazy oaf but an object worthy of study (p. 137B) and later a partner in self-analysis (p. 160M); and serious subjects like politics and war arouse unanswerable questions in her probing mind.

Under normal circumstances, Anne's intelligent appraisal of herself and others would have been perfectly remarkable, as she comes to grips with the multiple problems arising in the life of every young girl in the middle years of adolescence. But when we realize that this is a girl faced with the shocks and strangeness of living two critical years in a most unnatural environment and confronted by realities ordinarily not experienced by other girls at any age, we are amazed.

We are amazed at the courage revealed in her reactions to race hatred and violence (p. 4T), her attitude toward the hideaway that somehow is beautiful (pp. 17T, 32M), her calmness under ceaseless bombardment (p. 61T), and her awakening passion for Peter (p. 117M). Life must go on and be lived, regardless of time or place.

We are astonished at her penetration, already discussed at some length in the previous section. How wise she seems when she analyzes Mummy, Margot, and grownups (pp. 27B, 29M)! How superior she acts, in a girlish way, when she remains "calm" (p. 34M)! How hurt when she feels picked on (p. 39T)! How self-critical when she compares Daddy and Mummy (pp. 40–41)! How womanly when Peter's glory has faded (p. 221M)!

But there is also the little girl—the wondering, open-faced, curious, smug little girl next door who is the bane of all little boys' existence. What maturity for a thirteen-year-old (p. 2B)! What a woman of the world (pp. 5T, 10B, 117T, 118M)! What a worrisome student (p. 5B)! What a confident jokester (p. 6B)! What naïveté (p. 125M)!

And then there are her humor, her feeling for other people as she gazes through an open window and sobs for hungry children, her disarming innocence as she discovers her physical self, and her unfailing optimism even to the moment when violent hands ripped apart the slim barricade that had kept her alive. Here indeed was a human being who, far beyond her years, had the wisdom and understanding so few of us ever reach, though we come to the "sear and yellow leaf" of an average lifetime.

Part II

A. IMPROVEMENT OF WRITING SKILLS

MANY A GREAT WRITER, in discussing how he developed his own unique style, frankly confessed to the debt he owed to authors whose material he had studied and imitated in the early stages of his career. In reading a book, you, too, can pick up valuable hints which will aid you in strengthening your writing skills. It would be unwise, of course, to attempt to incorporate every feature of an author's style into your own. Even if you could do this, you would not want to lose your own individuality. You can, however, concentrate on a few of the most effective techniques used by a writer and get useful suggestions from them.

Anne Frank offers, in effect, some valuable suggestions to other young writers who would like to improve their skills:

1. *Keep your descriptions organized!*

Whether it is a room, a person, or a scene of action you are describing, try to present a picture that is logically arranged. Start from the left and move to the right, or go from top to bottom, or reverse either pattern, or proceed from the more prominent details to the lesser ones, or vice versa. Usually, there is no one design superior to another, but some specific arrangement should be clear to the reader so that he can visualize easily.

Observe how Anne describes the building (p. 15T). She uses the *bottom to top* technique, pausing on each floor to give the general layout. You start at the front door next to the warehouse, move upstairs to the "office," pause to note some additional rooms, go up four steps to the showroom, the kitchen, and the water closet. In this fashion you gradually are brought up and into the Secret Annexe.

Or examine how Anne, by a series of sketches framed by a room, presents the tableau of sausage-makers (p. 52T); or study the bombing scene (p. 81M), or "going to bed" (p. 85M), or the "timetable" (p. 89T). Each passage is a fine example of organized, detailed description.

2. *Use* understatement *to heighten an effect!*

It is startling to realize that a teen-age writer like Anne had mastered the technique of stimulating sharp reader reaction by creating a contrast between relatively mild words and events calling for exclamation marks. She talks of her fear of being discovered and shot and says, "That is not exactly a pleasant prospect" (p. 19B). The understatement of the century! Weren't your emotions stirred by the crushing simplicity of "there are many who wait for death" (p. 57M) or the plaintive words "Whoever wants to follow a slimming course . . ." (p. 70M)?

Some actors, like writers, have gained great critical favor by their habit of underplaying their roles rather than "tearing a passion to tatters." In fact, the "ham" on the stage is generally the one who is unable to say even "good morning" without making a dramatic climax out of it. Try low-level writing on occasion; your simple words may leave a stronger impact than if they were all superlatives.

3. *Try short, crisp dialogue to liven up a scene!*

When a dramatist writes a play, he has the job of converting practically all narration, description, and action into dialogue. If he does it skillfully, the whole story springs to life in sharply etched acts and scenes. Every writer should recognize and take advantage of the dramatic values inherent in dialogue. When people talk, a greater sense of reality is achieved.

Notice how effectively Anne creates an interlude in the potato-peeling chores by recording Mrs. Van Daan's efforts to attract attention (p. 93M), how delicately she introduces the subject of kissing in the conversation with Peter (p. 160T), how modestly she considers her own appeal to Peter (p. 166). In each instance, the crisp dialogue carries the scene far more strikingly than if it had been presented in straight description. A good practice exercise for you, occasionally, is to try to convert a scene involving people entirely into dialogue. You can thus train yourself to use this writing device with confidence.

4. *Introduce a personal touch into your writing!*

You may have heard people talk of a conversational style. This is generally achieved by the use of asides, interspersed remarks, personal references, and parenthetical expressions. Some examples from the *Diary* follow:

"as far as I was concerned" (p. 14T)

"But *she* is not spoiled!" (p. 29T)

"Rather vague, don't you think?" (p. 36B)

"substantial person (he looked fatter than he is!) . . ." (p. 52T)

"have had glasses . . . (phew, what an owl I shall look!) . . ." (p. 75M)

You can find many more such personal touches in Anne's prose if you look for them. They add great charm to writing, if not overused, and they manage to bring the reader very close to the author.

B. VOCABULARY DEVELOPMENT

1. *What words should you try to learn?*

a. If you meet a word for the first time, do your best to work out its meaning from the sense of the sentence or paragraph in which it appears. If this is impossible, don't worry about it. Even if you miss a word here and there, you will still be able to follow the main ideas. There is no point in wasting time trying to learn every new word you see in every book you read.

b. If you come across a word that looks vaguely familiar (perhaps you've seen it two or three times be-

fore), circle it lightly in pencil, *but keep on reading!*
Don't destroy the continuity of your reading by rush-
ing to a dictionary for each strange word. Again, do
what you can to locate the general meaning from the
context and, if you have some spare time later, just
look up the precise meaning and check out how the
word was used in the original sentence. That's all!

c. There will be some words that you will meet for
perhaps the fifth or sixth time. These are the ones
worth doing something about because you now have
proof that they are used frequently. *Underline each of
these,* but keep on reading. After you have finished the
book, select the 30 or so underlined words that you
have seen most often before and would like to add to
your permanent vocabulary. Work with these in the
manner suggested in the exercises that follow.

2. *Typical Vocabulary Exercises*

We have selected 30 words that you probably should
know better because they are popular with good writers and speakers. These may not necessarily be the
ones you have underlined yourself, but they will serve
to illustrate how you should practice with any words
that you are trying to master. Proceed this way:

- Look up each word in a good dictionary.
- Say it aloud; note its spelling.
- Check the source of the word, its etymology, its
  breakdown into prefix, stem or root, and suffix (if
  any).
- Go back to the original sentence in the book and
  decide what meaning was most appropriate.
- Now divide the set of words into three groups:
  a. those that can most easily be remembered

because their interesting history provides a good clue to their meaning.

b. those that come from a "family" of words, all of which have a common root and can be remembered by association with one another.

c. those that had best be mastered directly, but for which you can perhaps invent your own clue or association.

NOTE: We will work with groups of 10, but your own choices might vary in number within groups.

Group a

1) List each word and next to it write out its "story" and current meanings:

scrounging (p. 4B): Formerly a slang word that has become respectable. It probably was derived from *scrouge* (to squeeze, press) which suggests the penny-pinching Scrooge of *A Christmas Carol.*

looking for and taking without permission, pilfering

chattels (p. 14B): Has a common origin with *cattle,* once the chief property of the average free man.

personal or movable property (as opposed to real or land property)

hypochondria (p. 22B): From the Greek, referring to the abdominal region of the body, where, supposedly, anxious feelings arise—*hypo* (under) + *chondros* (rib cage).

abnormal concern over health (usually accompanied by imaginary ailments) *furbelows* (p. 129M): Originally used to identify fringes or ruffles, then applied to any useless ornamentation.

showy trimmings or ornamentation

scandalous (p. 188M): variously traced to French, Latin, or Greek, generally indicating *stumbling* or *climbing;* in short, an obstacle in the path of righteousness.

anything offending or shocking moral feelings

boisterous (p. 199M): From the Middle English *boistous* (rough in quality). Just think of a lot of *boys* shouting at the top of their lungs.

loud, noisily good-natured

abyss (p. 212B): From the Greek *a* (without) + *byssos* (bottom), hence anything very deep down.

bottomless pit, measureless depth

purgatory (p. 226B): Has a common origin with *purge* (to cleanse). According to theology, a place between Heaven and Hell where people's sins are atoned for by suffering, their souls thereby being cleansed.

state or place of temporary punishment, any state of suffering

finicky (p. 229M): Really an extension of *fine,* but in a derogatory sense—too fine!

too dainty, fussy, too particular

impeccable (p. 234M): A *peccadillo* is a small sin or
  fault (from *peccare*, to sin). Anyone or anything without even a little fault is practically perfect.

  without defect or error, faultless, flawless

2) Now compose a matching exercise, mixing up the
words, the clues, and the current meanings in three
columns. Later, for practice, you rearrange the items
to match!

Word	Clue	Meaning
scrounging	little boys	measureless depth
chattels	cleansing place	morally shocking
hypochondria	sinless	pilfering
furbelows	fine	flawless
scandalous	rib cage	too particular
boisterous	Scrooge	health-anxiety
abyss	cattle	useless decoration
purgatory	fringes	personal property
finicky	no bottom	noisy
impeccable	stumbling	state of suffering

3) Check the use of the words in the original sentences in this book.

4) Construct an original paragraph, using the current meanings and listing the new words beneath the
paragraph. Underline the meanings and, for later re-
view, substitute the new words in place of the meanings.

"La Divina Commedia" (Divine Comedy), the mas-
terpiece of the greatest of all Italian poets, Dante
Alighieri, was written around 1300. It describes Dante's supposed experiences in the three great regions of
the Beyond. First he descends to the *bottomless pit* of

Hell (Inferno), where he witnesses the punishments being meted out to those whose conduct had been *morally shocking* on earth or who had spent their time *pilfering* for personal gain, not being *too fussy* about honesty or decency. After leaving the *noisy* souls of the lower region, Dante ascends to Mount *Place of Suffering*, where he imagines he receives purification of remaining sins. Here he rids himself of such petty qualities as greed for another's *personal property* or too much concern over himself, perhaps even *health-anxiety*. Stripped of the *useless ornamentations* of earthly passion, he enters the Garden of Eden, at the top of the mountain. Now, practically *sinless* in mind and soul, he can proceed to the third region, Paradise, and glory in the presence of God.

scrounging	chattels
hypochondria	furbelows
scandalous	boisterous
abyss	purgatory
finicky	impeccable

5) For the next month or so, make a daily effort to use one or more of these new words in your speaking or writing activities. A good practice is to put a word on a card each day as a reminder to use it that day.

Group b

1) List each word, the meaning of the stem or root (the main part of the word), and the current meanings.

2) Now, by trying out various affixes (forms that may be added before or after the root, as the case may be), try to identify other words from the same source.

A friend with a good vocabulary may be able to help you. Otherwise, consult a good etymological dictionary.

enTHRALLing (p. 23B)

THRALL (slave)
enslaving, strongly influencing, fascinating

SEE: thrall, thralldom, enthrall

VERitable (p. 50M)

VERUS (true)
true, real, actual

SEE: verify, veracity, verisimilitude

PEDantic (p. 79T)

PAIDOS (child) + AGEIN (lead, teach)
petty about minor details of learning, narrow-minded

SEE: pedagogue, pedant, pedagogy

irreVOCable (p. 89M)

VOCARE (to call)
unable to be recalled or undone, unalterable

SEE: vocal, vociferous, revoke

imPENETRAble (p. 103T)

PENETRARE (pierce into)
unable to be entered, pierced, or solved

SEE: penetrate, penetrable, intrude

STAGNant (p. 131T)

> STAGNARE (cause to stand)
> *without motion, not flowing, sluggish*
>
> SEE: stagnate, stage, stationary

conFIDant (p. 151M)

> FIDERE (to trust)
> *trusted friend, sharer of secrets*
>
> SEE: confide, fidelity, infidel

inCESSantly (p. 157M)

> CESSARE (to cease)
> *without stopping, endlessly, constant*
>
> SEE: cessation, ceaseless

QUELLed (p 174B)

> QUELLEN (to kill)
> *made fall, put down, crushed, quieted*
>
> SEE: qualm, kill, kill-joy

JOCular (p. 192B)

> JOCUS (joke)
> *joking, humorous, full of fun*
>
> SEE: jokester, jocund, jocose

3) Repeat as with *Group a.*

4) *The Practice Paragraph:*

The classroom scene is repeated daily. For some the lesson is *fascinating* and a *real* adventure in learning. Others find the talk too *learnedly fussy* and can barely keep awake as the voice of the teacher drones on *endlessly*. Since their minds are like *motionless* pools of water or *unable to be pierced* jungles of indifference, they seek entertainment elsewhere. Soon *joking* comments are being muttered to a *close friend* and the destruction of attention seems *unalterable*, even though the whispered uprising may be *put down* by a sharp tongue.

impenetrable	enthralling
pedantic	irrevocable
veritable	stagnant
confidant	incessantly
jocular	quelled

5) Repeat as with *Group a*.

Group c

1) List each word, its current meanings, and a *clue* of your own that enables you to establish a good association. The dictionary will help in most cases.

2) Construct new sentences of your own if the word has other forms that are frequently used. Be sure to make these meanings clear.

enhance (p. 3T)

to make greater in value

CLUE: higher, fancier

blithely (p. 5T)

gaily, joyfully, cheerfully

CLUE: lightly
The fool disregarded the advice with *blithesome* stupidity.

loathe (p. 18M)

to dislike intensely, hate, detest

CLUE: low regard
It was a *loathesome* creature, green and slimy.
His *loathing* twisted his face into a mask of hate.

piqued (p. 23T)

offended, excited, stimulated

CLUE: picked at
Her *pique* at our indifference showed in her angry eyes.
A *piquant* wit can enliven a dull evening.

bickering (p. 29M)

quarreling, wrangling

CLUE: kicking at
They *bickered* over the spoils for hours in hot fury.

urchins (p. 33T)

mischievous boys, ragamuffins

CLUE: dirty chins

gruesome (p. 82T)

causing fear and loathing, ghastly

CLUE: GRR!

fatuous (p. 115T)

stupid, silly, foolish

CLUE: fathead
Fatuity stems from an empty mind and a loose mouth.

scoff (p. 220T)

mock, scorn, jeer at

CLUE: laugh off

exuberant (p. 235M)

overflowing, high-spirited, lavish

CLUE: (uber) *over* or above normal
Our *exuberance* was suddenly checked by the sad news.
He spoke *exuberantly* of the new job and bright future.

3) Repeat as with *Group a*.

4) *The Practice Paragraph:*

Our appreciation of Anne Frank's great courage is *made greater in value* when we see her going about her daily chores *joyfully*, despite rather depressing surroundings. Her *overflowing* spirits are not even dampened by the frequent *quarreling* of the Van Daans, nor does she permit Mr. Dussel's *foolish* comments to upset her too much. Unmindful of her own hard lot, she finds her sympathies *stimulated* by the sight of street *ragamuffins* begging for food. Let no one *mock* at any madman who seeks power by teaching one group to *hate* another. Instead, let his evil be exposed and his *ghastly* influence destroyed. Only then will the sacrifices of people like Anne Frank have meaning and purpose.

loathe	piqued
bickering	scoff
urchins	exuberant
gruesome	enhanced
fatuous	blithely

5) Repeat as with *Group a*.

VOCABULARY REVIEW

When you have finished with the preliminary work for all 30 words, compose a multiple choice exercise for later practice:

1. scrounging	a. saving	b. dividing	c. pilfering
2. chattels	a. property	b. windows	c. losses
3. hypochon- dria	a. pain	b. dope	c. health- anxiety
4. furbelows	a. toys	b. showy decorations	c. rags
5. scandalous	a. worthy	b. shocking	c. tall
6. boisterous	a. noisy	b. dull	c. restful
7. abyss	a. peak	b. card	c. bottomless pit
8. purgatory	a. school	b. cleansing place	c. damnation
9. finicky	a. careless	b. too hard	c. too fussy
10. impeccable	a. flawless	b. lovable	c. sinful
11. enthralling	a. routine	b. fascinating	c. laughable

12. veritable	a. imagined	b. false	c. real
13. pedantic	a. mentally petty	b. wise	c. heavy
14. irrevocable	a. tense	b. unalterable	c. favorable
15. impenetrable	a. open	b. high	c. not to be pierced
16. stagnant	a. rushing	b. still	c. pretended
17. confidant	a. sharer of secrets	b. certain	c. sure
18. incessantly	a. rapidly	b. endlessly	c. briefly
19. quelled	a. urged	b. rang out	c. checked
20. jocular	a. gay	b. sad	c. tough
21. enhance	a. disgrace	b. enrich	c. lower in value
22. blithely	a. moodily	b. lazily	c. happily
23. loathe	a. love	b. detest	c. load
24. piqued	a. stimulated	b. tested	c. ignored
25. bickering	a. quarreling	b. coaxing	c. following
26. urchins	a. choir boys	b. puppies	c. ragamuffins
27. gruesome	a. solemn	b. ghastly	c. lovely
28. fatuous	a. silly	b. wise	c. weighty
29. scoff	a. cry at	b. sigh at	c. laugh at
30. exuberant	a. lively	b. asleep	c. stingy

C. SPELLING EXERCISES

As YOU ADD WORDS to your vocabulary, you will want to be able to spell them correctly so that you can use them freely when you write. Follow these steps to make the words *part of you*, bearing in mind that you must make a *habit* of spelling each word correctly (as must be done with any word you want to master).

1. Ask a friend or relative to dictate the vocabulary paragraphs in each group of the preceding exercises, after you have substituted the new words for the meanings.

2. Make a list of the words you misspell in the dictation in this fashion:

—Write the word so that the difficult part for you (the part you misspelled) stands out. Use colored pencil, large letters, any device that helps you SEE THE WORD! For example:

FUR BELOW s

Stare at the image of the word for ten seconds and then try to reproduce the *difficult part* in your *mind's eye,* on a wall, anywhere.

—Now compose a *bond,* some association or clue that reminds you of the difficult part, or use a spelling rule (if a good one exists) as your bond. All this helps you THINK THE WORD! The sillier the bond is, the better.

The FUR BELOW the hem creates FURBELOWs.

—Finally, write out the word in large letters and *trace it with your finger* (not pen or pencil), saying each letter aloud as you trace it. No pauses during the tracing, no stops, only smooth follow through! Dot the *i's* and cross the *t's*. Do this three times. Then turn the paper over and without looking down, write the word *as you sing a song or recite some jingle*. This is important. If you can spell a word while your mind concentrates on something else, you have begun to FEEL THE WORD, to make the spelling habitually correct.

furbelows

3. Take one word a day, no more. Practice three times, all three steps, with each word each day. Space your practice—morning, noon, and night.

4. When you have accumulated 10 words, compose sentences and have someone dictate them, *after you have practiced with them all*, as a final check on your progress.

Here is a typical group of 10 words from our vocabulary list:

HYPO CHON dria
>   Mr. HYPO CHON suffers
>   from HYPOCHONdria.   *hypochondria*

b OIST erous
>   The bOISTerous boys will
>   hOIST their voices.   *boisterous*

ab Y SS
>   Y is there double SS in
>   abYSS?   *abyss*

fi NICK y
>   NICK is a fiNICKy per-
>   son.   *finicky*

ve RITA ble
>   RITA is a veRITAble
>   queen.   *veritable*

enthr ALL ing
>   ALL of the show was en-
>   thrALLing.   *enthralling*

impe NET r ABLE

> We were ABLE to see
> that the NET was im-
> peNETrABLE.

impenetrable

stagn ANT

> The ANT was caught in
> the stagnANT water.

stagnant

b LITHE ly

> The LITHE dancer
> bLITHEly danced.

blithely

g RUE SOME

> You will RUE SOME the
> gRUESOME scene.

gruesome

Sentences

1. His *hypochondria* threw his mind into a *veritable abyss*.

2. The *gruesome* remains were found in some *stagnant* water of an *impenetrable* swamp.

3. The *finicky* will call these *furbelows*.

4. The *boisterous* group *blithely* ignored the *enthralling* scene.

D. IDEAS FOR DISCUSSION OR REPORT

A WRITER USUALLY does more than merely tell a story. He tries to express his ideas on human life as well. This is particularly true of Anne Frank, who had so much to say about people, especially herself. Here are some suggestions that might lead to fruitful discussion or worth-while reports.

1. Anne describes her first opportunity to "talk things out with Peter" (p. 159B). Why was it easier to talk "beside the open window in the semidarkness"? What made it such a "wonderful evening"? Why do boys feel differently about kissing parents than do girls? What other teen-age reactions are indicated that are typical of most adolescents of fifteen or sixteen?

2. For one of the rare times in the *Diary,* Anne finds that her Daddy has failed her (p. 231T). What are some of the things about his daughter that Mr. Frank apparently doesn't understand? To what extent are his attitudes typical of most fathers? What are some of the things about her Daddy that Anne doesn't understand? To what extent are her reactions reasonable? Unreasonable? Typical?

3. Anne talks of herself as a "little bundle of contradictions" (p. 235T). Why are most human beings two, or even more, different people? Why do teen-agers fear laughter more than anything else under certain conditions? To what extent do we ever reveal our inner selves to anyone? What cure, if any, is there for this apparent desire to erect walls between ourselves and other people, however close they may be?

4. Anne describes her first big "crush" (p. 118M). Which of Anne's attitudes toward boys are typical of girls, which not? Which are commendable and which not? To what extent was this first love characteristic of all such adventures? How long do we tend to remember the faces and personalities of those whom we grow fond of in our early years?

5. As you read about Mr. Koophuis, Miep, Elli,

Henk, and the others "on the outside," you get some idea of the risks taken by many natives in occupied countries in their efforts to help their persecuted friends. What leads some people to consider it their duty to fight all enemies of democracy and human dignity, while others look on either indifferently or even approvingly? What is the chief flaw in human nature that accounts for the existence of prejudice and active hostility toward alien groups?

6. The constant quarrels with and by the Van Daans are discussed repeatedly by Anne. She asks whether there would be trouble with "whoever one shared a house with" (p. 123M). Do such differences arise whenever people share quarters? Give examples.

7. Anne describes what a mother should be like (p. 114B). Do you agree with her in every respect? Why?

8. Why does Peter's clumsiness (p. 149T) attract Anne's interest?

9. Anne talks of her hobbies (p. 176). How suited are they to her age and personality? Which of them would you be interested in pursuing? Why?

10. It seems strange to find two sisters, living as Anne and Margot do, writing letters to each other (p. 162). Yet, is it really strange? Why was it easier for them to communicate on paper than face to face? To what extent does the same situation apply to Anne's letter to Daddy?

E. SUGGESTIONS FOR FURTHER READING

1. Books that provide additional background material:

Gunther, John, *Inside Europe Today*.*
Hersey, John, *The Wall*.*
Koestler, Arthur, *Scum of the Earth*.
Pauling, Linus, *No More War!*
Shirer, William L., *Berlin Diary*.
Shirer, William L., *Rise and Fall of the Third Reich*.
Van Paassen, Pierre, *Earth Could Be Fair*.

2. Novels that deal with young people or with the problems mentioned in *Anne Frank: The Diary of a Young Girl*:

Crane, Stephen, *The Red Badge of Courage*.†
Fast, Howard, *April Morning*.
Hobson, Laura Z., *Gentleman's Agreement*.
Lee, Harper, *To Kill a Mockingbird*.
Maltz, Albert, *Cross and the Arrow*.
Miller, Arthur, *Focus*.
Schwarz-Bart, Andre, *The Last of the Just*.
Uris, Leon, *Exodus*.

---

*These books are available in *Giant Cardinal* editions.
†This book is available in a *Washington Square Press* edition.